DELHI

BUNNY KNOTT

Backwards into Delhi

THE MARLBORO PRESS

TMP

Manufactured in the United States of America

Library of Congress Catalog Card Number 89-60941

ISBN 0-910395-52-7

The Marlboro Press
Marlboro, Vermont

This book is dedicated to
my mother
who urged me to write it; to
Meb and Fariyal Pirani
who named it and criticized it constructively; to
Mark Proctor
who convinced me I could do it
and encouraged and supported me
from beginning to end; and to
Ed
who lived it with me.

CONTENTS

Backwards into Delhi

DELHI

Street Sleepers

The big plane droned above utter blackness. Although we had crossed from Pakistan into India some time before, there was not a light to be seen. Pressing our noses to the glass, we peered down through moonlit skies to the velvet darkness of the land below. Once we spotted a ribbon of moonshine that must have been a river far beneath us, but still the landscape lacked the tiniest point of light that might indicate that people inhabited this vast country.

I let my mind wander back over the past year of planning for our journey. It had all begun in Thailand two years before. Ed and I had been playing double solitaire in a train station at Hua Hin near the Malaysian border, waiting for the Magic Arrow train which was to take us to Penang, when we were joined by a French couple about our age. The woman spoke good English, and soon we were involved in a spirited conversation that continued after we boarded the train. All four of us were somehow employed in the education field, with our summers off, and we were all dedicated travelers. With so much in common, it was natural that we liked each other right away, and the hours which we passed in the dining car, drinking beer and comparing notes, flew by like minutes.

At last I asked the woman, "What is your favorite country?" and her face lit up. "Ah, India!" she replied, her eyes shining.

I was astonished. "India?" Somehow I had never thought of that country as a tourist destination. "What is so wonderful about India?"

"Ah," she said, "You go zhere. You will see. Eet ees wonderful. So interesting. So colorful. Zhe people are so friendly, eet ees cheap. You go zhere. You will see."

Back at home, I started thinking about what she had said. I began to pick up books from the library about India, and started to prowl used book stores. I read *An Area of Darkness* by Naipaul, and *Land of the*

Black Pagoda by Lowell Thomas. I read *One Man's India* by Arthur Stratton and a book by Gordon Sinclair, *Footloose in India*. Most of these books portrayed India as a country of pitiful poverty, heat, dust, and starvation. Then I read the grossly unfair *Mother India* by Katherine Mayo, which really made the country sound like an earthly version of Hell. I was intrigued and repelled at the same time, and I couldn't shake the fascination which had taken hold of me.

Talking Ed into going to India was more difficult than it had been to talk myself into the trip. He was dubious, and when he looked over the books I had been reading, he was convinced that we should simply forget the whole idea.

"Let's go to Great Britain," he said. "I've always wanted to see England and Scotland. We've seen most of Europe and a good chunk of Asia, but we somehow passed over England. I want to go there."

I put off my dreams of India and we did go to Great Britain the following year. When we returned home, I got out my books again, and pored over maps of Asia.

"You got your wish, now I want mine," I pleaded. "I want to go to India. I'm sure it isn't as bad as it is painted in those books. Anyway, Mark Twain said that India is the most fascinating country in the world."

"I guess we can go, if you want to so much," Ed agreed reluctantly. "Whatever you want to do, honey."

Happily, I began our preparations. I wrote to the best known travel agency in India and arranged to get Indrail passes to cover most of the time we planned to be there, and made train reservations in advance to all the places we wanted to see. The travel books I had picked up all advised that this was necessary because Indian trains are invariably crowded and tickets hard to get at the last minute, or even at a week's notice.

At last June had arrived, and we locked up our apartment, said goodbye to our family and friends, and started on the long series of flights that would eventually land us in the country that I both longed for and feared.

The first stop was New York, where we boarded our Air India B747. After only five or six hours, we were already tired of being locked into a cramped airplane seat, and we had eaten two meals on the previous flight, so the dinner served by an exquisitely beautiful stewardess in an orange silk sari was not as welcome as it might have been. Afterwards I rose to join the line at the restrooms.

A diminutive elderly lady in a grey sari was ahead of me, and after a minute or two, an old gentlemen who might have been her husband spoke to her and tried to step in front of her. She spoke sharply to him in Hindi, and he got behind her (but in front of me).

"Excuse me," I said to the lady, "is this gentleman your husband?"

"Certainly not," she said.

The old man turned to me. "She go first," he said, indicating the lady.

"I go second," I said, and stepped in front of him.

"I never did like Englishmen," he muttered behind me.

"I am not English," I said, and could not repress a giggle. This little exchange restored my good humor and provided me with an amusing story to tell Ed when I returned to my seat.

I settled down for a sleep, but our stop in London, and an unexpected stop in Rome, interrupted my slumbers. At last we took off for the last leg of what seemed like an endless voyage, over the deserts of Turkey, Iran, Afghanistan, and Pakistan. Gazing below at the barren terrain washed in the mellow light of late afternoon, we saw the occasional road like a thread winding its way through the low hills. Only once in a great while did we spot a hut; they and the few roads were the only signs of human habitation. Eventually night fell for the second time on our journey, and at last I had got an hour's sleep before we crossed into India and approached New Delhi.

A change in the pitch of the great turbines broke the train of my thoughts and told us that we were letting down for our landing. Suddenly ahead I saw that the sky was suffused with the lights of Delhi. Our adventure was about to begin.

As we descended the steps onto the airfield, the "feel" of India settled over us: the hot, soft air, the smell: dung smoke, flowers, and rich vegetation. We crossed the field and entered the long, low building ahead of us. Inside, despite the lateness of the hour (it was 2:00 a.m.), the crush of people made it seem like midday. We attached ourselves to one of the long lines in front of the Customs windows. After interminable formalities, we emerged at long last onto the street, and were at once surrounded by shouting taxi drivers, who pushed and shoved in their eagerness to be chosen.

We named an obscure guesthouse in Old Delhi where we had reservations; one that had been recommended by our travel book as being both clean and cheap. At first none of the taxi drivers seemed to have heard of it, but finally one came forward who nodded his head when we asked if he knew where the "Mughal-e-Azam" was. We climbed in thankfully after stowing our suitcases in the trunk.

3

As soon as we closed the taxi doors, the heat became stifling. Quickly we rolled down the windows to let the fresh air cool our faces as we moved down the deserted streets of New Delhi. Mile after mile we drove down park-like boulevards lined with oleanders and big ficus trees. Lawns extended on either side, silvery in the bright moonlight. But nowhere could we see the crowded rabbit warrens of human habitation that we expected.

It was a long time before we came at last through a gateway into another world: Old Delhi. Here were the narrow streets, the houses crowding each other, vying for position. Gaudy Indian movie posters on the walls looked somehow sinister in the blue midnight. Pools of yellow light splashed on white bundles lying in the gutters and on the sidewalks. What *were* they? Of course: the street sleepers of India! They lay close together, each wrapped in a white sheet, like so many corpses. Their thin coffee colored legs stuck straight out from the wrappings, reminding me of bundles of faggots partly covered.

My fuzzy, sleep-starved brain could barely take it in, but even so I became aware that we were turning corner after corner, up one street and down another.

I whispered to Ed. "Do you suppose we are lost? I have a feeling that our driver hasn't the least idea where the guesthouse is."

"I've suspected that for some time," he said, "but what are we going to do about it? I haven't any idea where we are." He tapped the driver on the shoulder. "Are you sure you know where the Mughal-e-Azam is?"

The driver waggled his head and shrugged. "Hotel," he said and then lapsed into Hindi.

"Good God," said Ed. "He hardly speaks any English."

We were sitting there, desperately wondering what to do, when the driver pulled up and stopped beside a little knot of men on a corner. Getting out of the taxi, he huddled with them for several minutes of rapid conversation. Finally he returned.

"Okay, okay." He waggled his head happily and ground the gears. We lurched off in a different direction, and, after several blocks, stopped at a dark and shuttered facade on what looked like a main street. Getting out, our driver tried the door. It was locked—padlocked, in fact, as we saw when we got out to look, stepping over several sleepers on the sidewalk. Our driver and Ed pounded repeatedly on the door, waking everyone within earshot, but with absolutely no result from within. At last we gave up and told the driver to take us to another hotel, our second choice. Of course, there we had no reservations.

Fortunately, our second choice was only a couple of blocks away, open, with lights shining from the lobby. We stumbled up the steps thankfully and booked an available room. I filled out the lengthy registration form while Ed argued with the taxi driver over the fare.

"Little burglar wanted eighty rupees," he grumbled when he caught up with me. "I haggled him down to fifty. That's not much less than we'd have to pay back home."

"Never mind. It was a hell of a long way, and he did spend a lot of time looking for the Mughal-e-Azam."

"Well, he said he knew where it was," Ed pointed out, and then the elevator arrived. We hauled our exhausted bodies into our room and collapsed in the beds unbathed, where we slept like the dead until we were awakened by an unearthly sound.

I struggled out of sleep, disoriented, dimly aware of the lovely music from out of the night. It was still dark, and the room was otherwise still. The beautiful sound rose and fell, and I lay there listening until it stopped. I realized at last what it was: the cry of the muezzin from a nearby mosque. It was so quiet because the air conditioning was off, and I became aware that the room was overpoweringly hot and stuffy.

I went to the window, opened it wide, and leaned out into the cool, fresh morning. Dawn was just breaking in the east, and roosters were crowing somewhere below. People were beginning to get up from their charpoys which, because of the heat, they had placed on the flat roofs of the old houses; monkeys swung hand over hand along the balconies and roofs, and the streets started to fill with people. The street sleepers had vanished in the growing daylight, and in their places a couple of stately cows browsed through the gutters, looking for scraps to eat. Below our window was a well at which two little boys bathed in buckets, while young mothers, carrying their babies on their hips, brought brass water jugs to be filled. Ed joined me there at the windowsill, and we watched the action below until the power came back on and the whirr of the air conditioner lured us back to bed for another few hours of sleep.

At ten we were ready to hit the streets, but breakfast was the first priority, so we tried the hotel dining room. It was empty, but after a little wait, a shy young boy came in with a grease-stained menu.

"Let's try Indian food," I suggested. "I don't feel like having eggs and toast, and there isn't much else."

"What's *puri badji*?" Ed asked the waiter. The boy swallowed and rolled his eyes. He waggled his head from side to side, in a gesture that was becoming familiar.

5

"Sir, we have eggs and toast," he suggested hopefully.

"No, we want an Indian breakfast," I put in. "Let's try the puri badji. Do you have it?"

"Yes, yes. But eggs and toast very good."

"We'll have the puri badji," said Ed, firmly. "And coffee."

"What kind of coffee?" I asked suspiciously. "Nescafe?"

"Yes, yes. Very good Nescafe."

"I'll have tea," I said quickly.

"I'll have tea also," said Ed.

The bewildered boy wandered off, and we sat in the quiet room, with only the whirling fan for company. Eventually he reappeared with spotless linen napkins, knives and forks, and glasses. He poured water for us and left. We eyed our glasses longingly, but didn't taste the invitingly clear water. ("Don't drink the water" is the first rule in the Indian traveler's handbook.) Another long wait followed. At last the waiter brought us our puri badji.

It was good—a very large serving of potato and onion curry accompanied by two fried rounds of unleavened whole wheat bread that were puffed up like miniature basketballs, and tea that was strong enough to require hot milk and sugar. When the bill came, the total amount for our substantial breakfast was less than we'd have expected to pay for a cup of coffee each at home.

Out in the street, the sun was blinding after the relatively cool dimness of the restaurant, and the heat was like a blow. We walked the several blocks to our original hotel, which the book had listed as the "Mughal-e-Azam". When we found it, we noticed that it had a large sign in English over the sidewalk, "5-Star Guest House" which we hadn't noticed the night before. No wonder the taxi drivers hadn't heard of it. We found out later that the "Mughal-e-Azam" was the name of the little cafe below the guest house itself.

This time we found the door open. Walking in, we climbed cool, shiny cement stairs to the desk on the second floor. There the manager was effusive in his apologies when he heard why we had not arrived as scheduled.

"Oh, sir," he said, shaking his head, "our boy must have been asleep. He was waiting for you at the bottom of the steps by the entrance door. He was still there this morning, asleep, when I arrived. Oh, do forgive us. Of course your room is waiting for you still. Please come with me." Somehow he forgot to explain why, on the night before, the door had been padlocked from the *outside*.

We followed him up more steps and down a hall, then along the edge of the roof. Most of the rooms faced stepped terraces which looked out over Old Delhi. Our room, on the topmost terrace, was hot when we entered, but as soon as the "air cooler" and the fan were turned on, the temperature dropped until it was quite comfortable. The air cooler was an interesting appliance. It was really nothing but a large box set into the wall. A four-inch layer of straw formed the outside surface, and a large fan directly in front of that drew air from the outside into the room. Water continually dripped through the straw, and the resulting evaporation effectively chilled the air. In a humid climate, the "air cooler" would not have worked at all, but in Delhi's dry atmosphere it was quite adequate.

The room was spartan in its simplicity—cement walls and floor, very hard twin beds with crisp sheets, a wardrobe, and a suitcase rack. The attached bath was merely a concrete cubicle with a shower head in the ceiling, a washstand, a toilet, and a blue plastic bucket with an orange plastic dipper in it, which hung by its handle from the water faucet on the wall. Everything was very clean. The price quoted was less than a third of what the other hotel was charging us.

After retrieving our luggage and getting installed in our new room, we were finally able to start taking our first good look around Delhi. We decided to go to the Red Fort and from there to Chandni Chowk, the old bazaar area. Emerging into the street again, we hailed the first "rickshaw" we saw. It was pedalled by a thin old man who insisted that he could propel both of us together with no trouble.

"Okay-okay," he said in his limited English, and motioned us both aboard. We squeezed our ample bottoms onto the narrow seat and off we went, our chauffeur straining with every revolution of the pedals. Slowly his shirt became damp with sweat, and the muscles stood out on his spare calves. I found myself holding my breath each time he thrust down on the pedals, and a glance at Ed showed that he was doing the same. It was agonizing. I couldn't relax and enjoy the ride.

"I can't stand this," said Ed. "Stop!" Obediently, our driver pulled over to the side, and Ed dismounted.

"You stay there," he said, "and I'll get another rickshaw."

Within a few seconds, another came along and Ed climbed aboard. This time my driver was able to move along with no trouble. The breeze blew over me as we wove between the pedestrians, the bicycles, and the cows; and my perch, well above the street, afforded me a wonderful view of the passing scene. The two rickshaws arrived at the Red Fort almost at the same time. Ed asked the drivers how much we owed them.

7

"Eight rupees," his driver said, and mine echoed, "eight."

"Damn it," said Ed, turning to me. "I completely forgot to settle on the fare before we started out. I know it shouldn't be more than three, according to the book." His face was grimly set as he got out the bills he carried in his front pocket.

"Too late now," I said. "I guess we'll just have to chalk it up to experience. At least we'll know next time—don't be mad."

"Mostly I'm mad at myself. It's not as if we'd never taken a rickshaw in Asia before. It was just as bad in Thailand."

Grumpily he led the way to the gate and purchased our tickets into the Red Fort. It was a pleasant surprise to find that the admission amounted to about three or four cents in American money each.

The builders of the fort had made the entrance gate an imposing twenty feet high, to allow elephants, complete with howdah and passengers, to pass through it. Inside, the grounds were beautifully maintained, with lawns and flower borders along the neat brick paths. Elegant Indian women in saris of brilliant colors, often with flowers in their hair, strolled with men who were smartly dressed in white shirts and dark slacks. I was impressed with the good looks of the people; there were more beautiful women and handsome men in this crowd than in a comparable group of Westerners.

"You know," I remarked, "I can't get over the prosperous appearance of most of the people here. Where are the poverty-stricken masses we were always reading about back home?"

"I know. I don't think that India is going to be as bad as we—or at least I—expected. Delhi looks just as good as almost any other mainland Asian city to me. Of course, we probably haven't seen any of the slums yet. I'm sure there are some. And of course, there *are* the street sleepers."

We spent the afternoon gawking at the exquisite architecture of such buildings as the Pearl Mosque, a little jewel of white marble in its setting of green lawns and emerald ashoka trees. Most of the other buildings were of rose red sandstone so hard and dense that the carvings of flowers and arabesques have been unaltered by centuries of blazing sun and monsoon rain.

The heat was intense, but I soon became accustomed to it and would hardly have noticed it except that I was often thirsty. I wanted a drink of water, but I knew there was none available—at least, none that we ought to drink. We made do with bottled pop, which was at least well-chilled. I was standing at the edge of a nicely-kept lawn, drinking my second bottle of "Limca" in a row, when I saw two men pushing a lawn mower, while one man pulled it with a rope.

"Look at that," I giggled, "power mower, Indian style."

Ed laughed too. "Well, it's a labor-intensive country," he said. "It makes sense to employ a lot of people and pay each of them a small wage rather than to invest in machinery to do the work."

When we had finished our sight-seeing at the fort, we left by the main gate and started up Chandni Chowk, the "Silver Street," so called because of the silver bazaars along both sides. It was crowded with shoppers and strollers, but very few tourists were to be seen. We wandered along, staring at the strange and wonderful sights: men having their hair cut, their chins shaved, and their ears cleaned right on the sidewalk by itinerant barbers who squatted with their tools spread out on a cloth beside them; men making jewelry in the open thresholds of the little shops, soldering gold and silver and setting stones which they chose from trays of glittering gems; men hammering the finishing touches on copper and brass kitchen pans and utensils on the sidewalks, while people flowed around them as they worked; open-fronted eating stalls with *tandoor* ovens where meat and bread were cooked in front of onlookers. The ovens looked like huge clay jars, with charcoal fires in the bottom. Meat was threaded on a skewer which was thrust in from the top and rested in the coals; it cooked very quickly. Most fascinating was the way bread, called *naan,* was cooked in them. The cook placed the flat, raw dough on a padded "mitt" and slapped it against the red-hot side of the jar, just as it sloped away in its outward curve. The naan hung there free, attached only at the top, and turned golden brown before our eyes, acquiring by its own weight the characteristic "leaf" shape. The cook knackily removed the bread with a large hook, thereby sparing his fingers. We stopped in at one of those little restaurants, and sampled the juicy skewered "lamb" (which is actually goat) and deliciously crisp naan.

There were beggars in the street when we left the restaurant, and several followed us persistently, demanding "baksheesh" in harsh, high voices. We said no and shook our heads, but they kept on following, sometimes accompanying us for a block or two.

"How can we get rid of them?" I said in exasperation. "They aren't starving or crippled, or I'd want to give them something. I know that the government wants to put a stop to begging. But they are so persistent, I feel like giving them something just to get rid of them."

9

"If you do, every beggar in sight will want some too. Look at that, Bunny. They aren't following that young Western traveler across the street. He doesn't even look at them, and he doesn't say no, either. Maybe we are doing this all wrong. Try to look right through them and don't speak."

We had hit on the right method, all right. If we had the strength of character to ignore the beggars completely, they gave up almost immediately. But if we weakened and made eye contact, we were lost. Eventually we became quite good at ignoring beggars, but it took a lot of practice, and even at the end of the trip, we would sometimes forget, betrayed by our curious eyes.

At last, tired out, we looked for rickshaws to return us to our hotel. This time Ed settled on the fare before we started out, and I climbed onto the high, narrow seat, with the expectation of enjoying myself thoroughly all the way home. Immediately my driver took the lead, turning down an incredibly narrow alley, and barely missing pedestrians, cows, and stray dogs as we whistled along. After a particularly narrow squeeze, I laughed aloud, and I caught a glimpse of my driver's white teeth as his dark face split in a delighted grin. Instantly he speeded up to a furious pace, and I held onto my seat with both hands as we careened down one tiny alley after another, while pedestrians leaped for the safety of doorways on either side. Even the normally placid cows stepped aside in alarm as they saw us coming, the whites showing around their soft brown eyes. Once I turned to see if Ed was still behind us—he was, hanging on for dear life—but I didn't dare take my eyes off the road ahead for more than a moment. I was helpless with laughter, and my driver, hearing it, was inspired to an even faster pace. When at last we arrived at the hotel, we were all exhausted, our drivers from the tremendous effort of propelling us at such a speed, and we with the laughter we hadn't been able to stop. Weakly climbing down, we gave each driver a large tip and shook hands all around. They waved as they left, still grinning, and we turned to enter the hotel.

Our room, once the air cooler had been operating for a short time, was a cool, peaceful refuge from the crowded street that we had left. We bathed, changed into fresh clothes, and lay down on our beds, intending to rest for just a little while before going out again to see Delhi after dark . . .

At some time in the middle of the night I woke briefly feeling chilly, pulled the covers over me without bothering to get undressed, and slipped back into sleep. We woke up to broad daylight and the sun streaming in the window.

"What shall we do today?" I asked dreamily, still lying on the bed and wiggling my toes. I turned over all the delicious possibilities in my mind as I lay there . . . what could be more wonderful than waking up in a nice little hotel room in India after a ten-hour sleep, knowing that I had nearly three months of similar mornings ahead of me, and wondering what adventures we would share that day!

Ed was lying on his bed too, pouring over *India—A Travel Survival Kit* and *India on $15 and $20 a Day.*

"How about the Railway Museum? It sounds good—they have one of the largest collections of antique railway locomotives in the world. And do you want to go to the zoo? It says here they have fourteen white tigers!"

"God, yes! You know how I love zoos, and remember that article *National Geographic* had about the white tigers? I've wanted to see them ever since. I want to see the Qutb Minar (however you pronounce it) and the Iron Pillar too. I think they are in the same area. Do you think we have time for all of them? It's too bad that we have to leave for Jaipur tomorrow morning. I wouldn't mind staying another day here."

Ed had put down the books and was looking over a large map of Delhi. "Zoo first. Then the Q . . . whatever-it-is Minar and the Iron Pillar. Back to Connaught Circus for lunch and then the Railway Museum in the afternoon."

By that time I was up and brushing my teeth with soda water from a bottle we had purchased the day before. "What about breakfast?"

"Breakfast downstairs I guess, in the Mughal-e-Azam."

But the little restaurant below the 5-Star Guest House was closed for some reason, so we made do with a package of commercially packaged cookies called Glucose Bisquits and a bottle of pop each which we purchased in a tiny stall just down the street from the hotel.

The zoo was in New Delhi and a long way from Old Delhi and our hotel, so we chose a three-wheeled scooter-taxi to take us there. The driver let us off at an imposing gate, and after paying the fee, we started down the broad path into the zoo, noticing that there were few other people around. It was blazing hot, for we were completely in the open at first, and we thought that might have been the reason for the lack of people. Soon, though, we came to the cages, and realized why Delhi Zoo was not a major attraction: it had a decidedly neglected appearance; it had been allowed to go to seed. It was depressing to notice the number of empty enclosures all overgrown with weeds, the fences rotting around them. We followed the signs to the section where the white tigers were kept, and instantly forgot the sorry state of the rest of the zoo.

What beautiful beasts! They were semi-albinos, with wonderful pale blue eyes and fur as white as snow between stripes which were coal black. The first one we saw was a magnificent male who lay regally on his side, head erect and paws extended, whose long, feathered tail twitched gently as he watched us with those crystal blue eyes. Two others paced the extent of their enclosure, which was well kept with green grass and several large trees to provide shade.

As we leaned on the surrounding fence, admiring the tigers, a small boy approached us.

"Mem and Sahib wish to see baby?"

"We would love to see the baby!"

He beckoned and we followed him around the side of the tiger house which adjoined the enclosure. Suddenly the little fellow stopped and put finger to lips meaningfully, then looked around with exaggerated innocence. We glanced behind us surreptitiously and noticed a zoo keeper watching. Trying to appear nonchalant, we walked along the fence, pointing to the tigers in the enclosure and pretending that the tiger house itself was of no interest to us whatsoever. The ploy was evidently successful, because the zoo keeper wandered off. The little boy, who I guess was an apprentice zoo keeper, quickly led us to a small door in the tiger house, unlocked it, and we went in, closing the door behind us. Inside were several cages containing tigers that were separated from us only by fragile looking iron bars and a couple of feet of space. The largest cage contained the baby and his mother.

He was only four months old, with blue eyes, big ears, and a "horse face," which seemed to be a characteristic of the white tigers. Ed bent toward him to take a close-up picture, and he rose, arched his little back, and spat at Ed, drawing his pink lips back from needle-sharp teeth, and pawing ferociously at us with one little clawed foot. His mother yawned and then eyed her fierce little one approvingly through half-closed lids. *She* wasn't going to get excited on such a hot morning. She reached out to pat him with one great paw, and he sank back against her and relaxed, turning his little face toward the fan that sat in front of the cage blowing a constant stream of cool air on the occupants.

We stayed until the fetid smell of raw meat, pretty high in the hot climate of Delhi, drove us out into the fresh air. It had been wonderful to

12

see the beautiful cats at such close range, and we tipped the little boy twice the price of admission (ten rupees) for providing us with such a thrilling experience. I think he was nearly as thrilled to get such a large sum as we were to see the tigers.

We continued our circuit of the zoo, seeing only a small herd of Axis deer before we made another exciting discovery. A fenced pool of thick, emerald-green water which lay beside the path upon which we walked suddenly made snorting noises at us. We stopped and peered into the depths, whereupon a large horn followed by a broad back rose to the surface of the water. Funny little ears rapidly fanned, sending droplets in every direction, and two piggy eyes stared into ours. The one-horned rhino seemed to be half hippopotamus as he exhaled, blowing bubbles in the water, and then raised his head again just enough to take a breath. He was certainly enjoying himself in the cool water, and I almost envied him, until I noticed again how thick and green it was. The one-horned rhinoceros, native to India's jungles, is on the endangered list and is a very rare sight, even in a zoo. We felt privileged to have seen one at all.

A giant red-headed crane peered disapprovingly at us from his enclosure as we left the zoo. He had a grey back and pretty white frills like pantaloons above his knees. Standing almost six feet tall, it was the largest bird, except for ostriches, that we had ever seen, and he exhibited a lordly dignity as he stalked along on his long, black legs.

"That's not a bad tally," remarked Ed, as we passed through the gate. "Three animals that we have never seen before. It doesn't matter that the zoo hardly had any others."

It was a good distance from the zoo to the Qutb Minar, which was a strange tower, eight hundred years old, and unlike any we had seen before: fat at the bottom, the fluted pink sandstone tapered as it rose. This would seem an obvious idea, but as far as I know, it is the only one of its kind. It was beautiful in its setting of green lawns and shiny green trees, and we lingered for a while before walking through a portico and across a broad expanse of stone paving to see the Iron Pillar.

The pillar, a slender column twenty-four feet tall, was a few hundred years older than the Qutb Minar. It is a mysterious fact that the metal has never rusted, and remains as pristine as on the day it was placed on its platform. A legend says that the person who can encircle it with arms *behind his back* will always have good luck. I was anxious to try.

Pressing my back to the warm metal, I tried to touch the tips of my fingers together on the other side.

"Am I close?"

"Nah. Nowhere near. Let me try."

Taking my place, Ed put his arms around the pillar and strained to get them together. His fingers were at least six inches apart, and though I grabbed his hands and pulled, I couldn't get them any closer together.

"Ouch. Take it easy."

"They're pretty safe promising good luck to anyone who can do it," I said. "No one has arms that long!"

A grinning young man approached.

"Sir, I show you. It is easy. Take the position once again."

He raised Ed's arms *above his head* and told him to try again. Magically his fingers met on the other side with little effort.

"Here, you try, Bunny."

My fingers met behind the pillar as well, and I felt quite ridiculously happy, considering that anyone knowing the secret would be just as successful.

We returned to Connaught Circus for lunch, as it was already past one o'clock and we were starved after our sketchy breakfast. After walking up and down a few streets near the circus, looking for a place to eat and trying hard to ignore the beggars who seemed particularly persistent there, we found a cool and quiet restaurant and ordered club sandwiches and mango juice, feeling guilty as we did so.

"They will probably have tomatoes in them and we'll die of salmonella," Ed said gloomily.

"Maybe not. They probably cater to lots of tourists here and know we're not supposed to have raw vegetables."

Of course the sandwiches contained tomatoes, but they looked so good and tasted so delicious that we finished them down to the last crumb, tomatoes and all.

"Maybe we should take a couple of Pepto Bismols," said Ed, prudently. We had read that the popular patent medicine had special properties which could actually prevent "Delhi belly" if taken as a precaution.

"Uh-uh. Not me. I hate the chalky taste. I'll wait to see if I feel sick first."

"I think I'll take a couple anyway. You got some?"

"Sure." I fished them out of my purse.

I was lucky that I didn't need "P.B.s," as we called them, in that instance. I knew that I should have taken them, but as long as I felt well, I was inclined to take chances. Later, of course, the odds would catch up with me.

14

When we returned to the hotel after all our sightseeing, we realized that our bodies had not completely adjusted to Asian time, for we were so tired that we gave up all thoughts of going out to dinner, and simply went to bed at dusk. After all, we had to get up early to catch the "Pink City Express" to Jaipur in the morning.

CHAPTER 2

Pink Elephants

The "Pink City Express" was a coach train that left Delhi early in the hot morning, heading southwest for Jaipur. It was going to be just a preliminary jaunt on our train journey—a mere day trip lasting a few hours.

The Delhi station had been busy, and comparatively ordinary. To us it looked much like any other Asian railway station, and we got aboard the train and into our very comfortable plush seats without incident. The car was full of Westerners, mostly British and French, plus one family in the American diplomatic service who were living in Delhi. We started to chat with the Americans in the desultory way one does on a train, and I let my eyes wander out the window as the train slowly chugged out of the station.

What were those men doing? A little group of them were squatting in a circle on the railroad right-of-way, chatting to each other. Beneath their bare bottoms were piles of—it couldn't be!—yes it was—shit. The words died on my lips as I stared, fascinated, until they were passed. There was another! And another group of three or four. I touched Ed's shoulder, and he followed my gaze.

"They're shitting," I whispered.

"Nah. They're just squatting there talking," said Ed, and started to speak knowledgeably about squatting being a natural and comfortable position to many Asians, and then his voice trailed off as he realized that they were, after all, shitting. He sat for a minute, like me, staring nonplussed at the unusual sight. Then he suddenly reached for his camera—too late. The last of the shitters had disappeared behind the train as we headed out for open country.

"I'm going to do a photo essay on shitters," said Ed happily. "It'll be the most popular part of our slide show when we get home."

The American family had been watching us with amused expressions.

16

"You'll see it everywhere," said the diplomat. "India's villages and suburbs, for the most part, have no sewage systems. The ugly black pigs you see everywhere are India's waste disposal units. They are herded through the areas of wasteland which are used for public 'outhouses,' and they do a damn good job of cleanup."

The country outside was flat and uninteresting, burned brown by the pitiless sun. Little mud and thatch villages sat close together, most of them separated by a mile or less of scrub desert. It was depressing to see, at this, the end of the hot season, and we turned with relief to conversation with our new friends, for we were eager to learn more about this strange country, especially from people who had been there awhile. The time passed swiftly, and soon we pulled into Jaipur Station.

Emerging into the blazing sunlight of the street, I was disappointed to find that Jaipur seemed just like any other city in Asia, with square, dull buildings of a uniform cream color. Where were the fabled pink buildings, the wedding cake decorations that I had read so much about? We looked around for a taxi or rickshaw, and soon were haggling with two rickshaw drivers over the price of a ride to the Bissau Hotel, which we had chosen from our guidebook. Eventually I found myself perched on the high, hard seat with my suitcase at my feet, starting down the crowded street. After going a couple of blocks, we turned a corner and passed through an enormous rococco gate, and the pink city lay before us.

Surely it was a dream, that impossible jumble of lacy pink, coral, terra cotta, rose- and peach-colored buildings, interspersed with large green trees. The streets were filled, not with cars, but with camels, cows, bicycles, rickshaws, strolling men and women in brilliant turbans and saris, and occasionally even an elephant with a painted face. Monkeys swung along the building fronts singly and in groups; some sat on the roofs watching the street. We raced through those incredible rosy streets entranced by the sights, the sounds, and the smells of incense, cow dung and flowers. We seemed to have been magically transported to another time, to a different world from the everyday one we were used to. I felt like Marco Polo, or Sheherezade, and I caught my breath with delight.

At last we came to Chandpole Gate, one of the nine city gates which enclose the rose pink city, and to the end of our fairytale ride. Outside the gate, the buildings became cream-colored again, and we turned down a muddy and crowded lane lined on both sides with fruit and vegetable stalls. Black water buffalo and white zebu cows jostled each other; little, dainty spotted goats picked their way through the crowd; hawkers cried out to the passing throng. The ditches along the sides were full of vegetable peels and indescribably filthy looking water. At an open space, pigs and dogs rooted through a pile of refuse, and I began to have my doubts about the location of our hotel. But before long, the lane became quiet and residential, and we pulled up to the Bissau.

The Bissau Hotel had been the guesthouse of a local prince; a charming, low, buff-colored building just outside the city gate (and therefore not pink), set well back from the road, with spacious green lawns and a fountain that splashed invitingly. A peacock haughtily paced up and down the lawn, and dozens of small birds were bathing in the fountain. The whole was shaded by huge peepul (pipal) and neem trees and sparked with the bright red of canna lilies. It was a cool, quiet oasis, especially after the noise and squalor of the lane.

We were met on the steps by a beautiful young woman carrying a box of ochre pigment from which she gave us each a *tilak* mark on our foreheads before showing us to our quarters. This mark is not, as is often thought in the West, a caste mark. It seems to have religious significance, but is often merely a decoration (smart young women have plastic "stick-on" tilak marks in different colors to match their costumes).

The room to which we were shown was simple but charming, with an "air cooler" like the one we'd had in Delhi. After freshening up, we went into the airy courtyard. We sank into comfortably cushioned rattan chairs, and, feeling like "sahibs" from the British Raj, ordered tea.

"Black tea, madame?" asked the turbanned attendant.

"No, milk tea. Readymade chai." I answered, quoting our book, and Ed nodded in agreement. We were looking forward to trying the national drink of India, which one of our handbooks had highly recommended. One part each of water and milk are boiled together and a handful each of tea and sugar are thrown in. The mixture is taken off the heat and stirred until the desired strength has been attained, and then it is strained off into the cup. Sometimes on special occasions, spices such as cinnamon, cloves and cardamom are added to the milk-water mixture. It sounded good to us.

"Not black tea?" our waiter hesitated, waggling his head from side to side.

"Milk tea, please," Ed answered, and the waiter moved away, glancing back once or twice.

"What do you suppose that was all about?" I asked. "I know that Indians always drink milk tea."

"Beats me. Let's look over our guidebook and see where we'll go today."

As we pored over our book, I vaguely noticed that a small boy, carrying a brass can, passed us on his way out to the lane. After a considerable time, he returned, carefully carrying the can, which was now full of milk. He disappeared into the building, and some time passed before our attendant reappeared with our tea and a steaming pitcher of boiled milk. As he poured, I repressed a giggle, and soon I was struggling to contain my laughter. "What is the matter with you?" Ed demanded, after our attendant had left. Wiping my streaming eyes, I told him my suspicions.

"I'm sure he went out to milk a cow for our tea," I said, weakly. "And then they had to boil it. No wonder they hoped we'd order black tea!"

Lunch in the dining room was lacking nothing, however. The food was Indian and absolutely delicious. We wolfed it down hungrily and hurriedly, as we were anxious to get started on our sightseeing. We had decided on the City Palace and the famous Observatory as our starting points.

Leaving the cool, green quietude of the palace grounds, we picked our way down the crowded lane. On foot it seemed less horrifying, somehow. A crowd of noisy children were playing tag until they saw us, then they stopped and shyly watched us as we started to pass them. Among them was one of the prettiest children we had ever seen, a dark-eyed princess in a bright red dress, about eight years old. Long black hair fell in deep waves over her shoulders, covering the torn sleeve of the tawdry dress, the color of which set off her eyes and her white teeth. Ed got out his camera and we asked the child if we could take her picture. Instantly all the children crowded around, eager to have their pictures taken too. Rather thoughtlessly I waved them off because we wanted her alone. Politely they moved away while we got the picture we wanted, and then happily posed for us afterward, when we took their picture to make amends.

We enjoyed our afternoon's sightseeing at the beautiful City Palace, where the most fascinating of the things we saw were two enormous silver jars which had been made to carry Ganges water for the Maharana of Jaipur to Queen Victoria's Diamond Jubilee Celebration (the old boy refused to drink or bathe in anything else). They are nearly five and a half feet tall and are the two largest solid silver items in the world.

In one of the upstairs rooms was a display of rich fabrics and articles of clothing worn by the various maharajahs and maharanis. There we saw the enormous tent-like clothing of one maharajah who was so fat that he caused the deaths of several wives on their wedding night from the weight of his body upon them. There was a photograph of one of the doomed maidens in the display. She had been a beautiful creature, dainty and petite, and I wondered at the venality of her father, who must have known of the awful fate awaiting his child when he arranged the marriage with the maharajah. I was abstracted and a little sad after that, and at first I was uninterested when Ed excitedly called to me that he had discovered a wonderful display.

"You've got to see this, Bunny. It's the greatest display of arms I've ever seen. I just looked in, and when I saw what they've got here, I had to come back for you. You'll get a real kick out of it."

He dragged me down the hall and into a section of the palace devoted to arms of every kind. The great thing about the display to me was the decorations on the pieces—the knives, swords, and even the rifles were so beautiful they could have been worn for jewelry. Heavy gold and silver set with diamonds, pearls, rubies, sapphires and emeralds graced the handles, and even the gun barrels were overlaid with precious metals and gorgeously engraved. Ed had been right; I loved it.

We also marvelled at how well-kept the grounds and the buildings were, and at the exquisite architecture, which even surpassed the beauty of Italy's public buildings. But the real wonder was, even though it was the height of the summer season for the western world, there were no crowds, and almost no tourists. We had the beautiful buildings, the lovely gardens and fountains nearly to ourselves.

After we had finished with the City Palace, we walked across the street to the wonderful Observatory, built by Maharajah Jai Singh in the eighteenth century. The place looked like a set for a futuristic science fiction movie, with its towers and staircases that ended in space, and the strange sunken hemispheres of marble designed to plot the movement of the stars. We climbed to the tops of the narrow flights of stairs which give one a breathless view of the area. We were most impressed with one enormous sun "clock" which told the time of day to within ten seconds. A double-curved strip of white marble, with the hours, minutes *and seconds* engraved on the lower edge, swooped dizzyingly beside a red sandstone staircase. I climbed up the steep stairs to where the shadow of the sun hit the marble, and I could actually see the shadow move along, counting off the seconds! It was strange to think that the maharajah who built this, over two hundred years ago, is completely unknown to Westerners, though he was undoubtedly one of the foremost astronomers of his time.

We returned to the hotel hot, tired and frazzled after the strenuous day. I started shedding my clothes the moment the door was shut behind me, on my way to the bathroom for a well-earned cold bath. During the Indian autumn or monsoon, water is never *cold*, only mildly cool, and it always caused a shiver of pure pleasure when I lowered my hot and sweaty body into a deep tub at the end of a long day. A bath and a change of clothes seemed to stimulate our appetites, and we would be ravenous when we approached the dining room. After dinner we would go to the library, which was furnished with antiques and memorabilia from days of the Raj, ostensibly to discuss our plans for the following day, but after a few minutes, our eyes would begin to droop and by eight-thirty we would both be ready for bed. This became the pattern of our days in India: to bed by nine, and up at seven.

The following day we set out early for our eagerly-awaited visit to Amber, the seventeenth century palace set high on a hilltop north of Jaipur. This time we hired a three-wheeler to take us there, as it was about an hour's drive through the open desert. Our driver, whose name was Sembu, steered us into an "emporium" along the way.

"Only a minute, madame," he pleaded. "No need to buy, just look."

"Why not," we said, mentally promising ourselves that we would buy nothing. Of course, we weakened after about two minutes, and I had a wonderful time picking out gorgeous little mirrored birds to give to some of the children back home. Later we discovered that a driver gets a percentage of any purchases made by his customers, but I'm afraid that we didn't add much to Sembu's pockets that day, because all the offerings in the emporium were so inexpensive.

Our drive took us past the sewage disposal pond for the city of Jaipur, which, as a good-sized Indian city, was on a sewage system. The water hyacinths which covered the surface of the water with lavender blooms purified the water naturally, without benefit of aeration apparatus. The pond itself, set amid the desert hills, looked like a charming lake.

"Look!" said Ed as we rounded a corner. The stone palace of Amber rose high above us, seeming to grow right out of the rock. Below it lay a placid lake, with one tiny island upon it. On the lakeshore just below the road, an elephant bathed all alone, his wet skin shiny black. This magical scene was suffused with early morning sunshine, making the barren hills around us pinky-gold. We were both silent as we approached the little village at the foot of the hill.

Our mood was shattered by a mob of hawkers the minute we stepped out of the three-wheeler. They crowded around, at first physically

21

preventing us from moving, but giving ground slowly as we steadfastly ignored them.

"Postcards!" "Peectures!" "See the preety beads," they carolled in their sing-song voices. Our driver rescued us by shooing them away (no percentage there!) and showing us where to buy tickets for our elephant ride to the top. We mounted the flight of steps to the platform from which we were to board our elephant, followed closely by the hawkers.

Out of a doorway in the great wall facing us, the huge lumbering elephant approached on padded feet, a mahout astride his neck, and an open howdah strapped to his back. He had an unusual face; pink, with dark grey spots on it almost like freckles. He lurched into position alongside our platform and leaned against it. Gingerly I sat down on the cushion, facing outwards, with my feet on a footrest which hung down from the side. The mahout snapped a safety bar over my knees and then the elephant turned around and presented his other side to Ed, who sat down with his back to me. We set off at a slow, measured pace up the steep path to the palace. I had the outward-facing side, so I enjoyed a sweeping view of the well-maintained gardens and the lake beyond. It was a popular pathway, with throngs of Indians on foot and, behind us, other elephants carrying other groups of two or four. I was glad that we weren't walking up the unshaded path, as the sun was already hot in the cloudless sky.

Amber is a wonderland of mirrored rooms, marble platforms, well-kept green courtyards, and airy turrets which hang far out over the valley floor below. Exploring it was fun because the guards let us go where we wanted, and never made us feel that we couldn't touch anything. We even went into the old, unused section and explored the crumbling, dark, passages, rank with bat smell, and climbed to the highest pinnacles—alone and unwatched. We found one graceful turret at the top where we stood as swallows darted and swooped all around us, making us dizzy.

The morning slipped away while we enjoyed ourselves like children exploring an abandoned house. The sun was overhead and Ed's watch said it was nearly noon before our stomachs told us we had stayed long enough.

On the way back to Jaipur we decided to stop in at a bank before lunch to cash a few travelers' checks, as we were nearly out of rupees. Our driver let us off at the "foreign exchange" bank near the railway station and promised to wait for us.

The bank was large and crowded with long lines of people at most of the tellers' wickets. The windows, set high in the walls, were merely iron grills without glass in them, and little birds darted in and out freely, fluttering around their nests which were built on top of the hanging light fixtures. No one paid them any attention. Clerks scurried around behind the counters carrying piles of papers from one desk to another, and other employees busily wrote at their desks. Dusty papers were stacked everywhere, up the walls and on tables. At least a dozen fans whirled lazily overhead, keeping the air moving and the temperature to a bearable level.

We approached a counter that did not have a long line in front of it.

"Pardon me, we would like to cash some travelers' checks," said Ed to the pretty young lady in a chic flowered sari who sat behind the counter.

"No problem, sir," she smiled, and opened a little gate. We followed her to the office of a portly man in a wilted white shirt and tie, who motioned us to sit down, pulling up a chair for me.

"Would you like a sweet soda?" he asked.

"I would love one," I said, amazed, "thank you very much."

He called to a clerk and spoke to him in rapid Hindi. After a little wait, the clerk brought in two glasses of cola and three identical forms. While we sipped, the portly man, who seemed to be a person of some importance, filled out all three forms, carefully reading each one over as he finished it. At last he handed Ed the stack of papers.

"Sign your name twice on each form," he said, "and then your wife must sign each one twice as well. May I see your passports, please?"

He read each passport and then turned to the visa pages and read them. We signed each form as requested, one signature just below the other.

"Please wait here," he said, smiling, and left. We finished our drinks and sat. The whirling fans and buzz of voices lulled me into a soporific state and I dozed.

"Now if you will please take these tokens over to window number twenty, they will take care of you," the manager said as he reentered the office. He shook our hands and ushered us out of the office. We took the heavy bronze tokens over to window number twenty, noting that nearly everyone had left the bank. The clerk inside the cage was counting stacks of money. He accepted our tokens and handed them to another clerk who took them away. We sat down in a couple of the chairs that lined the walls and waited. The fans droned and I sank into another doze. Finally the clerk called out to us and we stepped up to the cage to collect our money. He counted it carefully, turned it over, and counted it again. Then he counted it into Ed's hand, and we were free. The clerk followed us to the door, opened it, and locked it behind us. The bank was then closed until four o'clock.

"That took exactly forty-six minutes," said Ed, as we approached our three-wheeler. Our driver had climbed into the back seat and was draped over it, one leg crooked against the side wall, the other dangling outside, sound asleep. "Next time I think we'll try the hotel desk instead."

"They won't give us as good a rate," I protested.

"Who cares. Wake up," he said to Sembu.

After lunch at the hotel, we set out to explore Jaipur. We had our rickshaws drop us off on a main street, and then turned off it right away into an interesting narrow alley before I realized that there were open concrete urinals on either side of the entrance. Both were occupied, and I averted my gaze and passed them. A lingering whiff followed me for a few steps before we came to the "Saree Bazaar." Open stalls, raised above the six-foot wide stone street, lined both sides. Each had walls and floor padded and upholstered in white muslin, and gorgeous saris in all colors hung in the entrances and were stacked against the walls. Customers were comfortably seated inside many of the stalls, choosing from piles of glowing material. We paused to watch a mother and her pretty young daughter choose a wedding sari of scarlet silk, encrusted with golden sequins so that it sparkled with points of light. Many a shopowner called out to me as we passed, hoping to make a sale to the tourists. As I lingered at one stall, Ed tugged at my arm.

"We're sightseeing, not buying," he urged. "Come on."

"It would be different if I were looking at antiques," I teased.

He grinned guiltily, but continued to urge me on. Shopping for clothes is not his favorite pastime.

A beggar dressed up in a gaudy outfit and with a painted face, carrying a begging bowl of gigantic proportions, accosted us. He was so unusual that Ed took his picture and added to the collection of coins that half-filled the bowl. A passerby stopped to tell us that the beggar was the most successful in Jaipur.

"Does his costume mean anything?" I asked curiously.

"No. He just dresses up like that because more people give him money," said the young man, laughing.

Further along we came to the *pani puri wallahs* stalls. Pani puri is a popular snack in India. It is a puff of fried dough, like a cream-puff, but filled with tamarind water. The spicy, tart liquid is a piquant counterpoint to the rich pastry. I bought and ate one despite Ed's protests and was none the worse, although pani puri is reputedly just about the worst thing for a tourist to eat, because of the water, no doubt unboiled, which is used to fill them. Down another street were the sweets sellers—all the delicious sticky sweets of India—*gulab jamun, jalebis, barfi,* and other less well-known varieties, attractively displayed on open tables. They were usually covered with flies, but that never seemed to bother the Indian customers, for those stalls did a brisk business! Beyond them were men making candy—they beat pans of milk and sugar into a froth, and, squatting there with their bare feet on the padded muslin, scooped out little gobs of the fluffy white foam onto the muslin in rows of mathematical neatness with motions almost too quick to follow. The sweets hardened into the delicious little mounds which are given to worshippers in the temples. Rock candy, plain granulated sugar, and cakes of brown sugar were sold in this section.

Stepping carefully over piles of garbage for the cows, piles of shit for the pigs, and drainage ditches of disgusting black water, we picked our way past temples, holy men, monkeys, machine shops, ledger binders, book presses, and bakeries. This was triple-distilled India—filthy, gorgeous, poor, fascinating! All manufacturing and cooking took place on the street in little open stalls and we could watch to our heart's content. Everyone smiled and seemed pleased that we were taking such an interest. Everyone was happy to have his picture taken—even holy men willingly posed for our cameras. We found a Nandi temple, where I bought a leaf packet of jasmine and other fragrant flowers for one rupee (about ten cents) from an old woman selling them for the temple. I only had a two-rupee coin, so I gave it to the ancient crone, collected my flowers, and turned away, feeling that she could probably use the money anyway, but she followed me with the change. We went into the temple and enjoyed the atmosphere and the sweetness of the incense and flowers. Because I didn't deposit my offering flowers at the brass image of Nandi the Bull, but kept them instead, I got a tongue-lashing from the old lady as we left. Fortunately, it was in the local dialect, so I didn't understand what she said. Judging by her intonation, it was probably pretty colorful.

At the lacy wedding cake building known as the Hawa Mahal (Palace of the Winds) several snake-charmers sat on the sidewalk with their baskets of black cobras before them. They played their flutes and the snakes swayed, looking convincingly lethal. They had been defanged, though, poor things, and would only last a year or so on the milk diet which was force-fed to them. Without fangs, they could not swallow mice. There must have been an endless supply of cobras out in the hills, however. There seemed to be no lack of snakes or snake-charmers in Rajasthan.

We called a couple of rickshaws and spent a lovely half hour zipping along the rose pink streets. The low sun tinted the beautiful tattered buildings. Whole families of monkeys scampered along the house fronts, and leapt from tree to tree. The shining green ashoka trees were full of swallows settling down for the night and chattering to each other about it. The streets were full of people, all out for their strolls in the cool of evening. The smell of incense and of *bidis*, the pungent Indian cigarettes, perfumed the air. We passed a wedding procession with a big brass band—the groom, with Christmas-tree tinsel in front of his face, sat on a gaily caparisoned horse with his little brother on the pommel in front of him. The brightly dressed crowd behind him clapped and laughed in happy celebration.

But India could be cruel too. A horsedrawn tonga collided with a bicycle, and the poor horse's hind foot became caught in the spokes of the bike. He reared and neighed, trying to free his foot, and then fell, screaming in pain. When we passed by later, he was lying there dead with his elderly owner still sitting by him, crying.

My driver, a wicked looking youth whose bloodshot eyes proclaimed an indulgence in *ganga* (marijuana), enjoyed going fast, and at each stop we had to wait for Ed and his slower charioteer. We spun out our ride for as long as our change held out, and finally pulled up at the hotel just as dusk settled over the most beautiful of India's cities.

ABU

CHAPTER 3

The Train

We were sorry to leave the delights and comforts of Jaipur, and both of us were secretly more than a little worried about the trip we were about to embark upon. It was to be the first stage in our train journey around India, and we had no idea what to expect. Our next destination was Mount Abu, a hill station high in the mountains above the Rajasthani desert. Our train would be waiting in the station, according to the itinerary put together so long ago in California.

We caught a three-wheeler to the station. It was very hot, and the dust hung in the air like haze as we stepped out of the taxi and dodged several beggars who hung around the station entrance. I made the mistake of saying "no" and making eye contact, which made me the immediate target of all the beggars. "Damn," I thought, as they followed me into the station. "Why can't I get used to looking right through them?" The well-dressed Indians milling around the platform had no trouble ignoring the beggars, but then, they were seldom accosted anyway.

The station had a smell that would become familiar in the weeks to come; a mixture of dung, diesel oil, tea, and, unexpectedly, flowers. Flies hovered just above the cement floor, settling for an instant and then taking off again, changing places with one another in a flurry of activity. They kept crawling over my bare feet in open sandals, and I had to stamp at intervals to discourage them.

I looked around, fascinated by the strange atmosphere of the station, while Ed searched for our carriage. People were lounging around on the floor, instead of standing or sitting on benches as they do almost everywhere else in the world. The men often lay right on the cement, but the women were usually comfortably seated on large cloths which they spread out around them, bags and boxes of food and supplies making little barriers between themselves and other family groups. Children

27

played and slept on the cloths, sometimes eating sweets from little paper bags, or suckling their mothers. Large white cows amiably trod through the open spaces between the families, picking their way carefully so as not to step on stray babies. Mangy curs sniffed around the corners, looking for dropped bits of food to eat, peeing on the supporting posts, and slinking away from passing men, who were apt to kick out at them irritably.

I had been standing there alone for quite a while when I began to fear that somehow our train might leave without us. Ed was out of sight, and I was growing tired of standing with both suitcases and my smaller bag at my feet, worrying that a passing thief might snatch one before I could stop him. Suddenly I was conscious of the heat, and the sweat running down the sides of my face and between my breasts. Suddenly I was tired, and longed to get on the train, sit down and relax. The flies buzzed around my feet, a little beggar woman was whining "Baksheesh" at me, and I wanted to cry. Where, for heaven's sake, was Ed?

At last he appeared, smiling. Obviously he had found our carriage. He grabbed our suitcases and led the way down the platform.

"Look," he said, indicating the window of a carriage with a large 1 written on the side.

There, posted in the corner of the glass, was a handwritten list of the first-class passengers. Our name, in spidery handwriting, was halfway down the list.

"That's why we had to make our reservations so far in advance," he chuckled. "They don't have computers."

"Or typewriters," I thought.

Since we had avoided the porters who prowled the station, we had to heave our suitcases before us up the steep steps of the carriage. Then we dragged them behind us down the narrow corridor until we found our compartment.

"This is it," Ed said, and I entered the hot, dark, airless little space.

When my eyes grew accustomed to the dark, I saw dusty grey upholstered benches—one on each side of the compartment. Two half-naked, bearded *Sennyasi*, or holy men, sat cross-legged on the right hand bench. Each was dressed only in a spotless loincloth. Their wrinkled old legs were crossed comfortably under them and their grey beards reached down their hairy chests.

The other bench was empty. Ours. The windows were tightly shuttered, the small table between them was broken and hanging forlornly from one hinge, and several flies circled around in the middle of the compartment. My heart sank as I thought of the weeks of travel ahead of us. Tears stung my eyes and I sank down on the empty bench. Ed eyed me sympathetically and set about opening the windows and raising the shutters. Instantly the gloom was dispelled and a faint breeze stirred.

I felt better at once and dusted off the bench, while Ed stowed our suitcases under the seats. Perhaps it wouldn't be so bad after all. I looked around, noticing that the windows were horizontally barred, and contained both shutters and dirty glass panes. These could be fully raised, allowing maximum breeze. The bench we sat on had a back that could be lowered, converting it into a reasonably wide bed. Above our heads was another bunk secured to the ceiling with chains in the corners. Little steps to the upper bunk were inset into the wall on the corridor side. On the ceiling were four fans, one for each bunk, which could be tilted for the best effect. As I gazed at them, they began to whir. Their steady hum was soothing, and the air moving across our sweaty faces was sweetly cool. Without them the compartment had been almost unbearable.

I became aware that the two old holy men were eyeing us balefully. "Goodness," I thought, "they certainly don't approve of us."

This was borne out almost immediately, because they gathered up their seating cloths, their begging bowls and their brass water bowls and quit the compartment, leaving it to us and to the flies eddying in the sunlight streaming through the window.

After what seemed like a long time, the train jerked into movement, and we rolled slowly out of the station. The pink and cream buildings of Jaipur gradually disappeared behind us, and then the Rajasthani desert, cruel in the blinding sunlight, glided past. Strange angular cacti had been planted in thick rows, making fences to contain the thin white cattle and the little goats that picked at the poor bits of vegetation that still survived. The monsoon was overdue, and the desert seemed to wait breathlessly for the rain. Leaning my arms on the window sill, I stared out at the barren landscape, wondering how anyone could manage to scratch a subsistence out of such soil.

Darkness fell suddenly at seven o'clock and we began to feel hungry. Was there a dining car on the train? We had no idea, so Ed set out to find one. After a time he returned, looking rather grim.

"No dining car," he growled "and I'm starving."

There was no bedding anywhere in the compartment either. It looked like it would be an uncomfortable night, and our gloom deepened. At this point, the conductor stuck his head in the door, and asked us something incomprehensible in Hindi. Shaking our heads, we signed that we could not understand.

"English?" we asked hopefully.

"No, no." He pointed to his mouth and rubbed his stomach.

"Dinner!" we exclaimed at once. We nodded with enthusiasm, hoping that he would understand.

Smiling, he waggled his head from side to side and disappeared down the passageway.

"Jesus, I hope you're right," groaned Ed. "My stomach thinks my throat has been cut. But I don't see how we're going to get dinner when there is no dining car or kitchen on the train."

Just then the train ground into a large station and we distracted ourselves by watching the activity on the platform. Vendors approached the train holding up trays of sweets and tea. We were afraid to try the sweets, as we had been warned against buying food from stalls or from street sellers, but we ordered chai from a thin youth who passed it through the window to us. It came in heavy glasses and I peered at mine dubiously; the glass looked as though it might have been hastily rinsed out but it certainly didn't appear to have been thoroughly washed.

"Thirty paise," said the youth, and Ed handed over a one-rupee coin, receiving several coins in change.

"Well, it's certainly cheap enough," I remarked, and gingerly tasted my tea. It was delicious. "What the hell," I thought, and started to drink it.

Just then a small boy appeared from the passage, carrying two metal trays. Dinner! He indicated that we should pay him, so Ed produced a handful of small bills and coins, and the little boy selected a few, after placing the trays on the seat.

I got my tray and inspected it. A large pile of rice was in the big compartment in the center, and there were two curries in the smaller spaces, yoghurt, and a serving of pickles. A stack of chapattis topped the mountain of rice, and I chose one of those to start. As I munched on it, I looked around for fork or spoon; there were none.

"When in India, do as the Indians do," I said as I dug in with my right hand. It was easier than I expected, and I soon learned to scoop up clumps of rice and dip them into the gravies. I managed the large pieces of meat and vegetables with the help of my chapattis. The curries weren't too bad, and the chapattis were certainly delicious.

"I think," said Ed with his mouth full, "that meals on this trip aren't exactly going to break us. So far this evening we have spent just over a dollar for the tea and both dinners."

As we ate, the train left the station, and soon we were rocking along again in the warm, dark Indian night. After we had finished eating, we put our trays down on the end of the seat, turned out the lights and watched the moon rise. Not a light was to be seen anywhere, yet we passed village after village, ghostly in the moonlight. We had heard that only about fifteen per cent of India's villages have electricity.

At the next station our trays were collected by the little boy, and we saw him leave the train with them balanced on his head. Meals ordered by the passengers were picked up at one station, and the empty trays dropped off at the next. I supposed that the boy with the empty trays simply caught a ride back on the first returning train.

A new conductor poked his head in the door. "Do you need bedding tonight?"

We were relieved at this latest evidence that India's train system is much better than it seems at first glance. At our affirmative, he disappeared onto the platform, and soon reappeared with a pair of incredibly shabby and dusty bedrolls, which we received in exchange for fifty cents worth of rupees.

"God, I hope it doesn't have bugs," I said, as I unrolled mine. It opened to reveal a crisply ironed sheet and pillowcase, both immaculate. The pillow enclosed in the clean pillowcase was dirty, lumpy and thin, but I quickly covered it up again and spread the bedding out on my top bunk.

At this point we were joined in the compartment by two young men, nattily dressed almost identically in white shirts with open collars, tight, dark-colored bell-bottomed pants, and pointy black shoes. They smiled shyly, lit cigarettes, and watched us with their large dark eyes.

"How in the world am I going to undress and get into bed," I thought "with them watching me?"

I rummaged through my traincase for my soap and sponge and started for the toilet at the end of the car. The door creaked open to reveal a tiny cubicle with dingy walls and an "Asian style" toilet (a stainless steel trough in the floor) at one side. A tiny steel sink, long unpolished, was on one wall, with a small dim mirror above it. Despite the rather grim appearance of the little room, there was none of the urine smell I had expected, and no evidence of waste or dirt. It was dampish, however, with drops of water on the walls and floor. Looking up, I discovered a shower head in the ceiling. Removing my dress and underwear, and thankful that I was wearing rubber thongs, I promptly took a shower, letting the cool water run over my hot, sticky body. I dried myself with my sponge, lacking a towel, and then washed it with soap before putting on my dress again.

Returning to the compartment, I decided that this was not the place to demand Western comforts, and simply climbed into the upper bunk wearing my cotton dress. It was none too clean, but it was comfortable enough and certainly preserved my modesty in the too-public compartment. I pulled the sheet over my legs and collapsed into instant sleep. It had been quite a day.

Sometime in the night I was awakened from a confused dream by loud cries. Disoriented, I lay in my strange bed for a long moment, wondering where I was and why it was so hot. More cries brought me to earth and I realized that the train was stopped and that there were people outside making those alien sounds. I looked down from my perch and found that I was alone. Ed and the two young men had gone somewhere, and for a moment I panicked; irrationally I felt deserted in that foreign place.

I climbed down from my high bunk and looked outside. The platform was alive with strollers from the train, and vendors were plying their wares. I spotted Ed drinking tea and chatting with one of the men from our compartment. He looked up and saw me peering from the window, waved, and started toward me carrying a cup of tea. He passed it in the window and smiled.

"Beawar," he said, indicating the station. "It is two-twenty a.m. You've been having a good sleep."

"Haven't you slept?" I asked, as I sipped my tea.

"Nah," he said. "I can't sleep on trains."

"You're in trouble," I remarked. "We have eleven nights to spend on trains on this trip."

Just then the whistle blew and all the passengers crowded onto the cars. I returned to my bunk as the train shuddered and gathered speed. The motion and rhythmic noise was soothing, and soon I was asleep again.

"Wake up," said Ed. "We're coming into Abu Station."

"It's still dark," I mumbled. "What time is it?"

"Five o'clock."

Moaning, I climbed down and stumbled to the toilet. A splash of cold water on my face revived me somewhat, and soon we had our suitcases stacked by the door. As the train slid into the station, two porters climbed in the corridor windows and grabbed at our luggage. We made half-hearted efforts to regain them, and then, secretly thankful that we weren't carrying them, followed the men down the platform, keeping them in sight easily because they carried our cases on their heads. It was a long way into the station, up over a bridge over the tracks and down the other side. I was more thankful than ever that we had turned over our luggage to the turbanned men ahead of us, who carried our heavy cases as if they had been pillows, their sinewy legs as tireless on the steep stairs as they had been on level ground.

"Where you go?" one of the porters asked, as we reached the front door of the station. "Taxi?"

"We want the bus station," said Ed. "Bus for Mount Abu."

"Okay-okay." They set off at a trot, heading down the main street, which was just beginning to lighten with the dawn. We followed uncertainly. How far *was* the bus station? I wondered. I looked around at Abu Station, which was a rather forlorn little place consisting of a few cement or mud huts, some jerry-built stalls, and one reasonably modern building right next to the train station. Our porters turned in at that building and deposited our bags within.

"How much?" said Ed.

"Ten rupees, same-same," said the elder of the two hopefully, waving his hand from one to the other.

"Ten rupees each?" said Ed unbelievingly. "It's only supposed to be eighty paise per bag!"

"Ten rupees," said the younger porter firmly.

Knowing Ed's soft heart, I broke in. "Three rupees each! Three for you and three for you." I poked Ed.

"Give them three each and a little change," I whispered. "That's more than they'd get from Indian travelers."

Reluctantly, they accepted what Ed gave them, and shuffled away disconsolately. They had hoped for a full day's wages from the "rich" tourists.

"I guess we should carry our own bags," I said.

"But then we would have to fight them off at the beginning, instead of just quarreling over the money at the end. Besides, I hate to see you carrying that heavy suitcase up and down all those stairs."

We entered the station and Ed went to the window to purchase tickets to Mount Abu. The bus wasn't leaving for another hour, so we had plenty of time to get something to eat. I looked over the food displayed on the counter. Mostly it consisted of sweets and what Ed called "gedunk," or junk food. The buns and cookies were all well wrapped, so we weren't afraid to eat them. We settled down to wait for the bus.

We were busy talking and didn't notice that the station had emptied of people until we glanced out the window and saw the bus pull into the station yard. An enormous crowd had materialized from nowhere and they literally flung themselves at it almost before it had stopped. Some even climbed in the open windows of the bus as it stood there, rocking gently from the impact of so many people climbing in at the same time.

At once we realized that we should have been out there before it arrived. We grabbed our suitcases and raced out to the bus, hoping that a seat would be left. Once inside, we looked around at the interior, which was already packed with people. Yes, there was one! I quickly sat in the seat before someone else could. Ed made his way to the front, where he found a seat facing backwards behind the driver.

A conductor appeared to take our tickets, and told us that our suitcases must go on top of the bus. Ed went outside to see that they got up there safely and that they were properly moored; when he returned, he stopped by to say that there was no tarp over them, and that there were no ropes holding them down—only the railing, about eight inches high, which surrounded the luggage area.

"Jesus, I hope they don't bounce off the bus," he groaned. "I won't think of anything else all the way."

"Don't worry," I comforted him. "They'll probably be all right, but even if we do lose them, all our valuables are in our shoulder bags, and we can always buy clothes if we have to."

"To fit me?" Ed glanced down at his large frame. I had to admit it was unlikely that we could find anything in India to fit him. For that matter, I was considerably larger than any Indian woman we had seen so far. We both have large Western bones, well layered with flesh.

"I'm not going to think of our luggage *at all*," I said firmly, and hoped I could stick to my resolution.

I had an aisle seat, and the windows were filthy, making it difficult to watch the scenery as we bounced along, so I concentrated at first on our companions, who filled the seats and overflowed into the aisles. My seat mates (we were seated three abreast on a bench which would have accommodated only two in the West) were a young couple evidently newly married. They had eyes only for each other, though their hands were primly folded in their laps and they kept an inch or two of seat between them. A little ancient crone in a threadbare cotton sari sitting in the aisle next to me had made a seat of the large bundle she had brought

34

aboard the bus on her head and was obviously enjoying the ride. A whole family of seven people—father, mother, four small children and a baby—were in the triple seat opposite. Most of the passengers were men, and they amiably talked and joked, often jammed four to a seat. Everyone was cheerful, and they were very polite to the pair of foreigners sharing their transport. The young couple ate continually from paper bags of delicious-looking "gedunk," and they always offered me a sample of each new foodstuff as it appeared. I was dying to try some, so I accepted a small amount each time it was offered. Without exception, the various mixtures of cereals and peanuts were powerfully spicy, burning my mouth and lips painfully, but they were also very delicious, and often had a tang of lemon or lime to modify the heat. In return, I was able to offer my new friends cookies which we had bought in the station. I found myself enjoying the ride more than I would have believed possible, considering the crowding and the heat. Soon we started to climb; the road twisted and turned in tight switchbacks, the heat subsided, and the vegetation changed from desert scrub to larger and larger trees, draped with vines, that loomed above the road, blocking the sun.

At the first stop, we climbed out into the sweet-smelling morning. Birdsong accompanied us as we washed the outside windows nearest our seats with our packaged moist towelettes, which we had brought along for cleaning our hands.

"That's a use I never thought we'd put them to," I remarked. "Good thing we brought lots."

I nudged Ed as a couple of small men wearing only loincloths boarded the bus. Each carried a bow and a quiver of arrows, which were beautifully made. Later the nice young couple explained that they were Bhil tribesmen who lived in the desert below, and that they were going hunting in the forest further up the mountain.

When I started to get back into my seat, my seatmates insisted that I sit next to the window, and I was able after that to enjoy the wonderful scenery as we climbed up and up the mountain. We were travelling through high, cool jungle, and, once or twice, large black-faced monkeys with pale fur swung from branch to branch above us. Sometimes at switchbacks I could see out over the jungle, down the mountain to the flat, barren desert we had left behind. I tried to forget the luggage, and also to forget that the driver was very fast, and that the precipitous road had no guard rails. We bounced and swayed alarmingly, and, though signs said "Horn, please" at every sharp turn, our driver blithely ignored them and took the blind corners on the wrong side of the road every time. Fortunately, we met few cars, and eventually we arrived at the hill station of Mount Abu all in one piece, along with our luggage which had miraculously remained in place. Ed climbed up onto the top of the bus to retrieve it, a wide grin of relief on his face.

The bus deposited us in the middle of town. A fine rain was falling. Mist made the buildings and the lush vegetation appear and disappear, and the air was chilly and dank. I shivered in my cotton sundress, as I was already accustomed to the dry heat of the desert which we had left behind.

"What do we do now?" I asked Ed. It was very quiet and still. No taxis were in sight, though we seemed to be right in the center of town. Before us was a bazaar or marketplace, which was strangely deserted. Buildings straggled up steep streets on every side, but hardly anyone was in the streets.

"It's only 7:30," said Ed. "It seems like mid-morning to us after getting up so early, but it's not time for anything to be open yet. I'm sure there will be a taxi stand somewhere around. What hotel are we supposed to go to?"

"The Mount Hotel," I answered, checking my itinerary. "But I have no idea where it is."

"You stay here while I look around and ask about a taxi. I won't be long."

While he was gone I sat on our suitcases and looked around. It was peaceful, quiet, and damp. Cold, too. I shivered again.

Ed soon returned in a taxi, and after a short ride up a steep hill, we were deposited in front of a charming low house of white stucco, with a red tile roof. As we approached, we noticed that an old lady was drawing an elaborate design in rice flour on the landing of the steps. I started to walk carefully around it, but the old servant smiled toothlessly at me, took my arm, and guided my steps right through the middle of the design.

Our host, meeting us, explained that the *rangoli* was placed there afresh each morning as a sign of welcome, and that it was supposed to be walked on.

"Rice flour designs like these are very common in South India," said Mr. Adil. "I think it is a pleasant custom, and one that our guests appreciate."

Later on, after our naps, and over cups of hot tea, we discussed the day's program. Our guidebook said that the Dilwara temples did not

36

open until noon, so we planned to visit a smaller but older temple first, as it was still only ten o'clock.

We called a taxi and climbed up the stairs leading to the road. The sun burst through the mist and long fingers of yellow light reached the ground through the branches of the trees, picking out orange and pink flowers in the garden.

"No wonder this was a popular hill station with the British," Ed remarked. "They did have a talent for finding the good spots. I can't believe how cool it is here in the middle of Rajasthan at this time of year."

The skies were blue and full sunshine was reflected by the golden spires when we arrived at the Siva Temple of Achalghar, built around 900 A.D. We removed our shoes a little nervously and left them at the door in the wall surrounding the old stone buildings. The stones felt damp and gritty beneath our tender soles, and we wondered if we'd ever see our shoes again.

"We're going to have to get used to it. We've got about a hundred temples on the itinerary," I laughed.

A beautiful bronze statue of Nandi, the bull—Lord Siva's mount—, graced the inner courtyard. He was draped with jasmine and marigold garlands, and his metal hide shone like gold from the caressings of many worshippers. Several small shrines surrounded the courtyard, one with lovely Hindu carvings in a frieze around the cornice of the ceiling, but it was the "inner sanctum" of the main shrine that caught our interest. Worshippers rustled past, the womens' saris brushing the stone beneath their bare feet, as they crowded into the sanctuary.

"I wish we could go in," I whispered. "But all the books say we can't. Only Hindus."

Our taxi driver appeared and beckoned to us. To our delight, he led us into the sanctuary after a whispered consultation with the Brahman priest. I looked around as we waited our turn to approach the altar inside. We were in a tiny round cell, crowded with reverent people. The circular wall was a colorful confusion of flowers, red ochre paste, and gold leaf. Candles were the only illumination; the dreamlike atmosphere was due to their wavering light and the heady fragrance of jasmine mingled with incense. The altar, when some of the worshippers had left and we were able to see it clearly, was covered with flowers surrounding a deep pit in the center. Strange stone figures seemed to grow from the surface of the altar, so delicate and thin that the candles behind shone through them with a dull yellow glow.

The Brahman priest chanted for a while, and then tried to explain to us in Hindi the significance of the pit and of the figures. We nodded and smiled, not wanting to hurt his feelings by too obvious a show of ignorance. He smiled also, and dipping his forefinger in a pot of yellow paste, placed a tilak mark on each of our foreheads. Then he handed each of us a delicious piece of sweet fudge and said *"Prasad."*

"I wonder what 'prasad' means," I mused as we were putting on our shoes. "A special blessing or something?"

Later we asked Mr. Adil about our visit to the temple. He told us that *prasad* meant "something sweet from the temple." ("Damn," I thought. "I wouldn't have minded a special blessing.") He also told us that the Achalghar temple was very unusual—it featured the toe of Siva instead of his "lingam" (penis) as an object of worship, and also that the pit in the altar is said to extend all the way to the underworld and can never be filled with water, no matter how much is poured into it.

It was full noonday when we arrived at the famous Dilwara Temples, which had been built by the Jains a thousand years ago at the height of India's greatest period of artistic power. There was a ticket stand at the gate, where we stopped to buy our entrance passes, and where we had to check all leather goods in addition to our shoes. A large sign set out the rules for viewing the temples: no leather of any kind may be worn, as it is produced by the killing of animals and so is strictly forbidden. No loud talk or "unseemly behavior" was allowed; but the most unusual rule was the prohibition of menstruating women. (They are considered "unclean" and might defile the temples by their presence.)

Side by side, with suitably bared feet and beltless middles, we passed through the gate. Immediately we were pounced upon by a tall old man with greying stubble on both his head and chin. His khaki shorts and shirt barely clung to the bony protruberances of his shoulders and hips. He tottered along on splayed old feet, and when he smiled, he displayed pink gums from which one or two yellow snags still hung.

"Guide," he croaked. "I good guide." He talked on rapidly in a high, broken falsetto. Occasionally he said a word or two that we could understand, but most was lisped in an English—if it *was* English—that was completely incomprehensible. I looked imploringly at Ed, but I saw him weaken before my eyes.

"No," I thought. "Please, no."

"Okay," said Ed.

With a beaming smile, our "guide" led us into the first temple. A shining line of white marble elephants, about half life-size, met us in the entry hall. I started down the line, admiring the individual details of howdahs and harness on each elephant, and the varying expressions on their benign faces. Behind me I could hear our old tour guide, his voice rising and falling, and Ed's grunts in reply. Cruelly I kept well ahead of them, and entered the main hall.

Before me, upon a shining marble floor, rose column after column of exquisitely carved white marble. Each column, different from every other, was covered with figures of stalwart men, lissome women, animals and birds of every description. Frozen lotuses in the act of opening, horses caught while leaping, frogs just at the point of diving into marble pools, marvelous mythical creatures . . . a pantheon of gods, captured forever by their sculptors. Around the periphery walls were niches, and in them sat curious black marble figures with crystal eyes, a hundred versions of the Jain deity. As I stood there watching, two little laughing girls, their filmy scarves floating behind them, ran in and out of the niches.

I looked up and saw the most wonderful sight of all. The ceiling of the temple had been divided into sections, and each section was a shallow dome of carved decoration so beautiful and so delicate, it was difficult to believe that human beings had actually cut them out of rigid marble.

I wandered slowly through the temple, and then through two more of equal beauty, the satiny floors cool beneath my bare feet. Every now and again I would drift into earshot of poor Ed and our guide, but only once, briefly, did they catch me in a moment of carelessness. I endured only a couple of minutes of the guide's spiel before I fled, leaving Ed to face the music.

At last we started out to the entrance, the old man shuffling behind us, still talking. At the gate, Ed pulled out five rupees and offered it to the old man, feeling, as he said later, both virtuous and kindly for giving him what Ed considered to be a generous tip.

"Ten rupees!" our guide cried, for once intelligible. "Ten rupees!"

I laughed. "Live and learn," I teased. "You and your soft heart."

Grimly Ed gave the old man five more, and after he had gone, turned to me.

"The old bastard," he growled, "I couldn't understand a word he said! But I know one thing: from now on, no guides."

Late that afternoon, we walked around Lake Nakki, which is the focal point of the town. A woman was beating her washing with a stick along the shore, and swallows darted and swooped just above the water ("Gorging themselves on mosquitoes, no doubt," said I, slapping at one). Lovers strolled along the path around the lake, for Mount Abu is a favorite spot for Indian honeymooners. Ed took my hand as the sun set mistily behind the tall trees that surrounded the little lake.

"I love India," I said dreamily. "I really do. It is a different world from the one we've been used to."

CHAPTER 4

The Ecstasy
and the Agony

We took a public bus from Mount Abu to Udaipur after we discovered that the train connections were so poor that it would have taken two days to get there by rail. The bus was old, dirty, noisy and crowded. We were so new to bus travel in India that we did not realize that seat reservations were necessary, and so had to move from seat to seat as new people got on. Before the bus had even started, we found ourselves seated at opposite ends of the vehicle. Reservations applied only at terminals, however, so eventually as people left at stops, we got seats together. We washed our windows at the first opportunity and settled down to enjoy ourselves just watching the passing scene. When we started, it was comfortably cool in Mount Abu, but as we descended the mountain toward the desert below, the air became progressively warmer until, once more at the bottom, it was even hotter than we had remembered.

The rolling desert extended out ahead of us in the yellow sunlight, but in the west great black clouds had gathered on the horizon. I leaned my arms on my open windowsill and watched the clouds rolling toward us. A wind swept ahead of them, picking up the desert dust and hurling it at us, making me draw back and close my window. All up and down our side of the bus, people were slamming their windows shut against the storm, though the windows along the other side remained open. Suddenly a strong smell of damp earth filled the bus and almost immediately the skies opened and a cascade of water thundered over us, drowning out the sound of the engine. Windows were opened and faces turned to the raindrops, heedless of the wet. The bus slowed as water gathered on the road, making it a shallow river through which each wheel cut like the prow of a boat.

Though I relished the new coolness of the damp air, and though I noticed the pleasure on the faces of the other passengers, my heart sank with disappointment at the onset of the monsoon. I was looking forward to Udaipur, and I did so want to see it in sunshine. I suppose I had got my ideas about the monsoon from novels, because I thought that the rain would be more or less ceaseless for weeks or months. How wrong I was, for after a half hour's heavy downpour, the rain became a drizzle, and then ceased altogether. In a little while the clouds parted and soon the sun was pouring down on a steaming landscape.

Ahead of us a flash flood streamed over the road, and a cascade poured over the edge of the pavement. Below the road on our right a big truck lay on its side, looking obscenely like the dead cattle we had seen in Mexico, with their swollen legs sticking straight out. Our driver slowed the bus to a crawl, and we inched through the racing water, keeping well away from the edge. As we arrived safely on the other side, we waved to a little group of men, one of whom was undoubtedly the truck driver, and they waved cheerfully back. Their unperturbed attitude seemed to say, "Who cares about a little accident? The monsoon has arrived at last!" The ditches were brimming, and in one, a little group of women and girls were bathing and splashing each other with muddy water, laughing delightedly.

We stopped in a nameless little town where we were allowed half an hour for lunch. Little stalls for hot food were set up under the one big tree and the passengers all bought *pakoras* and *samosas* fresh and hot from a big pot of boiling oil. We hestitated to try them, but then we reasoned that germs could not live in such high temperatures, and we dipped right in with the rest.

After our lunch and a couple of bottles of Limca, we strolled through the town to the outskirts and were just about to turn around and go back, when Ed spotted a crowd of vultures just sitting along the ditch at the edge of the road a couple of hundred feet away. Curiously, we approached the big birds, expecting them to fly away as we drew near. They ignored us, intent on something down in the ditch, and we craned our necks as we approached, trying to see what they were so interested in. At the bottom of the steep decline, two bony dogs were tearing at the freshly skinned carcass of a large water buffalo. When the dogs saw us, they scuttled away, snarling back over their shoulders. Instantly, twenty or thirty of the huge grey birds lurched down the embankment and clustered over the carcass, hiding it from view. They tore at the flesh, rattling their feathers audibly in sort of a feeding frenzy, while the rest of the birds, perhaps a hundred more, sat hunched all around the carcass, politely waiting their turn. We would have waited for the "change of shift" but a blast on the horn of our bus summoned us, and we reluctantly boarded just as it set off again.

Three hours later we arrived in Udaipur, tired, hot, and half deaf from the noise of the bus. The rain was a long-ago memory, and the sun was in its accustomed place high in a pale blue sky when we descended shakily at the bus terminal. Ed climbed up to the roof of the bus to locate and hand down our suitcases, which were still slightly damp underneath from the downpour. A three-wheeler took us to a gate through which a road led to the jetty of the Lake Palace Hotel. Only taxis or charter buses were allowed past the gate, so we paid off our driver and dragged our luggage behind us up the road for a hundred yards. We reached the crest of a little hill, and the Lake Palace lay below us.

In the middle of the blue lake, which was surrounded by steep hills, the white marble palace floated like a dream, its minarets and turrets giving it a fairytale air. A single large green tree trailed its branches over the delicate walls on one side, and the sun glinted on the water. As we approached the wide steps which led into the lake, a launch detached itself from the hotel and chugged slowly across the intervening water toward us. It had a colorful canopy with scalloped edges and padded seats around the perimeter, and a motor which went "pocketa-pocketa" in the traditional fashion. We were helped in and settled ourselves at the front where we had a good view as the boat plowed through the choppy waves over to the Lake Palace. When we docked, uniformed and turbanned attendants grabbed our luggage and carried it inside while we walked empty-handed into the palatial marble lobby.

The Lake Palace Hotel was our big splurge of the trip. It cost about twice as much as our usual accommodations, but my feeling as I crossed the thick purple carpet was that it was going to be worth it.

The door of our room opened onto the central garden with its fountains and formal flower beds, but the windows looked out onto the lake and the City Palace across the water. The air conditioner hummed sweetly, the beds were soft, and the bathroom was large and tiled in gleaming white. After our long and dirty bus trip, it looked like paradise. Dropping my clothes along the way, I headed for the bath and turned on the cold water. It was hot, so I tried the hot water. It was also hot. I turned the cold back on and let it run, but after five minutes it was still steaming. Finally I filled the tub to the brim and took a sponge-bath in the sink, postponing my real bath until the water had cooled.

Meanwhile, we went out to explore the palace, taking our bathing suits with us in case the hotel had a pool. We found it at last, tucked alongside

43

the single large mango tree which we had seen from the shore. The pool was set into a marble pavilion surrounded by pierced marble walls which looked out over the lake. Little gazebos punctuated the wall in two places, each of them topped with three crystal finials which sparkled in the sun. There was a tiny lawn on one side of the pool, half shaded by the big tree. There wasn't a soul around. We spent the rest of the afternoon there, alternately swimming in the limpid water, and lying on cushioned chaise longues which had been thoughtfully provided for hotel guests. It was heaven.

When the shadows grew long, we returned to our room where I bathed in the now cold water and got into the one pretty dress I had brought that was suitable for such a grand occasion. We went out into the gathering dusk.

"It's still too early to eat," said Ed. "Let's walk around a bit more before we go in to dinner."

As we strolled through the gardens, I happened to glance up. A big bird flew over the roofs of the palace, flapping its wings in a peculiar way.

"Is that a bird? No, it's a bat! Good heavens, it's huge. Look, there's another!"

Ed said "Come on. I think we can get up onto the roof. I saw a stairway just outside our room."

As we emerged onto the roof, a marvellous sight met our eyes. Out of the hills behind the City Palace streamed a cloud of thousands of giant bats, heading our way. They came over the roof where we stood, only a few feet above our heads, flapping their huge wings in measured cadence. We could hear their cries, a faint chorus of squeaks as they passed overhead. The full moon shone eerily, silhouetting the sinister shapes against a glowing dark blue sky. Further out in the lake, hundreds more circled just above the water, their bodies black against the reflected radiance of the moon. We stood there watching until the last of them had crossed the lake and disappeared behind the high hills on the other side.

"Wasn't it wonderful?" I breathed. "I think they must have been fruit bats . . . what are they called? . . . flying foxes! I've never seen a sight like it before."

"What amazed me is that we could actually hear them. I thought their squeaks were supposed to be ultrasonic. Maybe it's because they are so large. They must have had wingspreads of three or four feet."

As we started toward the stairway, Ed stumbled over something, and started to laugh.

"Here's why your cold bathwater was hot," he chuckled. "The water pipes come right across the roof. During the day the sun must get that water nearly up to the boiling point. You'd better take your bath first thing in the morning."

We entered the nearly empty dining room and were ushered to a small table near the window. The only other occupants were three people at a large table next to ours. They hailed us.

"Why don't you all join us?" called the very red, very large man, while the two women smiled and beckoned. We moved to their table, glad to be able to talk to other Americans, and eager to hear how they felt about India.

"We're Ed and Bunny Knott from California."

"Alvin and Kate Neuman from Missouri," said the fat man, "and this here is Eileen from New York." He was kind and pleasant, and so was his plump and quiet wife. They looked like the well-to-do farmers that they were. Eileen was different; a little, skinny, dark woman, she jangled with heavy gold jewelry. Her voice was shrill, and her mouth was hard in a seamed, wrinkled face.

"Take this away, it is not what I want," she commanded the waiter imperiously, when he placed the plate before her.

"But Madame, is it not what you ordered?" he stammered.

"I don't like it. Take it away and bring me something that I can eat," she said in a loud voice, causing the headwaiter to come hurrying over.

"Madame," he said smoothly, "of course we will get you what you want. Do you wish to order something different?"

"I want something that I can eat!" she said harshly. "Bring me some chicken."

She drew herself up triumphantly. "And I want coffee now." She smiled, satisfied at the stir she had caused.

I turned to Alvin and Kate. "What made you come to India?" I asked. "How do you like it?"

"Well now, it seems a mite strange to us," said Alvin. "We wanted to see the world now that we've retired, so we found ourselves a guided tour. But you know," he smiled apologetically, "it's so different from home. Kate here is kinda homesick. And I don't much like the food. I'll be glad when we can have a good ol' American steak and potatoes."

Kate nodded. "We've been to Europe and then Egypt and now India. From here we are supposed to go to Thailand and Hong Kong, and then Japan and Hawaii. But I'd be happy just to go home now." She sighed. "I miss my grandchildren."

45

"Where is the rest of your tour group?" I asked.

"Just the three of us wanted to come to the Lake Palace, it was an optional extra," she said. "We had heard so much about it. The rest are in Delhi. It is beautiful here, isn't it?"

Eileen's chicken arrived. We all watched apprehensively while she tasted it.

"I guess it will have to do," she snapped. She ate a few bites, put down her knife and fork and lit a cigarette, tapping her foot impatiently.

"How do you like India?" I asked Eileen.

She tossed her fashionably coiffed head. "It's dirty and backward. I like the Riviera. They know how to treat you there. And I love the casinos."

"Have you done much travelling?"

"I travel all the time. I can afford it since my husband died. Next month I'm going to China. Then I'll spend a month cruising in the Caribbean. That's in October. I go to Switzerland for the skiing every winter."

Our dinners were excellent, but we found that we were not enjoying them as much as usual. Ed said that the sight of Eileen's smoldering cigarette butt in her plate of chicken positively put him off his food, and her conversation annoyed me enough to put me off mine. I kept thinking of the people whose vacations she would spoil. I'd had enough of her in one hour.

After they left, our food tasted better. When we looked over the dessert menu, I noticed that *paan* was available.

"Let's try it," I urged Ed. "My Indian cookbook at home has a section on paan. It is made of areca nut and powdered lime, sometimes with sweetened coconut, and maybe a little powdered tobacco and flavorings, wrapped in a fresh betel leaf. Do you want to try it?"

"I don't know," he said dubiously. "What about the fresh betel leaf? Would it be safe to eat?"

"I don't care. I want to try it. How about ordering me one?"

"Oh, hell. All right. I guess I'll have one too."

The paan came on a silver plate with a lace doily. Delicate silver foil partially covered the deep green rolled-up leaves. They looked awfully large, too big to pop into one's mouth. I picked one up and bit into it. A delicious flavor burst into my mouth—it was sweet, juicy, and fragrant. I chewed; it was heaven. I continued to chew, but the mass in my mouth did not soften or disintegrate. Instead, it seemed to swell, and soon the flavor left it. I chewed.

46

"Mmmph," I mumbled to Ed, through my full mouth, "I can' shwallow i'."

Ed gulped manfully. "I got mine down. Try."

"I can'. Shee you ou'shide," I muttered and fled. Once out in the garden, I removed the large plug from my mouth and deposited it under a bush. Paan may taste like heaven, but until they make it dissolvable in the mouth, I think I'll have to do without.

We spent the next couple of days relaxing, swimming in the beautiful pool, taking long boat trips around the lake and shopping in the town of Udaipur. We visited the City Palace, the largest palace in Rajasthan, and haggled for old silver in the bazaars. It was a lovely and peaceful interlude, and each evening we returned across the lake to the Lake Palace as the pigeons settled down for the night along the roof edges and the window sills, cooing and chuckling to themselves in the early dusk, just before the flight of the bats.

Then our time was up, and after a last, lingering look at our fairytale palace, we took ourselves to the railway station on a cloudy afternoon. Workaday India greeted us as we descended from our three-wheeler—a smiling lad knelt on the sidewalk kneading a mountain of dough on a ground cloth. I stopped to watch him, thinking that raisin bread was a strange thing to see in India, and then realized that what I had thought were raisins were flies. A large fruit bat hung from a power line just above our heads; his wings were horribly tangled in the wires, and his lips were drawn back from his needle sharp teeth in a death grimace. He was as repulsive in death as he had been graceful in life, and I turned away with a shudder. A couple of beggars followed us into the station, and a porter eagerly took our bags.

This time the train was a few minutes late, but soon we were settled down comfortably in a nice, clean compartment with the paperbacks we had purchased in Delhi. It started to rain gently, and the temperature was reasonably cool. The train wended its leisurely way through the low hills which were already turning green with the monsoon, and stopped at nearly every little town along the way. We ordered and ate our dinners at dusk, and then watched a thunderstorm for a while before picking up our books again. The Indian night was as black as the inside of a cave, relieved only by occasional flashes of sheet lightning or the flickering light of an oil lamp in the window of a village house. Our bedding hadn't arrived, and I started to snooze as I sat, the nodding of my head waking me now and then.

Suddenly a new conductor appeared at the door.

"Sir! Madame! Quickly, you must gather your bags and come!"

47

"Huh? What?"

"Come quickly, sir! Here, I take this bag for madame, you come now! This train will miss Bombay mail. We must get out!"

The train came to a shuddering halt as we hastily grabbed our belongings. Bewildered and still sleepy, we stumbled along the corridor and then jumped the long drop to the ground outside. The train started up behind us and disappeared into the night, leaving us standing on the tracks with the conductor and our suitcases. A single bright bulb burned above a platform on the other side of the tracks, shedding a circle of yellow light. There seemed to be no town nearby, not even a house; just a deserted platform in the middle of nowhere. We picked our way across at least four sets of rails and then Ed and the conductor thrust our baggage up onto the platform, gave me a boost up, and climbed up themselves. We stood there, panting slightly, looking around. Not another light showed anywhere; we could have been alone in the world with the frog chorus and the mosquitoes and the moths circling the single unshaded light.

"What now?' I thought, a little panicky with the swiftness of our transition from the known to the unknown.

"Fast train due any minute," said our friend. "Do not worry, madame. You will be able to catch your train to Bombay."

Then we heard it coming, and in a minute or two it thundered to a stop all the way across the tracks. We jumped the three feet down to the rails again, and ran across the several sets of tracks to the train. Our conductor tried the handle on the door of the carriage before us, but it would not open. He jumped up and pounded on it and then tried the handle again. It opened inward only an inch or two, but we could see that the train was packed with people and luggage. The whistle blew and the train jerked forward a foot.

"Oh my goodness, the door must open!" So saying, our conductor grasped handles on both sides of the door and jumped up. With both feet he kicked the door open, knocking one man over and moving a pile of suitcases and boxes back a couple of feet.

"Get in, madame," he screamed, and shoved me from behind as I grabbed the handles and hauled myself up the three feet or so to the first step. The train was really moving now, and he and Ed frantically shoved the suitcases in.

"Get in," I shrieked at Ed, who was running alongside holding one handle. He managed to grasp the other and swung himself up as the train gathered speed.

"Goodbye," our benefactor called as we chugged away. We stuck our heads out to wave to him, as he stood there in the middle of the tracks, all alone in the night.

Our fellow passengers greeted us with nods and smiles as we looked around the carriage. We were in a second class sleeper car and it was crammed to capacity. Wooden platforms stacked three deep against the compartment walls held five or six passengers each, most of them seated cross-legged in the Indian fashion. Standees filled the spaces between them; these were nearly all men, for most of the women had seats. I was pushed over to the nearest bunk, and a young man who had been sitting with his wife and baby daughter got up and indicated that I should sit in his place. I tried to demur, but he smiled and moved away, so I sat down gratefully. The pretty young mother and I played with the baby all the way to Ratlahm station. Ed and the young husband stood the whole distance, about a two-hour ride.

At Ratlahm we caught the Bombay mail with only ten minutes to spare. We had no bedding, so we dragged pieces of clothing out of our suitcases to lie upon. We laid our heads on Ed's rolled up underwear and fell asleep right away. It had been a pretty exciting night.

In the morning we woke to gentle rain and increased heat. The windows steamed up from the humidity, but since they were open anyway, we didn't care. We watched the lush green countryside approaching Bombay, so different from the parched desert that we had left behind. A flock of brilliant green parakeets flew alongside the train, looking like windswept leaves.

The slums of Bombay greeted us as we entered India's great modern city. They stretched for miles; dismal collections of cardboard and corrugated iron huts, with rivers of mud between them. Pigs wallowed and snuffled around in the mire, but there were no cows, for cows could not survive in those dreadful conditions. It was terribly depressing to see; but even here, the fortitude and resiliency of the Indian people were evident. Young men in spotless white shirts and shiny shoes, with hair carefully combed, emerged from the grim huts, looking like young men going to work anywhere. Women in rainbow saris hung up their washing and drew water from the wells, and little children crouched in the muddy doorways, playing with pebbles or perhaps some discarded bit of household trash.

Bombay's towering skyline appeared ahead of us, looking like Chicago as we approached. The station was huge and crowded, modern and uninteresting. Outside there wasn't a three-wheeler or rickshaw in sight, so we hailed a taxi. Our hotel was uninspiring; a dirty pile of yellowish brick that looked like it had been built in the twenties or thirties. Our room was large and hot, furnished in the style of the twenties and never redecorated. The furniture was decrepit, with white rings and cigarette burns on all the wooden pieces. A tacky sofa upholstered in torn maroon vinyl stood against one wall, and two dispirited beds, sagging in the middle, held up the other. Dirty walls and torn lace curtains completed the inventory. And it was *hot*.

"How do you turn on the air conditioner?"

"So sorry, madame, but Bombay has a power shortage. No air conditioning is allowed except in five-star hotels."

"Good heavens, it must be over a hundred in here. I don't see a fan. Is there one?"

"Well," he said slowly, "we might be able to find a fan for you. Do you need it right away?"

"Yes. Right away."

"I will try, sir. I'm sure you will be comfortable."

"And if frogs had wings they'd save their asses a lot of bumps," Ed muttered viciously, as the attendant closed the door behind him.

"Ed! I think he heard you."

"Good. How the hell are we going to sleep in this heat?"

He jerked open the window, but not even the faintest breeze stirred the curtains.

"What I hate is the smell," I said. You know what it reminds me of? That old refrigerator we bought for our cabin that had cockroaches in it. That same bitter smell." I opened the door to the bathroom and turned on the light. Dozens of cockroaches scuttled into cracks and drains.

"Yech!" I closed the door. "I'm going to hate it here."

A knock on the door announced the arrival of our fan, which was a relief to us, for we knew then that we would be able to sleep. A quick bath, even in the cockroachy bathroom, cooled us off, both literally and figuratively, and after a change of clothes we sallied forth to see Bombay.

It is a big city, modern and crowded. Good five-star hotels, which we couldn't afford, good restaurants, and good theaters distinguish this city, especially in the minds of expatriate Indians; but for us, it was a disappointingly dull place. There is little of Indian culture in the everyday life of Bombay; it is like a Western city in nearly every way. There are no cows, no pigs and few street sweepers (and the lack of the latter two is apparent in the streets, for the gutters are often filled with trash and worse). The warm, damp climate produces a dark mold which clings to the walls of buildings and drips from window sills and air conditioners, making all the buildings look dirty. The back streets here were not as interesting as those in other Indian cities; I suppose that city ordinances keep street sellers and stalls to a minimum—we hardly saw either in Bombay. We visited the Thieves' Market and bought some delightful small items of copper there, but that was the only bazaar we could find, though we combed the downtown streets.

Then we went to Malabar Hill to see the Towers of Silence where the Parsees, a Zoroastrian sect that originally came from Persia, put their dead out atop tall towers to be eaten by vultures. The towers are located on the top of the hill beside a lovely public park, and one of our books mentioned that people residing in the upper-class residential district that surrounds the towers sometimes find a hand or foot, or other ghastly souvenir dropped by the vultures, in their gardens or on their roofs! We enjoyed our stroll through the park, where the trees were full of screeching green parakeets and I kept an eye out for possible grisly bits on the lawns and paths, but fortunately my vigilance was unrewarded.

We had heard about Bombay's beautiful beaches, so after lunch we headed for India Gate and the waterfront. It was a rainy, grey day, though the temperature was over ninety. We walked along the waterfront near India Gate with the wind whipping off the Arabian Sea. Whitecaps piled up along the sea wall and we were dampened by the warm salt spray. It was exciting, and we decided to continue our walk back to the hotel along the waterfront instead of taking the main streets. South of the central part of town, the beaches became rockier and dirtier, and the buildings more dilapidated. Laundrymen laid their washing on the grass above high water along this section, and I wondered how they ever got the clothes so clean in lukewarm salt water. Certainly the water didn't look very clean!

Finally we had to leave the beach, for apartment blocks were built right out onto the sea wall. We turned down a sidestreet, and I noticed that a young man, neatly dressed in a white shirt and dark slacks, was sleeping on the sidewalk, flat on his back with one hand across his chest. He seemed to lie so comfortably there on the wet cement, and I remember wondering how he could sleep like that, with the flies crawling in and out of his nostrils and slightly opened mouth. It wasn't until we were nearly past him that I realized that he was dead. Tears of shock filled my eyes and my head buzzed, and Ed squeezed my shoulders in sympathy.

"How can people leave him like that?" I whispered. "We'd better report it to someone."

"No, Bunny. I was just reading about that in the English-language newspaper I got in the railway station. There is so much red tape that if someone reports finding a corpse, he can be tied up for days or even weeks as a witness. Even the local people are inconvenienced to such an extent that no one will report a dead body. And of course, no one but an 'untouchable' can touch a corpse anyway, so even if it is reported, it may be some time before they can arrange to have it removed. Don't think about it, honey. And remember that he can't feel anything."

"What do you suppose he died of?" I asked. "Certainly not starvation; he was well nourished—and, oh, Ed, he was so young."

"Maybe an overdose," said Ed. "Bombay does have a problem of drug use among the young crowd."

We returned to the hotel saddened and depressed. At dinnertime we chose a Chinese restaurant in Bombay's thriving Chinatown, but neither of us had an appetite. I was coming down with a cold; both of us were unaccustomed to the high humidity of the monsoon coast. That night we slept fitfully, waking frequently, bathed in perspiration. The fan kept the air moving, which gave a cooling effect, but the temperature itself was unaffected. My cold rapidly became worse. In the morning my head was stuffed and my eyes were hot.

"Led's go," I pleaded. "I hade id here." I sneezed violently into a wad of toilet paper. I was out of Kleenex.

"The only trouble is, we have our train reservations for tomorrow, not today. We'll have to stick it out today—but I bet the Tourist Bureau has a tour to the Elephanta Caves, and we do want to see them, don't we? Or would you rather stay in bed?"

"Heg do. I'd radder go eddywhere ded sday id dis dump."

At the Tourist Bureau we inquired about tours to the Caves, which were really one of our main reasons for coming to Bombay. We were told that tours to Elephanta were cancelled because of a one-day strike by the boatmen who operated the ferries. We were bitterly disappointed at this news, and tears of self-pity rose to my eyes.

"*Now* whud do we do?" I asked peevishly.

Calmly Ed asked the young lady behind the counter if there were any other tours we could take.

"Yes, sir. There is a nice tour of the Kinhera Caves which will start in fifteen minutes. Would you like me to put you down for it?"

"Yes. What kind of caves are they?"

"They are Buddhist caves, sir, very old. I'm sure you will enjoy the tour."

She was right—we did enjoy the tour, and my cold improved after a little while. The caves had been dug and lived in by a group of Buddhist monks around the time of the birth of Christ. They were interesting caves, for they included an ingenious system of water catchment channels and holding tanks, carved out of the solid rock. Funny, fat freshwater crabs sat like sentinels in these tanks, which held crystal clear water; the system was still working after nearly two thousand years. The monks' cells, however, were dismal little holes in the rock. They *looked* cold, even if they weren't. In the biggest cave, which contained a large stone figure of the Buddha, hundreds of little red bats hung upside down on the ceiling. I had always thought that bats slept peacefully all day long, but their sleep was certainly not undisturbed, for they continually changed places and quarreled over territory, squeaking and scrabbling. They were funny, interesting little creatures, but the bat smell in the caves which they inhabited was overpowering, and we were not tempted to linger.

After this pleasant day, our spirits were improved, and we could face another night in our hotel with reasonable equanimity. It was with relief and anticipation, however, that we left our hotel the next morning and set off for "Vicky Station" (Victoria Station, built in the "Indian baroque" style by the British) and the next leg of our journey through India.

COCHIN

CHAPTER 5

Painted Dancers

When we stepped off the train in Cochin we stepped into a tropical paradise of swaying coconut palms, sugar cane, lagoons and estuaries. We had left hot, damp Bombay behind as we traveled by steam locomotive through the jungly mountains south of Bombay, where waterfalls leap from every precipice during the monsoon season. It had been a beautiful and interesting trip, for the climate and topography changed drastically as we made our way to the deep South of India. Cochin was much cooler but even wetter than Bombay. The air was heavy on our bodies, like a thick, warm, wet towel. My hair clung to my forehead, and the perspiration ran in little trickles down the sides of my face and disconcertingly down my back, tickling as it went. My dress was continually damp around the neckline, and Ed's shirt was dark with sweat. The least breeze, though, instantly cooled us as though it were blowing over a block of ice.

We couldn't find a three-wheeler or rickshaw, so we took a taxi to the pier where we could catch a ferry to our hotel. The Bolghatti Palace had been built by the Dutch a couple of hundred years ago and then turned into a hotel after the British left.

The ferry landing led to a beautifully landscaped tropical garden, with red and pink hibiscus bushes blooming beneath large palms, and a generous stretch of lawn surrounding the big white gingerbread palace. We smiled at each other in pleased anticipation, and I squeezed Ed's hand. This was certainly an improvement over our last accommodations!

Our room was really a suite and contained a dressing room and bath in addition to the enormous bedroom. It was dusty and filled with ancient and slightly dilapidated furniture, and the bath was white marble with fixtures dating from about 1920. We settled in and ordered ice-cold beers which we drank sitting on our beds beneath the whirling fan. We decided to take a boat ride in early afternoon, and hired a heavy old rowboat piloted by an elderly oarsman. He slowly rowed us all around Bolghatti Island. I had Ed's umbrella as a parasol, for the sun was out and very powerful, but I managed to get a burn just from the reflection of the sun on the water. We passed fishermen's huts and strange structures that our oarsman explained were "Chinese nets"—great, tall, counterbalanced sails, made of netting, that looked like white moths all along the shore. These were lowered into the water by means of the counterbalance (a large rock), allowed to remain in the water for a certain length of time, and then raised by moving the counterbalance back. They came up full of several kinds of fish and shrimp, wriggling and flopping together in the middle of the net. Usually these fish were sold on the spot by the owner of the net or his wife, and I found myself wishing I had access to a kitchen so I could buy some and have them for dinner. As we moved placidly along to the creaking of the dripping oars, clumps of lavender-flowered water hyacinths drifted past, for we were in the fresh water estuary of a major river which joined the sea at Cochin. In the middle of the slow river, on some old snags, sat two ernes or sea eagles. They crouched and then slowly flapped away, dipping their large wings in the water with each stroke until they had enough speed to rise into the air. They were the first ernes we had ever seen.

Nice, neat little concrete homes, surrounded by palm trees, lined the shore. A few goats and ducks accompanied the many little brown children playing near the water. We waved at the children, but they were so shy that they ducked their heads and appeared ready to flee if we should come any nearer. Their parents waved and yelled cheery greetings to us in the local language, their teeth shining whitely in their dark faces. The people here were much darker in complexion than their cousins in the north, and they were also noticeably thinner. The younger women were some of the prettiest I had ever seen; each possessed a willowy grace of carriage and an air of charming innocence. They wore their hair in large, shiny chignons at the nape of their necks, and nearly all of them wore fresh white jasmine blossoms fastened just behind their ears. They favored cotton saris in pastel colors with the end draped fetchingly over one shoulder. The men wore white shirts and long sarongs which, in hot weather, they folded up above their knees with the hems knotted around their waists. Most people went barefoot except on the city streets. We had our oarsman let us off at the downtown pier, and set off to explore Cochin. It was a quaint town with an interesting bazaar section of little open-fronted shops near the pier. There was an amazing variety of strange-looking tropical fruits available, as well as fabrics, items made of coir (coconut fiber), and lots of plastic gewgaws. We wandered the hot, dirty streets, checking out the various little shops and returning the greetings which nearly everyone gave us. I think we were a real curiosity to the local people, for in our walks through local neighborhoods and bazaars, we never saw another Westerner.

We entered a large shop which specialized in metal wares and stood there admiring the gleaming rows of pots and pans. The corners of the shop were quite dark, for natural light from the open front was the only illumination, and from one of these came a frightful sound—a prolonged high-pitched shriek—which made my heart turn over. Through the gloom I could make out a man who seemed to be stamping on a sack on the floor, and quite unconsciously I moved closer. He looked up and saw me, and stopped in the act of stomping on the sack again. He crouched there, grinning self-consciously, and I realized what he had been doing, for the sack was squirming in a disgusting manner. There was a rat in the sack, and he was trying to kill it.

"Get him!" I said, and punched the palm of my left hand with my right fist (I hate rats more than anything.)

The little man grinned delightedly and applied his bare foot to the sack with gusto. We left with the ear-splitting shrieks still ringing in our ears, along with the laughter of the proprietor and his employees.

We spent the rest of the afternoon seeing the sights of Cochin, and at dusk we took a taxi to a private home with a small theater set up in the front yard. This had been recommended by our hotel clerk as the best place to see the famous "Kathakali" dancers. I wondered at first if he had been telling the truth, because there was no crowd of tourists, no crush of locals, only us and two French couples, who looked away disdainfully as we approached.

"What is the matter with the French?" I whispered to Ed after my "Good evening" had been ignored. "All together we are probably the only six Westerners within a hundred miles, and they won't even nod to us."

"Get a load of Vinegar Features over there," he observed. "She probably doesn't even say hello to her husband." He indicated one of the women who was standing sourly to one side, thin hip jutting, mouth pursed around a cigarette. She was wearing shabby trousers and a dirty T-shirt, and her hair was so short it was practically crew cut.

"And who ever said the French were chic?" I added. "They are usually the worst dressed people in any crowd, at least in Asia."

After a short wait, the lady of the house came out and invited us into an adjoining hut to see the dancers make up for their parts. We sat on wooden chairs under a couple of naked light bulbs and a fan (and one hundred and five mosquitoes) and watched the two dancers get ready. One of them was going to act the part of a woman, and was carefully making up his handsome young features with light flesh-colored paint. Then he delicately applied black lines around his eyes and on his eyebrows, and tiny white dots for highlights on his cheeks and forehead. When his face was finished, he strapped large breasts onto his chest and put on a fuschia sari with gold and silver borders. Finally he wrapped a pink scarf around his head and put on lots of gold jewelry. He looked gorgeous, and no one would have guessed him to be a man. He minced over to an empty chair and sat, carefully arranging his sari around his knees, while the other dancer got into his costume.

The "handsome prince" of the story had already finished his face, which was painted turquoise green, with a yellow triangle on his forehead, and red and white lines and dots in the triangle. His mouth was wide, smiling, and bright red, with circles in the corners, and on his chin was a white cardboard "beard" which was tied in the back of his head. His eyes were wild, wide, and rolling, with bloodshot whites, and he used them ferociously, even before the performance had begun. He put on a wig of coconut fiber which hung down his back nearly to his waist, and a tall headdress of gilt studded with jewels. A short, tight purple silk bodice with long sleeves and a short, very full skirt of brilliantly jeweled green satin went over many burlap petticoats. His feet were bare. His left hand had silver nails about four inches long. He was a fearsome sight.

The narrator introduced the musicians: one hand-drummer with a long, cylindrical drum, another drummer with a barrel-shaped drum and long, curved sticks, and the vocalist, who also had finger cymbals. The music was quavering and plaintive, quite agreeable to Western ears. Then the actor-dancers were introduced to the audience of six, and the "prince" demonstrated his control of eye, lip, and facial muscles. The narrator explained that Kathakali dancing is an avocation and not a profession, for each man must support himself by working at a regular job as well. Young boys begin at age five and must train for four hours a day for fifteen years before they can perform in public; a difficult and demanding regimen.

When the performance began, the "handsome prince" leaped and stamped, and the "beautiful girl" (who, in the story, was really a disguised demoness), slithered around the stage. They gestured theatri-

57

cally and used their facial muscles to tell the story. We found it easy to follow, even though we knew little of the Ramayana from which the story came. The music, sinuous and repetitive, lulled us into a semi-trance, as we watched, nearly mesmerized, ignoring the mosquitoes which whined around our ears. The dancers also seemed to be in a trance, for when the performance ended, it was a minute or two before they "came out of it" and returned to the everyday world. We sat for a minute or two, still caught up in the atmosphere, and then I turned to Ed.

"What time is it?" I asked, for I had lost track of the passing minutes, and was starting to feel the pangs of hunger.

"Eight-thirty," he replied. "We've been here for nearly two hours. It hardly seemed like ten minutes."

We preceded the others out to the dark road. Almost immediately, out of the night, a taxi appeared. We hailed it and reached for the door handle. The French people crowded past us and climbed in. The taxi disappeared and we were alone.

"What'll we do now?" I said peevishly, hating the French and getting hungrier by the minute. "I guess we'd better start walking."

We set off in the direction the taxi had taken, but after only a block or two another taxi came along and we gratefully climbed in.

At the jetty, no ferry was in sight, so we walked to a nearby hotel and Ed phoned the Bolghatti Palace.

"Oh, sir, we have been waiting for you to return. We send the boat right away."

In the Bolghatti dining room, we sat down in solitary splendor. Two youthful waiters leaned against the wall, and the fans rotated slowly above. Finally one youth detached himself from the supporting wall and approached us with a large, much-spotted menu. He handed it to us and gave us a brilliant smile. Then he crossed back to his side and propped his body against the wall again. We looked over the menu. It consisted almost entirely of Western food: fried fish, baked chicken, boiled vegetables.

"I bet it's all terrible," I complained, disappointed. "I wanted South Indian food, and it's all 'boiled British'." My hunger pangs were acute, and I felt irrationally sorry for myself.

"Never mind, we'll have a nice cold beer first, and anyway, I'm so hungry anything would taste good." Ed beckoned to the waiter and we ordered the set dinner "du jour".

Our beers came, along with some fried cashews, a local specialty. Ed had been right; my mood mellowed after a few sips, and after the first beer, we ordered seconds. We were downright jolly by the time our first course finally arrived, about an hour after we had ordered. It was freshly made cream of mushroom soup, and it was wonderful. We scraped the plates and looked hopefully and meaningfully at our waiters.

"Another beer, sir?"

"Sure. But we'd like the rest of our dinners soon."

"I can't drink another beer, Ed. I'll be too full to eat."

"Maybe that's all we're getting. Anyway, I can always finish yours for you if you can't."

The beers came, and after another long wait, juicy fried white fish with french fried potatoes. We ate it all and summoned the waiter.

"Bring us our check, please."

"Sir, the rest of your dinner is coming."

"Good heavens, there's more?"

"Oh yes, madame. It will be just one little minute."

We waited, while the fans slowly turned and we grew sleepy from our full stomachs and the beer.

Finally the waiter arrived bearing a large covered silver platter, and with a flourish, deposited it on the table. The cover was ceremoniously removed, revealing half a roast chicken, glazed new potatoes, and crisply tender beans and carrots.

"I may never walk again," Ed remarked, as we were helped to generous portions. "I suppose they'll bring us dessert next."

Fortunately, we were able to refuse dessert, and we did manage to eat most of our third course. We were aided by the fact that the food was simply wonderful—even our distended stomachs couldn't refuse that roast chicken.

"The service may be painfully slow, and the hotel may not be the cleanest we have ever seen, but by God, they sure can cook," said Ed, as we slowly toiled up the stairs to our room.

It was after midnight before we were bathed and ready for bed, and I was desperately sleepy as I untied my mosquito net and tucked it all around my mattress. I climbed into bed and wriggled around for a while, trying to get comfortable.

"This mattress is awfully lumpy," I said after a while.

"Huh? What?"

"Sorry, honey. Go back to sleep."

I turned over and curled my body around one particularly hard lump, and pulled up my knees to avoid another.

"That's not too bad," I thought, and started to drift off.

59

"Eeeerrrreeee," whined a mosquito at my ear, and I woke up with a start. "Wheeeerrr."

I got up and turned on the light, waking Ed.

"What's the matter now?" he demanded.

"Mosquitoes."

Ed got up and together we investigated the mosquito nets. There were several gaping holes in each, so we rummaged through my bag which contained the "drugstore" and found enough bandaids to patch them. After putting calamine on our bites, we crawled back into bed, adjusted our bodies around the lumps, and sank into sleep at last, lulled by the whirring fans and the faint whine of mosquitoes as they hurled themselves against the now impregnable nets.

We woke early the following morning; the beds were too uncomfortable for sleeping late, and the back of my leg just at the knee joint was terribly itchy. I craned my neck to see, and there they were, four bites close together, each about the size of a quarter and bright red. They were not mosquito bites; those do not last much longer than an hour on me, and even at their worst they are merely pale pink. These were angry looking, and boy, did they itch. I put calamine on them and tried to ignore them.

We planned to go to one of South India's famous beaches that day, but before we left, I looked over my clothes to see what needed washing before our departure the following day. I picked up the dress I had worn the night before and inspected it. It was my favorite, of heavy cotton, and therefore would take a long time to dry. Unfortunately, as it turned out, I decided that it was clean enough to be worn again, so I rehung it. We put our bathing suits on under our clothes and sallied forth.

The desk clerk was horrified at our plan. "Oh, sir, please do not swim during monsoon time. Very dangerous. Anyway there is no sand on beaches."

"Really? What happened to the sand?"

"At beginning of monsoon, one day, whoosh. All the sand goes away. At the end of monsoon, whoosh. All the sand comes back."

"No kidding. Well, we'll be careful."

"We won't swim, honestly," I said soothingly, seeing that he really was worried about our going. "We'll maybe just wade a little."

With unusual extravagance we hired a taxi for the day to take us to the nearest beach. The monsoon had set in again, and the wind was whipping up the waves, while showers swept over us in intermittent gusts. As we had been warned, there was little sand on the beach, just rocks, covered

60

with tiny oysters and little crabs, which scuttled away from our probing fingers. The water, roiled up from the waves, was muddy and lukewarm. We waited for a wave to wash up above our knees, and then dipped in briefly before it was sucked out again, just to be able to say we had been "in" the Arabian Sea. The current was strong, so strong that it was difficult to resist its pull, and then we understood the concern of the desk clerk. At noon we sat under soughing palms to eat the box lunch we had brought with us from the hotel. It was an interesting but uneventful day, a pleasant communing with nature on a deserted, windswept beach. We returned, tired and surprisingly sunburned, in time for another delicious dinner.

That night I took one of my precious sleeping pills, saved for emergencies, before entering the cozy torture chamber of my bed, and so achieved enough restful sleep to rise cheerfully in the morning and get under way for the next part of our trip. Ed, who looks on the taking of sleeping pills as a vice approximately comparable to the shooting up of heroin, suffered through the night and greeted the new day with a snarl.

By eight o'clock we were on our way. Ironically, the sun was shining out of a mostly blue sky (now that we were off the beach) and the tropical scenery was idyllic as the train made its way along the coast before it turned east and crossed the mountains out of Quilon. We passed palm trees, fields of manioc, watery rice paddies, and water buffaloes submerged to their nostrils in the ditches. Bright red hibiscus bloomed everywhere and the scent of jasmine drifted in through the open windows. The little houses, either thatched or concrete, were neat and pretty. Women and children bathed in the canals, and dugout canoes were poled by men whose skins were the color of black coffee.

Our train was very slow, and stopped often, affording the local people a chance to see the strange foreigners. We collected quite a crowd at some stations—but it was always a friendly crowd, for they smiled and waved at us, and the women held up their babies so they could see us better. We smiled and waved until our smiles grew stiff on our faces, and our jawbones ached. (Ed called it "mandibular paralysis".) The only fly in my ointment was the cluster of bites on my leg. They itched so much that I couldn't help rubbing them, and they swelled up hotly, bringing tears to my eyes.

"I swear they are something weird," I moaned. "I think they're bedbugs."

"Impossible, Bunny. If they were bedbugs you'd have gotten more bites last night, but you didn't. Only just that one group the night before."

61

"I know, but they can't be mosquito bites, for they are in an inaccessible spot and anyway they are too itchy. They're *killing* me. And why are they all in one spot?"

At this point, I needed some distraction, and I got it. We were joined in our compartment by a charming, bearded man wearing a business suit and tie. He smiled and introduced himself as Ashley Johnston, an Indian Christian from the state of Kerala, and an electronic systems engineer for the Indian Government. He was on his way to Madras where he was participating in a space shot to put a satellite into orbit. Since Ed had once been an electronics engineer in Silicone Valley before he became a teacher, the two happily began to talk shop, and I listened in. After a while we all began to compare lifestyles and experiences, and Ashley lit up a *bidi*, one of India's little clove-scented cigarettes.

"In my job," he confided, "we are expected to smoke Dunhills, even though they are prohibitively expensive. No engineer or executive in India would admit to smoking bidis, for they are supposed to be only for the poor people, so we all buy Dunhills and offer them to each other at work. But then we all go into the men's room and smoke bidis in secret." He laughed. "Even the top executive of the space shot group sneaks a bidi now and then. And we all have cars—but none of us drive them. Petrol is far too expensive. They sit in our garages and we all take taxis or sometimes even three-wheelers, but we never admit it."

At one of the stations, Ashley bought us Indian sweets and tea. We had nothing to give him except one of our ballpoint pens. We had heard that they were acceptable gifts in India, so we had brought plenty along. He was delighted.

"Pens are very expensive here," he said "and everyone hangs onto his until it has run quite dry. I have only one, and I do not lend it to anyone else. Thank you very much."

The country outside our windows had changed to semi-arid plains, for we had crossed the range of mountains which divides the lower portion of India in half. The wet, tropical west coast was behind us, and we had entered Tamil-Nadu, the southeastern tip of the subcontinent. The summer monsoon does not reach this portion of India, for the range of mountains acts as a barrier. Instead, the area has a winter monsoon, with winds from the east. It looked to us like southern California, with the backdrop of high peaks on one side, and the sea on the other. Low scrub and dry-country trees formed the vegetation, and the sun blazed down in a bright blue sky.

"Look," I cried, "a peacock!"—as one flew alongside the train for a short distance. This seemed as unlikely to me as seeing a unicorn galloping along beside us. It was a frequent sight on our journey, but I never quite got used to it.

At dusk we watched a flickering lightning storm over the mountains in the west, and it was fully dark when we arrived in the station at Madurai and said goodby to Ashley.

CHAPTER 6

MADURAI

Merry Multitudes

Ⓦe hadn't received an answer from the TNTDC (Tamil Nadu Tourist Development Corporation) to the letter we had written requesting reservations at the Tourist Bungalow in Madurai, so we were somewhat at a loss when we arrived in the city. I had dreaded this arrival, because this was the first place where we really didn't know if there would be a room for us. When we emerged from the station, a dusty taxi pulled up and the fare was settled upon. As the driver and Ed loaded the suitcases into the trunk, I looked around. The half-moon shone half-heartedly on the low, flat roofs of Madurai, weakly illuminating the wide street, which was empty of traffic of any kind. The town looked deserted and depressing, and suddenly I felt dead tired, overheated, and disgruntled. As we jounced along the uneven street, I found myself praying that the hotel would have a room—preferably air-conditioned—but at least *a room*.

We pulled up to a large, two-story building partly covered with bougainvillea, which looked black in the moonlight. Two sleeping clerks woke up, yawned and came to attention as I entered. I asked for an air-conditioned double, and they looked at each other and then waggled their heads simultaneously.

"No problem, madam," the spokesman said, and eventually they led us upstairs to a cubicle which was hideous with its stained mustard-colored walls and battered furniture, but which was mercifully cool and clean. We considered going out to dinner, but we were both exhausted from the long day's travel.

"I'm dead, honey," said Ed. "I don't even want dinner."

That was my feeling exactly, so we crawled into the hard beds and collapsed. Even the bites on my leg did not keep me awake for more than a few minutes.

In the morning, the world appeared a lot brighter when we pulled aside our tattered curtains and let the brilliant sunshine in. Loud recorded Indian popular music was playing over a loudspeaker somewhere, and in contrast to the previous night, the streets were full of people. We quickly got up and I dressed in my favorite heavy cotton sundress and tied a scarf around my head.

Out in the street, several rickshaws were hanging around, and we happily grabbed two. We hired the cheerful young drivers for the entire day at a set price and set off for the Meenakshi Temple, the largest and finest Hindu temple in India.

I had longed to see this temple ever since I was a child. I had read Richard Halliburton's account of it in *The Occident and the Orient* which had been a ninth birthday present from my father. Even though Richard Halliburton had been less than enchanted by the temple (he compared the Hindus and their temple unfavorably with the Muslims and their Taj Mahal) I had been fascinated with his description of the great towers covered with strange figures.

I first spotted one of the towers as we approached the temple from a side street. It was bathed in bright sunshine, which threw into sharp relief the thousands of brightly colored figures that romped in gay confusion up its sloping sides. The statues were nearly life-size, individually carved with loving care out of stone, and then painted in lifelike colors. There are nine *gopurams* (towers) altogether, the four largest, in the corners of the temple complex, were each over one hundred fifty feet tall.

Our drivers suggested that we leave our shoes in the rickshaws for safekeeping, and promised to wait for us on the street. We entered the main gate which opened through a small gopuram into a sort of courtyard or passageway which surrounded the main temple complex. We crossed this courtyard in the blazing sun, the stones burning hot beneath our feet, causing us to hop painfully until we reached the cool shadow under the wall. Another gateway through another tower followed, and then we were inside. It was dark there, and mysterious. Images of gods and goddesses, dragons and gargoyles were picked out in the light that streamed down from slits in the roof. These figures were often smeared with red ochre paste and *ghee* (butter oil), and draped with garlands of roses and jasmine. As we walked along, we passed sudden openings which revealed glimpses of the gopurams outside, shimmering in the sun, their thousands of figures—dancing girls, gargoyles, a joyous, fanciful mass of figures, all in riotous colors—peering down at us.

Outside the sanctuary, but inside the walls, were vendors selling bangles, toys, incense, offerings, and flowers. Leis of jasmine, marigolds,

65

and, surprisingly, roses, were piled on sellers' tables. The roses were exquisite, each a perfect, half-open bud. It was impossible to resist buying some. Sellers called out to us as we passed, and beggars sat in corners, hoping for a coin or two. Children played beside their mothers, while the ladies snoozed comfortably on cloths spread out on the stone floor.

We were denied the inner sanctums, unfortunately. Over these (there were two) were domes of real gold, which sparkled in the sun. They are so holy that no photographs are permitted, even at the official "photograph hours" between one o'clock and four.

The "tank" was situated in the center of the temple complex, open to the sky—a square pool of bright green water, colored by the algae inhabiting it. Stone steps led to the water from all four sides, and dozens of men, women and children were bathing in it, pouring water over their heads, drinking it, and, in some cases, submerging completely. The little children romped naked in the water, and the men were nearly so, for they had on nothing but loincloths. The women bathed in their saris, the cloth clinging wetly to their slim bodies. We watched a girl, when she finished bathing, climb back up the stairs, wringing out her sari, which streamed water in a series of little waterfalls down the steps. She then picked up a dry sari, and in a magical bit of sleight-of-hand, wound herself into the fresh one as she divested herself of the other. The walls around the tank were festooned with pastel saris drying in the sun.

On the terrace that surrounded the tank, a young Brahman boy was receiving his sacred thread, which every Brahman male above puberty wears over one shoulder and across his chest. We stopped to watch for a while, as the old priest performed the rites over the boy while the family stood and watched. There was much chanting and burning of incense, and an air of holy celebration, like a wedding, complete with flowers and sweets for the guests.

We lingered in the cool, dark passages, watching people performing *puja* (worship) at the various shrines. We gawked at the gargoyles and dragons that seemed to peer disdainfully at us from the pillars. We were intrigued with one erotically nude goddess, glistening with ghee and red ochre paste, whose genitals were worn shiny with the caressings of supplicants who begged for the ability to bear children.

At last we left the temple, intending to return during the hours when we could take pictures. When we went out to the rickshaws, we found that the one containing our shoes was gone. The other driver explained that a flat tire had been discovered, and that the driver had taken the rickshaw away to have it fixed. We climbed onto the remaining rickshaw and waited for a time in the shade of a huge tree that stretched its branches over the wall of the temple. After a while, the driver suggested that we return to the hotel and wait for the other rickshaw and our shoes there.

"You don't suppose he'd take our shoes?" I murmured nervously to Ed when the remaining driver was out of earshot.

"How many Indians do you think have size 12 EEE feet like mine?" parried Ed. "I don't think we have to worry."

As our strong young driver pedalled us along, seeming not to notice the double load, Ed spotted a liquor store. This was an unexpected sight, for in Tamil Nadu liquor is not sold to Hindus—and *everyone* is a Hindu, except tourists and visiting officials from elsewhere in India.

"Stop!" said Ed. "I want to buy brandy. I haven't had anything but beer to drink for weeks."

Our driver stood on the brakes and Ed disappeared into the store.

"Oh, madam. I would love to have a dreenk. Could my friend and I have a leetle dreenk of the brandy? We, being Hindus, cannot buy from store."

I assured him that we could spare a little drink for him and his friend, and when Ed returned, he laughed and agreed.

At the hotel, no more than ten minutes had passed before the second driver appeared with a hopeful grin and our shoes. We invited both men up to our room where we poured each a small glass of brandy. They downed it in one gulp apiece and grinned.

"VERY good brandy, mem, sir. Thank you very much."

They promised to return in one hour after we had cooled off with a bath and a change of clothes. I had noticed on the ride back that my bites were suddenly much worse, and now that we were alone I craned my neck to investigate. There were nine of them on the back of my leg—five more than before, and they were fresh and swollen. They itched unmercifully, and in despair I burst into tears.

"What are they?" I sobbed. "How did I get them, anyway? They weren't there this morning. What am I going to do?"

"Aren't you wearing the same dress you wore the night you got them?" Ed asked, in sudden inspiration.

"My God, you're right."

I went into the bathroom and got into the big old-fashioned tub. Sitting in the bottom, I slid out of my dress and underwear, and then stood up, examining my body for insects before stepping out of the tub. Then I ran hot water in and shook in half a small box of the detergent we used for clothes washing. I stirred my garments around and in a little while I had him: a small and insignificant-looking flea, whose drowned carcass rose to the surface of the water.

"Oh, you loathsome, virulent little beast," I muttered. "You must have been in the hem of my dress the whole time, and I think I must have acquired you at the Kathakali theater."

"Fleas don't affect you that badly at home, Bunny. It must be a super special Asian brand of flea. Little beggar wasn't very big though."

"Great things come in small packages. I sure hope I don't get any more like him."

My bites continued to itch for a couple of weeks after that, and even after we returned home to America, I had nine nickel-sized reddish spots on the back of my leg; it took months for the marks to fade away.

At one o'clock we set out again for the temple. The main gate was closed and locked, to our surprise. Fortunately, our drivers knew where to find the one entrance; into the wall was set a small door which was used by picture-taking tourists only. There was a dramatic change in the atmosphere and appearance inside. Gone were the crowds of worshipers, the sellers, the beggars, gone were the festoons of drying saris. The temple was dark and quiet, peopled only by sleeping priests or guards and a few tiptoeing tourists. Some of the slumberers lay side by side in the middle of the gateway into the inner temple, partially blocking the entrance. A group of British tourists stood listening to their tour guide, blocking the remaining space and making it impossible to go around the sleepers. I started to pick my way between the supine bodies, stepping carefully over their legs. Suddenly the tour guide broke off his talk.

"Don't *ever* step over a sleeping person," he said sharply to me, in a schoolmasterish tone.

For some reason this annoyed me terribly. Perhaps it was my itchy leg that made me irritable, perhaps it was his tone of voice, but I was furious. After all, it was *his* tour group that had made it impossible to walk around the sleeping Indians. I choked back an angry retort and continued to pick my way through the bodies. Ed followed.

"Silly twit," he said, behind me. "Ignore him."

(I haven't yet found out whether it really is a social gaffe to step over a sleeping person's legs, but I don't see how it can always be avoided, street sleepers being as numerous as they are.)

We took our photographs of the most interesting icons and gargoyles, and then made our way into the tank area. It was strangely changed without the cheerful crowds of bathers. The pool was not empty,

68

however, for hundreds of little frogs and a few small turtles hung in the water near the steps, basking in the hot sun. The golden temple domes glittered beneath the bright blue sky, and the silence was complete.

When we emerged onto the street again, we decided to walk around for a while. We poked around the streets, noting that the establishments here were proper stores, rather than the open-fronted stalls of north India, and consequently less interesting. There were more cars here and fewer cows and pigs.

While Ed was buying a copy of the Asian edition of *Time*, we were waylaid by two little beggar girls, one a pretty little mite about ten years old, who was dragging along her four-year-old sister. The elder approached me first with a winning smile and a practiced "Baksheesh, rupeeeee." I scowled at her and turned away (giving money to child beggars is strictly discouraged by the Indian government), and she turned from me to more attractive prospects. She pleaded with Ed in Tamil, all the while shoving her sister toward him, making the little one touch his feet and salaam. Little sister was only lukewarm about this—she took time out to pee in the ditch—but big sister never let up. Smiles alternated with agonized expressions of extreme hunger and pain, as she displayed an amazing repertoire of facial expressions and vocal colorations. Ed finished paying for his magazine and we started up the street to where our rickshaws waited, followed closely by the pair, while the ten-year-old kept up a steady monologue. We got into our rickshaws, but they persisted, and suddenly Ed burst out laughing, reached into his pocket for coins, and gave them each a rupee.

"Why did you give in?" I asked curiously.

"The little one was gnawing on my ankle," he said between guffaws, "I guess that's a new kind of begging!"

Whatever it was, it was certainly an effective method where Ed was concerned, and he continued to chuckle at intervals every time he thought about them.

We had our drivers take us on a scenic drive around Madurai, which is really quite a charming city, despite the first impressions of the night before. Many eucalyptus trees had been planted along the streets, for they are fast growing and do well in a hot, dry climate. Oleanders and bougainvillea were planted for the same reason, giving splashes of brilliant color to the residential areas, which were clean and attractive. We crossed a causeway over a meandering river that cut through a flood plain covered with green grass. The town *dhobis* (laundrymen) were set up there, and we stopped to watch them beat the dirty clothes with flat sticks on the rocks, mounding the clothes in piles and rhythmically pounding them, turning the mounds over and over as they worked. It reminded me a little of bread-kneading. They didn't seem to use soap, but the clothes got clean anyway, despite the rather muddy water in which they were washed. They were then spread out to dry on the grass; a pastel crazy quilt which extended as far as the eye could see.

Before we started out again, Ed's driver asked him if he wanted to try driving the rickshaw. Of course, Ed was delighted to have the chance, and the driver dismounted. I watched as Ed stood on the pedals and slowly started off. His rickshaw gradually drew off to the right, despite his best efforts to steer straight ahead. He gave up the driver's seat, a bemused expression on his face.

"I couldn't believe it, Bunny," he said later. "It was nearly impossible to steer, and *heavy*! You have no idea. I have the greatest respect for rickshaw drivers. They must have legs and arms of iron!"

When we were on our way back to the hotel, a little beggar boy ran out into the street and kept pace with our rickshaws, all the while pleading with Ed for a rupee. Again Ed ignored him, but the child persisted, racing along with us and continuing to plead. At last the rickshaw driver tossed the kid a couple of small coins. Ed was devastated.

"I've never been so embarrassed in my life," he groaned, later. "From now on I'm going to keep a pocketful of small coins so I can give to every beggar I see." He had to modify this, of course—we never did give money to the professional beggars that hang out at tourist centers and railway stations, but from then on we gave small coins to cripples, old *sennyasi* and, sometimes, to children.

That evening, after dinner, we discussed the next portion of our trip. We had been told by Ashley Johnston that we should really try to go to Ootacamund ("Ooty" to the British for whom it was the favorite hill station in South India) and also to the Mutamulai Game Preserve, for the two were situated close together in the mountains northwest of Madurai. We hadn't planned to go, but it seemed a shame to miss them when Ashley had said they were so interesting. Of course, we had no train reservations, but bus tickets were easy to get and cheap, and it wasn't very far. We decided to go. If we left early in the morning, shortening our stay in Madurai, and skipped Madras, we would have enough time.

At seven the next morning we were on an ancient bus, rattling through pretty, prosperous country cultivated with fields of sorghum, corn, rice and cotton. Every so often, we would drive through a pile of rice or millet which had been put on the road for the passing traffic to winnow. We got

70

a big kick out of this, especially when our bus driver, a real speed demon, went out of his way to drive right through the biggest piles.

We were fascinated to see that all the large trees in Tamil Nadu were numbered. The bark was scraped off a small section of the trunk, the exposed wood was painted yellow, and a number was then painted in black. The system of numbering was beyond us—sometimes the numbers would start at *1* and go up to *30* or so, sometimes they started randomly at *6* or *10* or whatever. Often numbers were skipped or doubled up. It drove us crazy trying to figure out the system, and despite our best efforts, we were never able to do so.

Just after noon, as we approached a town called Theni, I needed to use a toilet. I had put it off for quite a while, because we hadn't seen any ladies' rooms at the stops we had made (only men's rooms), but I couldn't put it off any longer. The bus pulled into a huge parking area, and we were allowed enough time to get something to eat, but my only thought was for a restroom. I walked around the perimeter of the parking lot, and finally found a door in a wall through which women were coming and going, but there was a window there for the payment of a fee.

"Five paise," said the attendant. Of course, I didn't have a cent with me, for I had left my purse with Ed in the bus. Back I went to get the money, and returned, paying the fee, which was the equivalent of about half a cent. By this time I was in desperate straits, so I hurried in through the door, and stopped short. The "ladies' room" was just a cement floor, open to the sky, with three raised platforms along one side. On each platform was a glistening pile of fresh shit. The floor was swimming in urine, for it was without a drain and there was no water available. I stood there for a moment, appalled, until my bladder insisted that it was going to rebel if I didn't hurry. I picked my way along the driest part of the floor to a corner which at least afforded me some privacy, squatted, and did my thing. There was nothing else to do, with a four-hour bus ride ahead.

We stayed overnight in an obscure town somewhere near the mountains, and arrived in Metapalyam, where we were to catch the cog railway steam train to Ooty, in mid-morning on the following day. The little train was the most attractive we had ever seen, painted blue and white, with bright brasswork and a tiny engine in the rear to push the train instead of pulling it, perhaps to keep the coal smoke out of the eyes of the passengers. We secured seats on polished wooden benches in the toylike compartment and settled down to wait for it to start out. After a little while I realized that nature was calling me again, and there seemed to be no ladies' room (or men's room either) on the train.

71

"Do you think I have time to go into the station?" I asked Ed.

"Sure," he answered. "I heard someone say it will be another ten minutes before we start. Just hurry."

I got off and looked around quickly. There it was! I hurried over to the nice clean ladies' room, entered a stall containing the usual Asian toilet, and closed the door behind me, which had an unusual bolt that seemed to slip into place automatically. I was still squatting when I heard a loud whistle, and a train started to chug. I was wearing trousers that had a drawstring waistband and I was in a panic as I hauled my resistant pants up over my sweaty rear. Not pausing to tie the drawstring, I held them up with one hand as I struggled with the lock with the other.

"Chug, chug, chug" went the train as it pulled out of the station, the puffs of steam coming ever closer together as it gathered speed.

I started to cry as I struggled with the lock, and in desperation I kicked the door. The bolt came off in my hand.

"Help!" I screamed, quite beyond reason in my utter terror.

Suddenly the door opened from the outside. A woman passenger had heard my cries and opened the door easily, there being no bolt, for in my panic I hadn't had the sense to turn the knob. Sobbing, I thanked the startled woman, thrust the bolt into her hand, and raced out to the platform, certain that I was too late, still holding my pants up with one hand.

The little blue and white train sat placidly on the track as if nothing had happened.

"What in the world is the matter," exclaimed Ed, when he saw my red eyes and dishevelled appearance. He put his arm around me sympathetically while I described my panic.

"I was terrified that I'd be left here without any passport or money. How was I ever going to catch up with you?"

"I'd never have stayed on the train without you, honey. But the train that left was on the other side of the tracks. Couldn't you tell?"

There was a suspicious quiver to his voice. I looked up to see his eyes twinkling.

"Hell," I giggled, beginning to see the funny side of it, "I was so scared my brain literally wasn't functioning."

I glanced down at my right hand, which had suddenly started to throb and ache. The middle finger was swelling rapidly, and had already started to turn blue. Somehow I had sprained it while trying to get the door unlocked, and I hadn't even noticed.

CHAPTER 7

Wild Elephants

OOTACAMUND

The little train chugged out of the station at Metapalyam into the foothills of the Nilgiri Mountains. First we passed through areca palm plantations, the trees standing tall in mathematical rows, with the sun slanting down through them in pleasing patterns of gold and green. As we started to climb, the plantations gave way to natural forests of unusual beauty. Scarlet hibiscus, tulip trees, and blue morning glories lighted up the verdant foliage that climbed the steep mountain sides, and the right-of-way was starred with wildflowers of all colors. The narrow train track wound through the canyons, following the contour of the land, scarcely disturbing the vegetation. The little engine gasped and panted as it pushed us along the precipitous track up a twelve-and-a-half per cent grade, at times going so slowly that I was able to pick a sprig of forget-me-nots from the bank as we passed.

Once I stuck my head out the window to watch as we crossed a curved wooden trestle over a merry mountain stream which threw itself down the canyon and created little rainbows in the sunshine. Looking back I could see all the way to Metapalyam and the areca plantations and even farther, to the flat yellow land that lay between the Nilgiri Hills and the sea.

We stopped at a tiny village perched on the edge, the buildings actually hanging out over the mountainside. Everyone got off the train and stretched his legs, and we walked back to watch the engine taking on water from an ingenious arrangement of wooden troughs that carried it from a nearby stream. We stuck our heads inside the little cab to see the firebox and the pile of coal from which it was fed. The birds were singing, the air was cool, and the sun shone. I got a rush of ecstasy from being alive on such a day, in such a beautiful place.

At seven thousand feet the countryside changed to more open forests of cedar and eucalyptus, and there the tea plantations began. Rows of bushes like fat green caterpillars crawled sideways over the hills, and women in bright saris pushed between the rows, carrying tall, heavy baskets strapped to their heads. They picked the tender new leaves at the tips of the branches as they slowly made their way along. The terrain became less steep, and gradually changed to a gently rolling plateau perched about seventy-five hundred feet above sea level. The air was crisp, so crisp that I shivered in my thin cotton shirt and trousers, and my feet were chilly in their open sandals, despite the cheerful sunshine.

We arrived in Ootacamund at twelve-thirty in a dense mist that had damply settled over the town, and grabbed a three-wheeler to the hotel we had decided upon, an Indian-style hotel belonging to a famous South Indian chain. It was situated in a charming garden, on a side hill overlooking the main part of town, and we entered eagerly, looking forward to Indian-style living for a change. The manager took us to see the room, which involved quite a long walk through the gardens past several wings of buildings. The room was high-ceilinged, rather gloomy, and with a decidedly rundown air. I was disappointed, but it seemed like too much trouble to search for another hotel, so we went back to the lobby and dismissed our three-wheeler. Ed went to the desk to sign in.

"You can cash travelers' checks, I suppose," he rather foolishly ventured, as he wrote in the ledger.

"So sorry, sir," the manager unctuously intoned. "We accept dollars or pounds only."

"We don't have any dollars, I'm afraid. We have rupees though."

"So sorry, we don't accept rupees from foreigners."

"You're kidding."

The manager shrugged and polished his nails on his shirt front.

"You mean to say we can't stay here unless we pay in American dollars?"

"Government regulations, very sorry," in a pleased tone of voice.

"Government regulations, hell. We've always been able to pay in either travelers' checks or rupees."

The manager shrugged again, clearly enjoying himself.

Ed gritted his teeth and a dangerous look came into his eye. I knew that look well, it heralded an explosion of temper.

"Come on, honey, let's go. We didn't like the room anyway."

I tugged at his arm and he relaxed and accompanied me outside.

"Next time maybe we shouldn't mention money until we are leaving," I suggested. "Then they'd *have* to accept travelers' checks."

"And we sent the goddamned three-wheeler away. There's no taxi around and we're half a mile out of town," Ed said wrathfully as we surveyed the situation. Our suitcases sat on the curb. They were pretty heavy and quite impossible to carry for half a mile. In the end Ed decided to walk into town to get a taxi or three-wheeler while I waited with the luggage.

I had no sooner made myself comfortable perched on the suitcases, when he reappeared in a regular taxi with two young men in the front—one the driver, and one to give him moral support, I guessed. In no time the baggage was stowed; one suitcase on the top and one in the trunk, and we were careening through town.

"We need a nice hotel that is not too expensive," I said hopefully.

"No problem, madam," grinned our driver's moral supporter, who turned out to be the interpreter. "We take you to good English hotel. VERY nice. Much better than Indian hotel."

We drove for a distance up a long hill and turned in at an imposing gate with a sign over it: "Ferndale". It was quite charming, and the double room we were shown was clean, bright and cheerful, with ruffled chintz curtains and bedspread. It even had a fireplace, the significance of which escaped me at first.

After a quick lunch in the dining room, which was in a separate bungalow, we picked our way back to the room over the dew-drenched lawn.

"I'm freezing, Ed," I said, examining my goosebumps. "I don't have a jacket or even a sweater. Who'd have thought it would be so cold here."

"Do you have anything you can wrap around you?" he asked. I rummaged through my suitcase, finally coming up with a dress-length of heavy cotton material which I had bought in Madurai. I folded it up until it was about the size and shape of a shawl, and draped it over my shoulders. Welcome warmth spread over my back and arms.

"My, I look glamorous," I giggled.

"Well, it's not too bad, and its better than your being cold."

We started off on a well-worn path that led down the hillside toward town. It was lined with familiar trees and wildflowers; cedar and eucalyptus, buttercups and forget-me-nots. The houses that we could see were English-style cottages with roses growing in the yards. It certainly wasn't very Indian, even though the people we passed were Indian in race, if not in clothing. As we walked, the sun peeked through the mist intermittently, and finally burnt it off to bathe us in lukewarm sunshine.

At the foot of the hill nestled a lovely lake, surrounded by large homes and open fields in which horses grazed. The path skirted the lake and passed a pretty white church with a tall steeple.

"I wonder if it was worthwhile to come here at all," I complained. "It is certainly very pretty, but not much different from England or parts of America."

"Well, maybe the town itself will be a bit more exotic."

This last was prophetic, for when we reached the "downtown," about a mile and a half from our hotel, we discovered an Indian town after all. The public buildings, such as the banks, hotels, and the city hall, were grandly British, but the town itself was truly Indian. The narrow streets were lined with open-fronted establishments selling old silver, silks, incense and spices —all the delicious Indian exotica that I had come to love. We prowled through these, looking for bargains—and finding them. After a while we found the public market, colorful with fruits and vegetables, although the fruits were cool-climate varieties like apples and pears, and the vegetables were carrots, turnips, spinach and other familiar kinds. Other stalls sold rice, millet, cottonseed for oil, and various peas and beans. In one we stopped to watch a youth grinding flour from whole wheat which he poured into the hopper of a noisy mechanical grinder. He and the other workers were covered with white flour dust. Another stall featured oil from the fragrant eucalyptus trees which had been planted in rows on the hills surrounding Ootacamund.

In the open square in the center of the market sat several women who were different from any we had seen before. They were large, strong, and handsome, and they had long hair which they wore in sausage curls in front of their ears, something like the hairdos of male Hassidic Jews. They dressed warmly in blankets and sat surrounded by their wares: mostly blankets and sweaters in bright colors.

"I think they are Todas, the hill tribe people of the Nilgiri mountains," I said. "They have a Semitic look, with those arched noses, don't they? Some authorities think they may be descended from one of the lost tribes of Israel."

We decided to take a three-wheeler back to the hotel instead of subjecting our tired feet to the long uphill walk. It was already nearly dusk in this southern latitude, and by the time we got back there was a decided chill to the air and a fine mist was falling.

"I feel like an oyster," I remarked, as Ed poured me a brandy in our room. "I don't suppose there is any heat."

"No, I asked," he said. "They only supply wood for the fireplaces in the winter."

I took a hot dipper bath instead of a shower. The dipper bath is an Indian institution, and consists of a tap, a bucket to fill with hot or cold water (depending on the climate), and a plastic dipper. I knew the procedure, so I started the hot water running into the bucket while I poured a couple of preliminary dippers over me, then I scrubbed myself down with soap (shivering during this part), and finally dipped out a veritable cascade of lovely hot water over me, using at least three bucketfuls. Then I put on two T-shirts and my dress, wrapped up in my makeshift "shawl," and we went to the dining room for dinner.

"Couldn't you please find us some wood for our fireplace?" I wheedled the waiter. "Our room is pretty cold."

"Very sorry, madam, we have no wood. But I can get you an electric heater," he said, waggling his head from side to side.

"We have to learn to ask the right questions," I remarked to Ed after the waiter had left to get our heater.

We inquired at the desk as to sightseeing tours to the Mutamalai Game Preserve, and were pleased to discover that we could book a tour for the next day which would pick us up right in front of the hotel. The first item on the agenda was to be a tour of the city, with a visit to the preserve in the afternoon.

The next morning we set off in a minibus with twelve others including the driver, all Indians. Across the aisle were two smartly dressed young men and a boy of about twelve, who wore a school uniform consisting of a white shirt, a sweater, and shorts above his plump knees. There were two other handsome young men, and two families with young children. None could speak much English except for the young men and the boy, who spoke better English than we did. They introduced themselves as cousins. One, who was a graduate electronics engineer, was visiting from England. The boy's name was Kumar, and he was taking a holiday away from school for a day to be with his relatives. He lived in Coonoor, just down the road from Ooty, and he and I hit it off right away.

The first few stops on our tour were points of interest around Ooty, including the Botanical Gardens, huge in area, and one of the glories of British Ootacamund, or "Snooty Ooty," as it was once called. The gardens climbed up the mountainside, terrace upon terrace of exotic trees and ponds, gorgeous lawns, and magnificent flower beds. I wondered what the ghosts of the British past would think of it now, for it had become subtly Indianized; "had suffered a . . . change, into something

77

rich and strange." The stone benches and statues were worn, a little crumbled with age. The borders and hedges, once rigidly prim, had been allowed to burgeon—a beautiful rose twined in loving embrace with a handsome laurel. Lush growth of ivy and honeysuckle covered the arbors, and fishponds were riots of waterlilies and water hyacinth.

As we descended the path, we both became aware that we were hungry, and we looked around for a booth or stall where we could get a snack for lunch, for this was to be an all-day tour. Just as we spotted a little cafe outside the gate, Kumar appeared.

"We're going now," he called. "The bus is waiting."

"Damn!" said Ed. "I wonder if we'll get a chance to eat."

We climbed aboard resignedly and took our seats. The bus proceeded into the downtown area, where it pulled into a long driveway and stopped.

"Lunch," the driver said. "One hour only."

We all trooped into a large dining hall that was nearly filled with people, and were shepherded over to three long empty tables. There were no menus on the table, and we looked around for a waiter to take our order. Almost immediately, one appeared bearing large *thalis*—shining metal trays containing small dishes of vegetable curries and various side-dishes, and placed them in front of us. They were included in the price of our tour. We ordered Limcas and tea, which were not included, and our new friends insisted on picking up the tab for them.

Our next stop was to be the Mutamulai Preserve. The little bus proceeded sedately through the bucolic countryside for a way, and then, after rounding a bend, plunged so suddenly down an incredibly steep road that it took my breath away. The road was hardly more than a paved path, only about six feet wide, and the grade was so steep that the driver was forced to keep the bus in low gear all the way, using his brakes frequently. I had the feeling that, at any moment, the bus would tip up on its front end and then continue to somersault, over and over, all the way to the bottom. The road had thirty-six hairpin turns, each numbered so you wouldn't forget where you were in the sequence. Once I got used to the feeling of sliding out of my seat, I enjoyed the ride, for the scenery was lovely, and the sunshine was warm. We were in wild country, for we were crossing part of the game preserve, and the only inhabitants were the birds and other wildlife. At last we reached the bottom, at only thirty-five hundred feet elevation—we had dropped four thousand feet in only a few miles! We crossed a river in which a mother elephant and her baby were getting scrubbed by their mahouts. I turned to Kumar, who had been snoozing next to me, in time to see him bump his head on the seat in front of us.

"Did you see the elephants?" I asked, seeing that he was awake.

"No," he said. "I was sleeping and bumping my head at that time."

After a short stop at a tea stall, we crossed back over the river, parked near where the elephants were bathing and walked over to the bank. Mother was lying on her side in the sparkling water while her mahout methodically rubbed her with his rubber thong. When he had finished one side, she heaved a mighty sigh and turned over in the water so he could do the other. The baby, who with his smaller bulk was already bathed, came over to investigate the strange foreigners. He snuffed me all over, and then reached up with his little short trunk and pulled me down close to him. I put my arms around him and he snorted with pleasure and rubbed against me. He was covered with long, stiff black hairs, to my surprise, for his mother was completely hairless. I wondered at what age they lose their hair, but never did find out, as the cousins didn't know, and the rest couldn't tell me. I could have spent a lot more time cuddling the baby, but the others dragged me away, for the afternoon was wearing on, and we still had the Game Preserve to see.

We entered the gates of the preserve and passed into the strange and wonderful world of the primeval forest. It was roofed with great trees. A little sunshine sifted through, dappling the ground, but there were few real breaks in the canopy. The ground was covered with knee-high grass and tender shrubs, but between this and the leafy boughs far above were just tree trunks, as far as the eye could see, and we could see a long way. It was ideal for spotting game, for there was no real cover.

Almost immediately we saw a group of about twelve beautiful axis deer. In their coats of reddish gold with white spots, they were conspicuous against the emerald background, and one of them carried magnificent antlers. They paid little attention to us until we stopped, then they leaped over the low bushes, and in a dozen springy bounds they were out of sight. The bus started moving again slowly, but after only a few yards, it stopped. The driver turned around and whispered, "Elephant!" We peered through the forest, and after a while we could dimly discern grey shapes among the tree trunks, but they were so indistinct we were disappointed. The driver pointed to the roof of the bus, and Kumar led the way outside, around the bus to the back, and up the little ladder to the top. Most of us followed him, and found that we could see the elephants much better from there. I was thrilled, for I had never thought we'd actually see a wild elephant. "Wait 'til we tell the folks back home,"

I said to Ed, jubilantly. "I never expected to see a wild elephant in India. It's too bad we're not close enough to get a picture!" We re-entered the bus after we'd all had a good look, and proceeded. Less than a mile farther on, off to the left and slightly above us, and only about seventy-five feet away, stood a herd of ten Indian bison, or gaur. They were great black beasts, with light-colored horns, nose, and "socks," making them very visible in the forest. The foremost animal, the largest male in the bunch, stood there slowly pawing the ground, as Ed dismounted and raised his camera. "Damn!" he said and climbed back in the bus. "That was my last picture and I underexposed it. Where's my film?" He hurriedly changed the film while we all got a good look at the herd. Then he went back outside and took his time about getting the picture. All the while, the gaur stood there, shifting their feet, clearly nervous. I was just wishing that Ed would get back in before one of them decided to charge, when he started to walk down the middle of the road ahead of us, looking off towards the left. The driver started the bus and followed him closely, and all of a sudden we saw three elephants, including a male tusker, up the slope on our left, just beyond the herd of gaur. They were a lot closer than the last bunch, and we could see them clearly. The tusker faced us, and started to pull up grass with his trunk and throw it over his shoulder, while rocking from side to side. I knew that this meant that he was agitated, and I was again wishing that Ed would get back in the bus, when they turned, and melted silently into the forest. Ed pointed up and to our right, and there, swinging through the trees, was a group of six or seven large monkeys. They were silvery in color, with black faces, and they swung easily from branch to branch and from tree to tree before they, too, disappeared. I was in a state of high excitement by that time—my breath was coming fast and my heart was pounding.

Ed got back in the bus and we set off again, each of us wondering what we would see next. Aside from a large herd of axis deer, however, for a long time we saw nothing at all, and we were actually approaching the exit gate of the preserve, when the driver stopped again. Off to our right this time was another group of three wild elephants, and as we were looking at them, our driver made a sudden exclamation. Following his pointing finger, we looked to the left, and saw a huge female elephant, not fifty feet away, in full view. She became agitated, and suddenly made a little charging run at the bus, shaking her head from side to side, and then made another, and another. She had obviously worked herself into a temper, and the driver started up, not wanting a maddened elephant butting the side of the bus. As we tried to move away, she ran alongside us for quite a while, shaking her head and trumpeting, her trunk held high, and her little eyes rolling in excitement! I felt that I could almost have reached out through the open window to touch her side, she was so close. Then we could see why she was so upset, for her tiny baby stood a little way up the hill behind her. When she got too far away from him, she stopped and let us escape. This was the end of our adventures, for we left the sanctuary only a mile further on. A beautiful peacock saw us out the gate, and we returned to the everyday world. The final tally: thirteen elephants, ten gaur, approximately thirty-five axis deer, half-a-dozen silvery monkeys, and one peacock. I think I was more excited than I'd ever been in my life. I felt a tap on my shoulder; the father of the family that sat behind Kumar and me offered us a snack, a delicious mixture of little puffs of cereal, nuts, and seeds, which was spicy and tangy. I wondered what it was called, for I had eaten it before and had been unable to find out the name. I always tried to learn the names of all the different dishes we had sampled. It was handy, when reading a menu, to know that *alu* meant potato, and *murg* meant chicken, for instance. I turned to Kumar. "What do you call this stuff?" I asked, indicating my handful of savories. He looked at me owlishly. "We call it 'mixture,' " he said. He probably never knew why I shrieked with laughter over that, and he was too polite to ask. We stopped for tea at a stall before tackling the road back to Ooty, and Ed and I bought tea for everyone in the bus. They had all been so nice to us that we wanted to do something for them. It was beginning to get on toward dusk when we started up the steep and twisting road back. Kumar had dozed off again, Ed was in conversation with the cousins, and the driver put on a tape of loud Indian popular music. I leaned my arms on the open window sill, put my chin on my arms, and dreamily gazed out at the steep jungle as we climbed. The music blared out over the noise of the laboring engine, the warm air stirred my hair, and I was absolutely perfectly happy. It had been a most wonderful day.

CHAPTER 8

Stone Elephants

MADRAS
MAHABALIPURAM

W e had managed to switch from a bus to a train at Bangalore and so arrived at the Madras station late on a stifling afternoon only thirty-six hours after leaving Ootacamund. We were not surprised to find it stifling, for we had heard that "Madras has three kinds of weather: hot, hotter, and hottest."

We wanted to stay at an Indian-style hotel for a change, despite our bad experience in Ootacamund, so we tried the Dashaprakash, which had a famous dining room featuring South Indian *thali* dinners, and was a "dry" Hindu hotel, with no liquor, meat, or pets allowed anywhere on the premises. Fortunately we had finished our little bottle of brandy in Ooty, so we had clear consciences and alcohol-free breath as we entered the dining room, which was as dim and cool as our room. We chose a booth along one wall and noticed that we were the only people there.

"I wonder if the food is any good," I murmured as the waiter approached with the menu.

"Too late to change our minds now," answered Ed cheerfully. "I'm so hungry I don't care if it's terrible!"

We ordered a thali dinner. The waiter took our order and almost immediately returned with our first trays of food: creamed vegetable soup, freshly fried potato chips, and, oddly, *ladoos*—sweet and sticky balls of cake with a heavenly flavor. These were followed by the main part of the meal: large trays containing six *puris* (fried rounds of unleavened bread), cabbage curry, a sweet tomato-and-green-bean dish, pineapple chunks and green chilies in a white sauce, a very hot and pungent red liquid curry that we could not identify, yoghurt in a little cup, *sambal* or hot sauce, ginger water, fresh carrot chutney, coconut chutney, and, of course, a large mound of the flavorful Indian rice. There were no forks or spoons provided, so we ate with our fingers, remembering to keep our left hands in our laps.

At last I mopped up the last of my curries with the remaining morsel of puri, and sat back satisfied. At this point an ancient busboy approached with a tray of steaming bowls, and stopped at our table.

"No, thank you," I smiled.

He deftly dipped a ladleful of pineapple and chilies into the emptied receptacle on my tray.

"No, no," I gasped helplessly, fluttering my hands over my tray, and then snatching them away as he swiftly filled all my dishes with the steaming mixtures. He waggled his head from side to side and gave me a dazzling smile as he attended to Ed's tray, finishing off with several puris for each of us. With a gallant bow he trotted off as I surveyed my replenished dishes. A trickle of perspiration streamed down the side of my face, caused as much by the prospect of eating so much more as by the spiciness of the food.

"I just can't eat any more, I'm stuffed," I moaned, "but to waste that much food! It's a sin, and especially in India. That tray would feed a child for a week."

"Well, I think I can manage to eat most of it," remarked Ed, as he happily started to plow through his second dinner.

I actually ate quite a bit more of mine before I gave up completely.

"It was certainly delicious," I said as I sighed and settled back, "I can't think why there is no one else here."

To my horror, the old busboy approached our table again, brandishing his steaming tray. Quickly we picked our trays up and moved them out of his reach. With a reproachful look he returned to the kitchen, sadly shaking his head.

The mystery of the missing customers was solved when people started drifting in just as we finished the bananas and coffee which were brought as our final course.

"We just eat too early for most Indians," remarked Ed as he checked his watch. "It's nearly nine o'clock now and people are just starting to come in. I bet it will be packed by ten."

After dinner we went out into the warm night and walked around the city streets looking for interesting sights. However, Madras is a bustling, modern city, and disappointingly prosaic, so soon we returned to our cool room and crawled into bed. My last conscious thought was, "I'll never get to sleep with such a full stomach."

In the morning we talked to the desk clerk about getting to Mahabalipuram, which is a small town south of Madras right on the coast, where the last remaining "beach temple" is located. He recommended that we take a tourist excursion bus, so we could see the temple town of Kanchipuram on the way to Mahabalipuram. Then we could, he suggested, have the driver drop us off at the Temple Bay hotel.

This sounded like a fine plan to us, and in no time we were waiting, bag and baggage, for the bus in front of the ITDC (India Tourist Development Corporation) office. A tall old man greeted the tourists as they arrived, and "practiced his English" on them and on us. He appeared to have no official status with the ITDC, but he tried to appear busy—and was quite obviously hoping for a tip.

When the bus arrived, we found seats in the very back, as we had been the last to buy tickets. I had settled myself on the seat and was preparing to enjoy the trip when the old man came down the center aisle carrying the handbag which I had left on the sidewalk.

"Oh, thank you sir," I gasped, as I frantically searched through it for a suitable reward. At last I found a five-rupee note, and Ed found another after digging through his pockets. It was little enough to pay for for the return of my precious bag; and he accepted it with a pleased smile.

"We are sure lucky," said Ed, "that the old man was there, and that he was honest enough to return your bag. All the travelers' checks were in there, and the entire 'drugstore'."

Mentally vowing that I'd be more careful, I settled back again and took note of our fellow passengers. Beyond Ed on the rear seat was a pale American girl with her companion, a deeply tanned blond young man with "beach boy" written all over him. Beyond them was a tall, cadaverous-looking man in his forties with stringy, greying hair that fell over his face, yellow teeth, and a rakish grin. He was dressed in the bare minimum; beltless jeans, a tattered vest over his naked chest, and rubber thong sandals. Two seats up and to the right were three young Belgian or French people, well dressed and handsome. The two young men appeared healthy and cheerful, but the girl kept a sweatshirt wrapped around her neck and lower face, despite the heat. She was a pretty blond girl, but she looked like death, with a ghastly complexion. In conversation later, she said that she had been suffering for over two weeks with a sore throat and a terrible headache, and that she felt very ill. She pulled the sweatshirt closer around her neck and shivered. I wondered if she had malaria, hepatitis, or just flu, and I wished that the cheerful young men would seem a little more concerned.

Ed was talking to the young couple next to us and I listened as the tanned young man, with a salesman's practiced smile, talked about his business contacts in India.

"My wife is from Connecticut," he said, "and this is her first trip to India. I'm originally from California, but I've spent a lot of time in India and Sri Lanka and I've come back here to start a business. I was going to college in Connecticut for a while, but I couldn't see how a degree could do me any good. There aren't any opportunities in America now. This is where it's at." He gestured at the passing countryside.

"My wife isn't too crazy about India, nor Sri Lanka either, but she'll get used to it." He went on at some length to Ed about the kinds of business opportunities that Asia afforded.

His pale little wife got up and squeezed in next to me, so that the men could sit together. She was sweetly pretty, with dark brown hair and a ladylike air.

"Hi," she said, "I'm Debbie. It's so nice to meet an American woman —I haven't had anyone to talk to for weeks, except my husband. Ricky is so happy to be back here, and he wishes I liked it better. I guess I'll get used to it, but the people are so strange, and the food doesn't agree with me." She glanced adoringly at her husband, who was still talking. "I met Ricky back home in Connecticut, and he was always talking about Sri Lanka and India. We were going to open a business in Trincomalee with some friends he had there, but . . . " she hesitated.

There was an awkward pause. To fill it, I said, "Were you in college together? Is that how you met?"

"Oh, no. I was a secretary when I met Rick. My girl friend introduced us. He just swept me off my feet—he's wonderful. We've only been married six months."

She paused again, and then made up her mind to confide in me. She said, in a whisper, "We took all our savings to start the business . . ." (You mean *your* savings, I mentally interpolated, remembering that Ricky had been in college.) "Five thousand dollars," she continued, "but he gave the money to his friends, and they disappeared with it." Her voice quavered. "We hardly have any left, and now I'm pregnant, and I'm scared. But Rick says I shouldn't worry, because he has some friends in Mahabalipuram and he can maybe get into some kind of a business with them . . ."

Her face started to work and I squeezed her hand and murmured something about everything turning out all right. She pulled herself together and was able to talk cheerfully for the rest of the trip.

After a while, Ricky moved up the aisle to talk to others and the cadaverous-looking man leaned over toward us.

"Good morning," he said to Ed in a cultured British voice, "I'm Pete. Where are you and your wife going?"

He was a delightful person despite his fearsome appearance, and we enjoyed his company, for he had funny stories to tell about his travels through Asia. He had been wandering around for eight years, drifting from country to country, avoiding the monsoon, mostly living on the beach. How he got money to keep himself going we never discovered, but we met many like him. Nearly always they were good company and often very intelligent. They had come to Asia, fallen in love with it, or with the drugs that are freely available there, and they never leave. I often wonder what happens to them in the end. Do they go home when they get older, or sick? Or do they just die somewhere on the road of an overdose, or hunger, or maybe of a disease like malaria or hepatitis?

After an hour's drive, we arrived in Kanchipuram, which had several great temple complexes much like the Meenakshi. The little bunch of Westerners mostly stuck together in a loose group as we explored the lovely buildings and courtyards. Ed and I enjoyed giving small change to the temple elephants who stood guard with their keepers at the main entrances. The great animals would daintily pick up the coin from our palms and hand it to the priest, and sinking to their front knees, they would bow in thanks. None of our companions gave money to the temple elephants, and I wondered why until I remembered—probably none of them could afford it.

The second stop was at Tirukkalikundram, a hilltop temple where two kites (vulture-like birds) come to be fed every day by the priests. They are said to be holy incarnations of gods, and they are supposed to fly there from Benares every day! This seems unlikely, as Benares is about two thousand miles away, but the fact nevertheless remains that for a recorded period of over three hundred years, and reputedly for centuries before that, two kites and two kites only have arrived on the temple platform for their daily feeding.

Unfortunately, the feeding had already taken place that day, so after our ritual visit to the temple, up an exceedingly steep and hot stairway, we returned to the little food stall at the foot of the hill, had a cold drink, and watched the hill tribe people bug the Indian tourists. They were trying to sell grisly little stuffed chipmunks, passing them off as "mongooses." The hill tribe people were dark and short, with curly, dusty hair, the men clad in loin-cloths, the women mostly in rags. One little girl of eleven or so had a repertoire of Donald Duck noises and a little song which she repeated monotonously and endlessly. She was still singing when the bus pulled away.

We rumbled into Mahabalipuram in mid-afternoon, the hottest time of a hot day. The driver stopped the bus at a driveway which stretched out as far as we could see across a broad field that shimmered in the sun.

"Temple Bay Hotel," he announced, and Ed and I looked at each other in dismay. Were we really going to have to carry or drag our suitcases for what looked like at least a mile?

Ed went up to discuss the situation with the driver and soon came back smiling.

"He'll take us down right to the front door," he said. "I'll give him ten rupees for his trouble. It's worth it."

The bus eased down the rutted sandy road until it pulled up on a concrete roundabout at the lobby. We dismounted thankfully and Ed and the attendant brought the suitcases down from the top of the bus.

Debbie came out with us and clung to me for a moment.

"Take care of yourself," I said, and found that my constricted throat would not let me say any more.

"We'll be all right," she said. "I'm sure we will."

She climbed aboard again and the bus roared off in a cloud of white dust. I could see hands waving dimly in the rear window before it disappeared in the blinding sunlight.

Ed patted my shoulder and said, "She can always wire her parents for the fare home," he said. "Don't worry."

"I know," I said, "it was just that she was so frightened. If only he had seemed more . . . responsible."

"He was a jerk, and he'll never survive in business here. She was a nice girl, wasn't she? What did she ever see in him?"

We were shown to our room and I looked around as the bellboy bustled about, turning on the air conditioner and opening the drapes.

"Good heavens," I exclaimed. "This is gorgeous!"

It was all in dusty rose and grey, and decorated in the Art Deco style of the 'thirties, with satin drapes over lace curtains. I entered the tiled bathroom, which was rather hot compared to the cool bedroom. I supposed that the air conditioning hadn't reached into it yet. A few mosquitoes circled lazily in the center of the room, and I hastily closed the door so they wouldn't move into the bedroom.

"Would you please spray the bathroom for the mosquitoes?" I asked the bellboy.

"No problem, madame," he said. He was back in a minute or two and gave the room a good spray, then closed the door and left. After waiting for a few minutes, I opened the door to allow the bathroom to cool off. Flopping down on my bed with a book, I waited for another period of time before entering the bathroom for my bath. It was as hot as ever, and a few mosquitoes lazily circled in the middle. Exasperated, I investigated behind the window curtain, to find that there was no glass in the window, just open wooden slats, and the screen that covered it was full of large holes.

"Hell! We'll have to keep the door closed all the time, and we'll be eaten alive whenever we go in there," I complained. This proved to be true, and our baths were necessarily short during our stay in Mahabalipuram.

"Let's go for a swim," I suggested, after we were well cooled off. "The beach looked divine."

We got into our bathing suits and went out onto the beach. A strip of white sand stretched out on both sides of us for miles, shaded with palm trees and lapped by little waves. The water was a limpid aquamarine, shimmering in the late afternoon sun. The only people on this beautiful strand were a German family who were crouched near the edge, building a sand-castle. The sand was clean and crystalline, crunching slightly beneath our feet.

We waded in, expecting lukewarm water like the sea at Cochin, and were delighted to find that the water was cool; really cool and pleasant, about eighty degrees Fahrenheit.

I was hanging in the water, waggling my fingers every now and then to keep myself afloat, when I noticed Ed peering down into the depths below with a gloomy expression.

"What's the matter, honey?" I asked. "Do you see a Portuguese man-of-war or something?"

"How far south of Madras are we, anyway?" he asked, worriedly. "I think it's only about thirty-five or forty miles. Remember when we were walking along the beach there, and we saw those signs which were posted every little way? 'Danger, sharks—No swimming allowed'—remember? I keep thinking about the headline I saw in the Madras newspaper that one fisherman was eaten by sharks and another had his arm bitten off. Shouldn't we be closer to the shore?"

"Ed, our book says this is the best swimming beach on the whole East coast of India. It said *everybody* swims here.

"Anyway," I added, "that book we have at home on sharks said that they are only attracted to people if they splash around, or kick their feet a lot when they swim. Just don't do the butterfly breast stroke!"

Ed grinned. "If I tried the butterfly breast stroke, I'd die of a heart attack before any shark could get to me."

We continued to bob around in the water for a long time after that until we'd finally had enough and emerged, uneaten.

Because the hotel was so grand, we dressed in our best for dinner. We joined the crowd of French tourists at the buffet and stared at the display of food. It was all Western: salads, cold and fresh, tray upon tray of them; chafing dishes of hot food, and a number of delicious-looking desserts and pastries.

"Look at the salads, Ed," I said avidly, gazing at the beautiful lettuce and tomato, jello, and cottage cheese and fruit creations, each one arranged for maximum eye-appeal. I hadn't tasted salad for weeks, and I longed for cold food.

"I'm going to have some," I said. "I don't care *what* our books say. Anyway, everyone else is eating them and I don't believe for a minute that they will hurt us." I loaded my plate and headed for the little table. Ed followed me, his plate also piled with salad. How we enjoyed them, especially the jello salad. After days of eating rich, hot and spicy Indian food, the cool sweet liquidness of jello tasted like heaven to me.

A round and cheerful-looking young man approached our table.

"Excuse me," he said, smiling, "would you mind veree much if I should share your table? My tour group eez too beeg and zhere is no room for me."

He proved to be a charming dinner companion, and kept up a steady chatter about life as a tour guide.

"Ah, norzhern France ees so cold and—'ow you say—rainee. I lov Eendia! I go home now and zhen, but mos' of zhe time I tak' one group aftair anozher, mos'ly in Sous' Eendia. Maybee som'day I get too old for zhis, I want to 'ave zhe wife, zhe cheeldren, but for now . . ." he gestured around the room ". . . I am happee."

"I take it back what I said about the French," I said to Ed, as we got ready for bed. "He was so nice. I envy him, guiding his tour groups. Wouldn't it be fun if we had a job like that?"

"Not really, Bunny. We can go where we please and do what we want, and we don't have to wet-nurse a bunch of persnickety tourists who want everything to be the same as it is at home. I like our summers just the way they are, and then I like going home again in the fall."

Wistfully I wondered if I'd ever get tired of traveling. Probably not, I concluded. *I'm* never happy to get home in the fall.

In bed I tossed and turned, sleep eluding me for once.

"What's the matter?" asked Ed, as I flopped over for the fifteenth time.

"I can't stop thinking about Debbie and worrying about what she is going to do when the baby comes. She is only a couple of years older than our daughter Betty, and I keep thinking about her alone and in a strange land and pregnant. And she didn't love India the way I do," I added.

He patted my shoulder sympathetically, and after a while I went to sleep.

We awoke early in the morning to a fresh, pale pink dawn, and were down on the beach before seven o'clock. The tide had risen in the night, and the gentle little waves lapped near the top of the steeply sloping beach and sometimes even broke over it. In the distance, we could see the shore temple rising right out of the sand, its strange and distinctive shape black against the morning sky.

We walked along the beach to the little fishing village which extended along the shore on the way to the temple. The mud and thatch huts were built well above high water, with waste land between them and the waves. This strip of land was used as a workshop at the northern end, and we walked over to where a nearly naked old man was standing, making rope. Three strands of hemp were held by three young men who stood far out, fan-like, from the ropemaker. Each of the young men was twisting his strand in a clockwise direction. The strands all came together in the old man's hand, while he twisted them into the completed rope, which was as smooth and even as if it had been machine-made. It made a fascinating picture: the old man, whose leathery skin was nearly black against the background of golden sand, his tangled mop of greying hair partially hiding the beads of sweat on his brow, magically molding the fat rope which fell behind his feet in a neat coil. He smiled in a pleased way at our interest, and allowed us to take his picture.

Further on, a young man was repairing the ropes of his one-man fishing boat. We had never seen a stranger craft, and we went closer to inspect it. It was really more a raft than a boat, only seven feet long, and consisting of three eight-inch-thick curved logs tied together with the tapered ends at the front, with a prow that curved sharply up. A short mast was secured a little ahead of center, using ropes loosely tied instead of nails or pegs. There were several other boats lying here and there in the sand that were constructed in the same way, but we couldn't look too closely at them as we walked, for we had to watch our step. Mounds of

90

shit dotted the sand, most of it, at least, I was relieved to see, well above high water. I hoped that somewhere in the tiny village there was a pig to take care of the sewage disposal.

As we approached the Shore Temple, the sand became clean underfoot again and we could concentrate on its exquisite profile. It was the last of the beach temples that once had decorated the beaches of Tamil-Nadu. The rest are now just faint traces in the sand. It was dedicated to both Vishnu and Siva, and in their honor long lines of fat stone bulls guarded the approach. These images were very weathered outside the temple, but were better preserved within. A sea wall had been built to shelter it from high seas, but unfortunately this was an eyesore, and effectively cut the temple off from the sea. Like most of the older type of Dravidian tamples, this one had no roof, but was open to the sky, yet once one was inside the temple there was a feeling of serene peace and protection, for the coal-colored walls rose high enough (though it was a tiny temple) to screen out the sound of the sea and the wind. The little carved figures upon the walls were ambiguous, for the centuries had softened their outlines, changing them into featureless little androgynous creatures, yet they danced in the sharp morning sunlight with joyous abandon.

The road into the town of Mahabalipuram was narrow and dusty, lined with stalls selling junk to the tourists, and other "tourist attrac-tions" of various kinds. An ancient crone dressed in rags led a fat dog by a string around the neck. He was saddled and bridled, and on his back sat a little monkey dressed up in a ridiculous brocade ball gown, complete with wig and hat. Both the dog and the monkey looked embarrassed and uncomfortable, as well they might, for it was a hot day for such goings-on. Further along squatted a snake-charmer with a mongoose on a chain by his side. I stopped to pat the pretty little creature, and the snake-charmer started to lift the cobra out of its basket.

"Fight, yes, Madame?" he grinned.

"No, no!" I cried, horrified.

Disappointed, he stuffed the snake back into the basket, but he was mollified when Ed gave him a rupee in payment for allowing him to take a picture of the little mongoose.

Although there were several Western-style restaurants along the road into town, none were open for breakfast, so eventually we found ourselves in the town square. There was an Indian restaurant there. We went toward it and peered inside; it was a huge, dark room with uneven cement floors and rackety wooden tables. It was packed with people and with waiters uncharacteristically rushing around with trays of steaming food. The din was terrific. We entered gingerly—this was something new in our Indian experience. A waiter took one look at our Western faces and led us into a small back room with only four tables in it, all of them occupied by Indian families. We were shown to two empty seats at one of the tables, facing a beautiful woman, her husband, who had a nose of heroic proportions, and their daughter, who looked to be about two years old. They nodded and smiled at our approach, and I deduced from this that they did not speak any English, especially when they started talking to each other in Tamil.

"What a beautiful woman," I remarked to Ed, "I hope that the little one takes after her . . ."

The waiter approached and distracted me before I could finish my sentence, which would have been ". . . instead of after her father."

We ordered *idlees*, which we wanted to try, and settled back to wait.

"What country do you come from?" asked the beautiful woman.

For once I was speechless.

Ed saved me by answering, and then I found my tongue and we had a lively conversation with the friendly family, until a waiter delivered their food. The dish they had ordered consisted of some kind of golden yellow, fluffy grain with fried cashew nuts scattered over it.

"It is *uppama*," said the woman, in answer to my question, "spiced wheat."

We continued to wait for our idlees for quite a while after our companions had finished their breakfast and left.

"I guess the waiter misunderstood or forgot our order," said Ed at last. "Let's order some of that uppama."

We hailed a passing waiter and after a short time, the uppama appeared. It was delicious, and we ordered coffee after it. The coffee was brought in a steel tumbler which was placed inside a steel bowl. You were supposed to pour it back and forth between the two to cool it slightly and mix the sugar in.

We were about to call for our check when the first waiter appeared with our idlees, which proved to be rice cakes with chutney.

"Oh, well," said Ed, "why not!" and dug into his second breakfast. I followed suit (the idlees were wonderful) and then we had a second cup of coffee.

The bill, when it came, amounted to fifty-five cents in American money.

Fortified, we set out to see the rest of the Hindu carvings of Mahabalipuram. The first stop was the plaza that contained the five

Rathas, little temples that were scattered around the sandy plaza, all facing the center, exquisitely carved, and in glorious condition. A stone elephant whose rotund form dominated the center portion seemed to be guarding the temples.

A short distance away were the wonderful temples hewn out of the huge rocks that overlooked the town. There were eight of them, and to see some of them one must climb up over large boulders. The place reminded me of my childhood—my family's favorite picnic spot had been a place called "Rock City" in Mount Diablo State Park near Walnut Creek, California. There the wind had carved natural caves in the sandstone, and children had scooped toeholds in the sloping rock to reach not only the caves, but sometimes the very top. Here my sister and I had played, carefully placing our feet in the toeholds and inching our way up the steep sides. I could still hear my father's voice—"Go carefully, girls. Make sure your foot is solidly placed before you move up." What wonderful parents they'd been, to allow us to climb in such perilous places. I remembered the exciting aura of danger and the heady feeling when we had achieved the summit.

I looked up at the toeholds scooped out of the pink Indian granite. "I'm going up, Ed."

"I'll be right behind you, honey."

It must have been quite a sight to the young Indian men who scampered up and down the boulders, and to their decorous wives and mothers who waited below: a well-upholstered greying female in a brightly-colored sundress, whose ample rump jutted out behind as she climbed up the steep rock! Once on top, a breeze cooled my sweating face as the familiar exhilaration came over me. The view of the crowded bazaar and town below was terrific and we lingered there for a while before heading for the temple that perched further along on the summit. There we hit a snag: the temple faced the other way, and our side hadn't a window or a door; nothing to break the smooth wall facing us. The rock fell away in a steep slope from the corner of the little building on each side, and there were no handholds on the side walls.

"Shall we go back?" asked Ed.

"It's such a long way around," I protested. Taking off my leather sandals and holding them in my hand, I faced outward, and, leaning back toward the wall, edged along in my bare feet, NOT looking down as I did so. The slope became less steep as I made my way along, and in a few steps I could walk normally. Ed followed in his rubber-soled shoes.

The temple, once we made our way to the door, was like the others in

93

the area; tiny, with a large phallic symbol inside, and figures carved at the entrance. Two others further down had beautiful life-size figures of Siva reclining (waiting for Parvati, his wife), and in each case his lingam, or penis, had been removed. (*Who* had removed them? The Muslims, great destroyers of Hindu art, had never got this far south. Were they in a British Museum somewhere? *Penises?* Or was the desecration ordered by some stuffy British official, worried that an English Memsahib might see them and be offended? We decided that it was probably the latter.

But what a pity! Hadn't they had *any* respect for their subjects' religious symbols?)

Around the back side of the rock was a large tank, about six or seven feet deep, ten or more feet long, and six feet wide, chipped out of the solid rock. It was half-filled with bright green water left over from last winter's monsoon. We sat down to rest by its side, facing West, away from Mahabalipuram. Before us stretched a river estuary, with tall palms along the banks and rice paddies beyond, and in one of them, water buffalo were slowly pulling a plow. The sun turned the partly flooded paddies and river into sheets of silver edged in green.

Our last visit was to the most wonderful carving of all: the huge rock face, covered with figures, called "Arjuna's Penance." Forty feet or more high, and at least as wide, the tableau dominated the area. We stood in real awe at this, the pinnacle of South Indian art. Realistic groups of monkeys grooming each other, elephants trumpeting, temple girls dancing, and other human figures and demons weaving together in a vortex of movement and form, were so lifelike, so supple, that it was hard to believe that they were made of rigid stone. Once again I wondered at the western world's ignorance of the glory that is India. Like Ed, I had never even heard of this artistic wonder. We had been brought up in a culture that reveres the history and accomplishments of Greece, Rome, and medieval Europe and ignores the great civilizations of Asia as if they had never existed.

That evening, we decided to go to a restaurant located near the Shore Temple that was reputed to have wonderful grilled lobster. Most of the tables in the little room were long, seating eight or ten, and scattered around them were quite a few young Western travelers, all of whom sat dispirited, unsmiling, staring into space. A few were eating, but most appeared to be simply killing time. A pretty young European girl with stringy, dusty hair, dressed in a faded sari, sat in a trance at the next table. Drugs? Homesickness? We had no way of knowing.

A smiling young waiter came from the kitchen, displaying two large live lobsters, and we ordered them grilled, with french fries. They came to the table appetizingly crispy around the edges and tender and juicy in the middle, but I found it hard to enjoy my dinner while being watched by the gaunt, bearded young men and sad girls who surrounded us. It was with relief that we left, and as an antidote, we stopped at a noisy, crowded Indian restaurant and had coffee before returning to the hotel.

CALCUTTA

CHAPTER 9

Blood and Hair

The train journey from Madras to Calcutta lasted a day and a half, leaving Madras in the evening and arriving in Calcutta just thirty-six hours later. We were a little nervous about our destination. I felt about it somewhat the same as I had felt about India originally, only more so: I feared it and was curious about it at the same time. We had scheduled only one full day there, thinking that we might not be able to stand any more. In the back of my mind on the whole trip had lurked the specter of Calcutta! (In my mind's eye, the name always had an exclamation point after it.)

I woke on the first morning at five o'clock after a fitful sleep. It had been a very hot and sticky night and the train had leapt and bounced along, but fortunately I had never stayed awake for long. Ed for a change had actually slept the night through. "Bed tea" arrived at seven and breakfast finally came along at nine.

I looked at what lay upon my tray—a delicious-looking omelet with onions and green chilis, two pieces of buttered toast and tea—and I found that I was decidedly not hungry. I took a few bites, but I had no desire for more than that. Ed was sitting opposite, eating his with obvious enjoyment.

"What's the matter?" he asked. "You're not eating. Isn't yours good?"

"Yes, it tastes fine, but I'm just not hungry. I think I'll just drink the tea." It came in a little pot that contained three cups and I drank it all.

"Are you sick?"

"No, honestly, Ed. It's funny, but I just can't force myself to eat anything. Otherwise I feel fine. And I want lots of tea, because I'm very thirsty." He was obviously worried because never in my whole life before had I been unable to eat.

I picked up my book, a delightfully romantic novel set in India, and lost myself in its pages until lunch time.

"Don't order any lunch for me," I said, when the conductor arrived for the lunch order.

"You're kidding!"

"I'm just not hungry."

The countryside flew by, flat and green with rice paddies, and quite dull. The only things of real interest in the countryside were the little huts built at the edges of the fields, to shelter the farmers from the sun or the rain as they watched their land. Perhaps they chased away marauding birds or browsing cows, or maybe even foraging beggars. What it was they guarded against we never discovered, but almost every field had its watchman. I gazed at the passing scene for a while and went back to my book, putting it down only in stations, where the sights were always interesting.

In one large town, where the train stopped for nearly half an hour, we watched a boy preparing food for one of the station foodstalls, squatting on the floor with a big pan of some kind of yellow foodstuff, picking it over and cleaning whatever it was. A pretty dog was sitting on her haunches, big ears pricked up, watching him intently. She seemed to be mostly whippet; she was pale golden brown in color, and almost fawn-like in appearance. The manager of the stall came out and shooed at her. She grinned at him, salaaming with her forelegs straight out, hind end up. The man smiled and left. Then the boy gave her a couple of hunks of the food, which she daintily ate, and resumed her sitting position. Another dog came along—a big, mean-looking male. Instantly she leapt to her feet, snarling, her lips drawn back from needle-sharp teeth, her eyes like slits. She snapped viciously at the other dog; he decided upon discretion and left. The boy finished with the pan, gave the dog another piece or two, and took it into the stall. Then he returned to his place with fresh vegetables, including green chilis. He cut these into inch-long pieces, with the dog an interested spectator. When he had filled a metal container with the vegetables, he brought out a pestle and started to pound the mixture. As he pounded, bits of the contents slopped out onto the far-from-clean cement floor. These he carefully picked up and returned to the pot.

"Oh, well," I said to Ed, laughing, "it will be cooked, anyway."

But the mixture was dumped into a serving dish and placed on the counter to be eaten fresh. Chutney!

Ed and I looked at each other and mentally chalked up one more thing we couldn't eat in India.

The afternoon passed slowly. At dinner time, when I still refused a

97

tray, Ed started to look grim. At the next stop he got off the train and disappeared. As soon as he left, I felt that restless, tight, lost feeling in the pit of my stomach that always lasted until he was safely back on the train again, and I nervously listened for the whistle that would tell me that he was left behind and gone forever. Instead, he was back within five minutes carrying a "hand" of finger-sized red bananas and several little square packages of cookies sealed in heavy waxed paper.

"You are going to eat at least one banana and some cookies," he said masterfully.

Meekly I did as I was told, I ate half a dozen of the sweet, crisp little cookies, along with tea which was brought to the window by a hawker, and then two bananas. They did taste good, and after a while I climbed into my upper bunk and fell into a sound sleep.

We woke just at dawn to a beautiful morning: warm, damp, and partly cloudy, with the sun frequently peeping through and splashing gold on the lush green countryside. Pretty little villages under huge, spreading peepul and neem trees, each village with its "tank" of muddy water in the center, lay only a few hundred feet apart. At one stop I watched women drawing water (drinking water?) from the tank as water buffalo submerged their fat and shiny bodies a few feet away. Dung smoke from the cooking fires, mixed with the sweet, earthy smell of flowers, drifted to our window: the scent of India. I sighed with pleasure.

"How do you feel this morning?" asked Ed.

"I feel fine."

"How about breakfast when we get to our hotel?"

"I'll just have more bananas and cookies now. And tea later. I'm still not hungry."

We arrived in Howrah Station at six-twenty, just twenty minutes behind schedule, after a journey of nearly a thousand miles. We hastily gathered together our belongings and dismounted behind the porters, looking around in trepidation.

Howrah Station was big and dark and crowded, with a dim glass roof high overhead, and, to my amazement, flower baskets hanging from the pillars. It was dirty, but no dirtier than other stations, and the crowds that milled around didn't look like they were starving, nor were they more ragged than anywhere else. We tried to observe with one eye as we kept our porters in sight with the other, while picking our way between the supine bodies of the sleepers.

Outside we caught a rattletrap taxi that actually had a working meter, and as we passed the infamous Howrah slums, we stared curiously out the window to see what was to be seen, but they appeared, at least to the untrained eye, to be no worse than those of Bombay. We were never to see more of those slums; all our books advised that it was dangerous to enter the area. The Howrah bridge into Calcutta was a spectral network of spidery steel packed with pedestrians, cars, bicycles and motorcycles, with an oxcart or two thrown in for nuisance value. A cacophony of horns, racing motors, and shouting taxi and truck drivers assaulted our ears, and diesel smoke and automobile fumes smote our noses. Far below, the sluggish Hooghly River, a branch of the Ganges, slid muddily between oily banks, carrying its burden of boats and ships of every description crowded together. Near the banks, naked men and children grubbed in mud up to their knees, looking for God knows what in the ooze. Oh, Calcutta!

Once we had crossed the bridge into the city proper, the way was easier, for the street became a wide boulevard. The Victorian buildings we passed were of stone and had originally been elegant, but their dignified facades were flaking and peeling, and mold had crept down from the roofs, leaving black trails like snail tracks. The dark clouds lowered overhead, for we were back in the land of the monsoon, and the streets were slick with greasy water.

We arrived at the Fairlawn Hotel on little Sudder Street, near the Museum, and were driven up a long driveway lined with flowerpots. The hotel looked like a Victorian mansion, with a large, square portico in front, under which we were deposited, and our room sustained the illusion, for it was quaint and chintzy, in a homey sort of way.

We went downstairs to breakfast just as the power went off, and while we looked over the menu, Ed asked a waiter the reason for the failure.

"So sorry, sir, but Calcutta power go off every morning for two hours, and every afternoon for two hours. Power shortage, so sorry. Very hot." He waggled his head from side to side sympathetically.

"It's not so bad here," I remarked, "since it is all open to the outside to catch the breezes." Really, the British had understood the climate of Calcutta, for french doors opened wide to the portico, and we could feel the fresh air on our faces.

After Ed had eaten his substantial breakfast and I had drunk my tea, we set out on foot to see the "New Market" which was near the hotel. It turned out to be anything but new: an enormous farmers' market and flea market, occupying several square blocks of old warehouses. It was possible to buy just about anything there, even meat, in the Muslim section. The only meats available were goat and chicken, and the thin little carcasses hung from overhead rails above every stall. The offal was tossed into shallow ditches which ran along the backs of the stalls, and the stench was terrific. This market was well attended by the Muslim community and also by the Chinese, a substantial group in Calcutta, judging by the number who were shopping there and in the huge fruit and vegetable market further along.

We stopped to watch and listen to a group of young Hindu street musicians who squatted on the curb, playing strange little instruments of various kinds, none of which we had ever seen or heard before. The melodies these instruments produced, all in a minor key, were strange, beautiful and mournful. The crowd of local shoppers watched and listened in the silence of appreciation, and a pile of coins on the ground cloth which was spread to receive them attested to the musicians' skill.

We spent the morning wandering through the antique and jewelry stalls, somehow acquiring a "market boy" (shill) whom we simply could not shake, no matter how rudely we spoke to him. He clung to us like a leech, trying to guide us into certain stalls, and unwilling to take no for an answer. We resolved to freeze him out with silence, but after ignoring him completely for at least twenty minutes without any result at all, I lost my temper.

"Go away, you miserable little creep," I shrieked at him in exasperation. "Get lost! Go away!"

"Oh, madam," he protested, and his eyes filled with real tears, "Oh, madam, you are breaking my heart."

I gave up at last, dissolving into laughter.

"Oh, hell! We might as well go back to the hotel. It's lunchtime anyway."

Happily, I was able to eat some real food at lunch, although my appetite was diminished. Later in our room, I looked at myself in the mirror and realized that I was decidedly thinner.

"Look at me, honey. I've actually lost quite a bit of weight! This was easier than any diet."

"You had lost weight even before you lost your appetite," said Ed, "and so have I. Look." He pulled his waistband away from his body a full three inches. "I've had to tighten my belt two notches."

This was an unexpected dividend; a reward (for what virtue?) and a delightful surprise. It is a fact that Westerners lose weight in India, and not necessarily because they get sick. We hadn't been sick at all, yet the flesh had simply melted away effortlessly, despite the fact that most of the time we had been eating more than we usually do at home. Whatever my malady had been, it seemed to be pretty much over, and I hadn't felt sick at all.

Our room was cool, for the power was not due to go off for a couple of hours, and we decided to take the opportunity for a nap. It seemed that we had only been asleep for a little while (though actually it was nearly two hours) when we were awakened by a strange thundering noise that filled every corner of the room. I lay there for a minute, wondering what in the world it could be, until I realized that it was the sound of rain. We got up and opened the windows, for it was hot and sticky in the room, the power having gone off as we slept. We watched the rain as it cascaded down, bouncing a foot off the window ledges, and falling in a solid curtain until it hit the ground below. The garden was awash with water—it had become a shallow pond, and the sodden flower heads were bent until they looked like they were drinking from a lake. The noise was pervasive; we had to shout to be heard above the thunder. A cool breath came from the open window, lifting the damp hair away from my forehead. We pulled up chairs and sat there by the window until the rain stopped, as suddenly as it had begun, about a half hour later.

We went out to a cooler, moist world of shiny streets and dripping trees and buildings. Outside the hotel grounds lurked a cluster of hand-pulled rickshaws manned by some of the most villainous-looking men we had ever seen. Two of them detached themselves from the group and came over to us.

"Rickshaw, sir? Rickshaw, madam? Only twenty rupees all day."

Seeing that it was already nearly four o'clock in the afternoon, and remembering that the desk clerk had told us that three rupees was about right for an afternoon's sightseeing, we demurred.

"Five rupees," said Ed firmly.

"Twenty rupees," repeated the villainous one. Ed cut the argument short by beckoning to two different rickshaws from the remaining group. The drivers immediately came over, grinning widely.

"Five rupees for the afternoon?"

"Yes, yes. Five rupees." They leered at the original two, who fell back with long faces, and we each climbed onto the high seats. My driver was a handsome youth, whose wicked face was marred, or enhanced, by a long scar which cut across his coffee-colored cheek, and whose beautiful white teeth were usually showing in a grin. He wore khaki shorts and a tee-shirt, once yellow, which slowly became soaked with sweat as he hauled me through the nearly impenetrable traffic. His sweat was the only indication of effort, for he loped along like an antelope, as if the

101

whole conveyance weighed only a few pounds, instead of the three hundred pounds that it actually did.

Hand-pulled rickshaws were something new in our experience; indeed, they exist only in Calcutta today, although in the past they had been found in every Asian country, from Japan to Malaysia. Several years before, the Indian Government had tried to outlaw hand-pulled rickshaws in favor of pedicabs, but the drivers had rebelled. In heavy traffic, the maneuverable rickshaws are preferable to the clumsy pedicabs, which need almost as much turning radius as an automobile. They are elegant conveyances; shiny black, with large wheels. At first I felt uneasily that somehow I was exploiting the sinewy young man between the shafts ahead of me, but after reflecting on the matter for a while, I realized that it was only a job, after all, and probably easier and more remunerative than, say, shoveling gravel on the roads, or pushing a plow. This was confirmed in conversation, for my driver was quite fluent in English.

"Madam, if they outlaw rickshaws, what should I do then? I cannot drive a taxi, for I cannot get a license. I must support my mother and young brother. Without the rickshaw, we would all starve."

"Where is your home in Calcutta?" I asked.

"My mother's house is outside of Calcutta in the country," he answered. "I live in my rickshaw."

"Do you sleep in it?" I asked, surprised.

"Yes, madam. It is not so bad. See, there is a top for when it rains, and the seat is quite soft."

"And quite tiny, too," I thought.

Later we saw many men asleep in their rickshaws, but to us they always looked terribly uncomfortable, draped over the narrow little seat with their rail-thin legs either propped against the side or hanging awkwardly out.

Our drivers took us alongside the Maidan, sometimes called the "lungs of Calcutta," a huge green park that had served as promenade, park, and sports ground for the British in the days of the Raj. It was full of strolling Bengalis taking the fresh air in the late afternoon, the women in their graceful saris, the men in shirts that were whiter than white. The sun occasionally broke through the clouds, sending shafts of radiance between the trees and turning the ground mist into a haze of gold.

The Bengalis were very different from the dark and gracefully languid people of the South. Their skins were golden brown, and they were short and sturdy with round faces. They seemed to be a volatile and voluble people, who often stopped to converse in groups, arguing and gesticulating in an animated fashion.

Calcutta is the center of the arts in India, and the Bengalis pride themselves on their intellectual achievements, and the quality of their theater and literature. Bombay may be the center of the movie industry, but the really fine Indian films which are shown in film festivals around the world are usually made in Calcutta. Poetry and literature are important to everyday life in Bengal, and Calcutta's poets and playwrights are justly famous.

Bengal is also the center of Kali worship in India, and it was here that human sacrifices used to take place at the Kali Ghat, which is the most important temple to Kali on the subcontinent. When the British came they stopped the human sacrifices, but animal sacrifices have continued to this day. Kali is an avatar, or one of the manifestations, of Parvati, Siva's consort. She is the Goddess of destruction and death.

We really enjoyed our drive around the downtown section of Calcutta, and we both wondered why it has such a fearsome reputation. To us, the city of some twelve million people was an exciting and fascinating spectacle, for it is alive and vibrant in a way that few cities are. It is true that there are many people living in the streets, for Calcutta is cursed with the arrival of an average of three hundred people *a day* from the countryside, most of whom have nothing but the clothes on their backs; but the fact that she can absorb and somehow provide, even minimally, for them all says something for her vitality. And however one pities the poor little families crouched under an old sari draped along a wall, cooking their meals over tiny fires built on the sidewalk, one cannot help but admire their fortitude and the cheerful faces they turn toward the world.

We stopped at a tiny open-fronted teahouse and bought ourselves and our sweating drivers tea, which we shared at a little table near the whirling fan, and then returned to the hotel. Despite the agreed-upon fare, we gave each a well-earned ten rupees plus a two-rupee tip and a ballpoint pen. Their pleased grins followed us up the driveway.

"I wish we had a couple more days here," Ed remarked, as we got ready for bed that night. "I've been looking over this guidebook, and it is a shame that we can't go to some of these interesting places."

"Like the Kali Ghat. I know. I've been thinking the same thing, but honey, we were so nervous of coming here . . ."

Reluctant though we were to leave, by seven o'clock the next morning we were at the airport for our flight to Nepal. While standing in line for our boarding passes, we discovered that the plane was delayed "until ten-thirty."

Resignedly, we sat down on hard plastic chairs to wait, after checking our baggage. The airport lounge was being redecorated, and a thick layer of dust and sawdust coated everything. A couple of workmen were scraping paint off the big plate glass windows, using pieces of broken glass which screeched earsplittingly as they were used. They were getting the paint off, all right, but each pass of the "scraper" left a long scratch in the glass, and the window was etched with deep grooves that covered the surface like crosshatching. Ed was amused at the uncaring attitude of the workmen, but I was appalled at the waste, for the windows, which were about twenty feet long and ten feet high, would certainly have to be replaced. It was depressing to sit there and watch the workmen ruin them, and my ears were beginning to suffer from the horrid screeching noises.

A ticket agent approached us with the news that the flight would be delayed until three o'clock in the afternoon. At first my spirits, already depressed, plunged to a new low, but after a minute or two I had a bright idea.

"Let's go back into town and see the Kali Ghat," I suggested. "We have plenty of time."

After finding a taxi-driver who could speak English and who promised to be our guide for the day, we located the Kali Ghat with no trouble. It was a low, dark temple with menacing carvings silhouetted against the sky, and a large courtyard surrounding the central sanctuary. On one side of the yard stood a gaunt, barren tree with branches like beseeching arms raised toward heaven. Something like Spanish moss hung on the branches, giving the tree an indescribably sinister look, and we went closer to see what it was. Black hanks of human hair were draped over every branch, looking like the icicles on a witches' Christmas tree. Some still had bits of flesh clinging to them, making me shudder in horror. Our driver explained that childless women came to this tree to pray to Kali for a child. As an offering, they pulled out a handful of hair ("Not just a leetle," he said) and laid it over a branch. If they were successful in conceiving, then they would return, find their own hanks of hair, and remove them. ("How in the world would they know their own?" I thought, and shuddered again.)

Our guide led the way across the courtyard.

"See, the sacrifice is here," he said, pointing to several little platforms, each with a shallow depression stained rusty red in the middle.

"Sometimes a goat, sometimes a cheeken," and he drew an imaginary knife across his throat.

We took off our shoes and picked our way across a muddy floor in the temple. The stones were gritty and damp, and my bare feet recoiled from their touch. I wondered how many damp towelettes I had with me.

Our guide held a whispered conversation with the Brahman priest, and then led us into the Holy of Holies. Before the altar sat several dozen worshippers packed closely together, swaying and chanting. Their eyes glittered in the candlelight, unblinking and unseeing. Sweat stood on their brows, and their expressions were ecstatic. I watched them sway in the flickering light, and I became lightheaded myself. I stumbled behind our guide toward the altar, and then I saw Kali. She was squat and black and horrible, with red and glittering eyes. Around her thick neck was a necklace of human skulls, and the cruel and avid smile on her hideous mouth made me draw back, repulsed. Around her shoulders were draped garlands of red flowers, and red candles surrounded her effigy, for red is the color of blood.

We stared in fascinated horror for a long moment before we followed our guide out into a fine rain, and I gulped big breaths of the fresh air. I had seldom seen anything to compare with the Kali Ghat for sheer horror, but I had to admit that it was one of the most interesting things I had ever beheld. And I have not forgotten it.

After the Kali temple, we went on to other sightseeing, but none of it made much of an impression on me, and the taste of Kali Ghat was still on my tongue when we returned to the airport.

KATHMANDU

CHAPTER 10

Land of the
Living Goddess

When we had planned our trip in the fall of the previous year (so long ago, back in that strange other world which seemed so far away now) my mother decided to take a tour of Asia to coincide with ours, and to take along her granddaughter, my niece Sue, a lovely eighteen-year-old. We were all planning to meet in Nepal, and Ed and I were arriving there just two days in advance of the two of them. We were looking forward to seeing them, of course, but also we thought it would probably be fun for them to see how we lived on our trips, in contrast to the deluxe treatment they would no doubt be receiving on theirs.

The plane dropped down toward the emerald valley that lay below us, flat as a table, surrounded by towering mountains. Giant clouds had gathered over the mountains; as yet the valley was bathed in sunshine. It was beautiful, but . . . disappointing.

"I thought Kathmandu was right in the mountains," Ed said, voicing my thoughts, " . . . sort of on the mountain slopes! This is as flat as Calcutta." But when we landed and started down the steps to the tarmac, the difference between Nepal and Calcutta immediately manifested itself. It was cool in Nepal; cool and fresh. A gentle breeze was wafting around us as we walked across the field toward the hangar, and the hangar itself was comfortable without air conditioning. We got to our hotel, the Panorama, in late afternoon. It had been added to several times; the result was a series of rabbit-warren passageways leading to different buildings. We were assigned to a room, number 58, and as Ed filled out the register I went ahead with the bellboy and the baggage. After several twistings and turnings and crossings of courtyards, we started up a stairwell that stretched up as far as I could see.

"What floor are we going to?" I asked.

"The seventh, madam."

"Good heavens! Haven't you got an elevator?"

"No, madam."

"Have you got a room lower down?"

"Yes, madam. I will show it to you."

We walked down a long corridor and he threw open a door into a large, dark, and dingy room with unmade beds. One curtain was torn and hanging, and the walls looked as if they hadn't been scrubbed since the hotel was built.

"I don't like this room. Do you have any more on a lower floor?"

"No, madam."

"Damn. I suppose you might as well show me number 58."

We started up the stairwell again; each floor had three flights of stairs. Twenty-one flights. I was panting by the third floor and by the sixth the blood was pounding in my head. I had to slow down, and finally emerged, gasping and sweating, at the top.

We were in a little elevator house on the roof. I followed the bellboy outside. The roof was paved with large blocks of concrete, furnished with wicker chairs, and edged with boxes of marigolds. The view was magnificent! The mountains surrounding Kathmandu seemed much closer than they had at street-level, and the medieval town stretched out around us, pink brick and timbered houses leaning crazily over narrow, twisting streets. Here was our dream of Kathmandu after all!

A penthouse room perched on the roof before us, and we went in. Windows all the way around, Tibetan rugs on the floor, and a yellow-tiled bath all seemed to say "Welcome!" I tipped the bellboy and started to settle in.

After a while Ed appeared, panting from the twenty-one flights.

"How do you like it?" I asked, waving my hand around the room. "We even have two *geckos* in the bathroom."

"It's great, but couldn't we have got one further down? We're going to have to climb those stairs several times a day."

"It's the fly in the ointment, isn't it? No. The room I saw on the second floor was gruesome. If we take the stairs slowly it's not so bad." I had been wandering around the room as I talked, and suddenly I spotted something written on the wall.

" 'Star Suite #58,' " I read aloud. "Someone else liked this room too. I wonder who it was."

"Probably a hippie. A *young, strong* hippie."

"Oh, honestly, Ed. You're not so decrepit!"

It was already dinner-time, so we went back down the twenty-one flights and out into the street. It teemed with people, and we noticed the

107

variety of types, races, and nationalities. To begin with, there were lots of Western tourists—Europeans, Americans, and Australians, and most of them were young travellers, bearded and backpacked. The men in this group outnumbered the women by about four to one. There were lots of Indian tourists also, mostly Sikhs from the Punjab, well-to-do, well-dressed, and turbanned. The Nepalese, small, slim and liquid-eyed, were in the minority in this section of Kathmandu, outnumbered by the tourists and the resident Tibetan refugees. The Tibetans were easy to spot, for they had round faces with high cheekbones and a proud grace of carriage. The women wore attractive dresses of wool suiting, crossed at the bodice, and almost touching the ground. The Tibetan men wore Western clothing. Colorful pedal rickshaws cruised the streets, expectantly pausing alongside prospective customers.

We hailed one, as it was starting to rain, and named a Chinese restaurant recommended in our guide-book.

"So long as it doesn't keep on raining," I said. "Wouldn't it be awful if it rained all the time we were here?"

"Don't worry, it will probably just rain for a little while and then stop, just as it has everywhere else."

The Chinese food was just what we had been craving, and the cozy, crowded restaurant was pleasant. We lingered over our dinner until it was late, emerging sleepily into a pouring rain that bounced off the cobbled streets and gleamed in the light that streamed from the windows. We looked around hopefully as we stood in the doorway, and our rickshaw, which had waited unasked in a shadowy corner, pulled up.

"Panorama Hotel?" the driver smiled. The pedicab had a folding top like a baby-carriage that didn't quite extend to cover our feet and legs. He tucked a waterproof tarp over our legs to protect them from the downpour. He opened an umbrella to cover his own head and shoulders, and holding it with one hand, steered with the other as he sped along. The driving rain, coupled with a ground mist eerily reflecting the lights from widely-spaced street lamps, the half-timbered houses half-leaning over the narrow cobbled street, and even the rickshaw, reminded me of old Sherlock Holmes movies in which Basil Rathbone and Nigel Bruce raced in a hansom cab to some sinister adventure.

"This is going to be fun," I panted, as we toiled up the twenty-one flights. "I think we are going to love Nepal. I just hope the rain stops."

We were awakened in the morning by pigeons stomping across our roof (this is no exaggeration; we could actually hear their little footsteps!) and the sun streaming in the windows. Out on the roof, Kathmandu lay before us bathed in bright sunshine. On the the rooftops of the tip-tilted houses below us, little boys were flying small kites in the wind. It was such a glorious morning that we skipped breakfast and hurried down to the streets.

We wandered up and down the twisting alleys, noticing how much dirtier these streets were than those of India. The children were dirtier too, with plump little hands and faces streaked with grime; often they had runny noses. They were certainly cute, though, and unlike the totally nude Indian tots, were clad in tee-shirts, their round, bare little bottoms showing below.

The architecture of the buildings verged on the fantastic. Some of the most miserable dwellings had gorgeous lines and riotous carvings, often of the most explicit erotica, over considerable portions of the facades, especially under and around the windows and over the doors. There were literally temples on every corner, halfway down every block, in back-yards, in front yards of homes and tenements. Most of the idols (Ganesh and Buddha were the favorites) were daubed with red ochre paste, partially obliterating their features and rendering them rather repulsive. The religion itself seemed to be a mixture of Buddhism and Hinduism with some purely Nepalese aspects thrown in. The little shrines were often crumbling with age and lack of maintenance (once we saw an exquisite little stone statue of Nandi the bull lying on its side almost in the gutter), but each had its garlands of marigolds and roses, and its sticks of incense fragrantly burning. Even the little children seemed to be deeply religious, and smeared red paste on each shrine as they passed.

Many of the little roofs over the windows of the houses served as platforms for the drying of red chilies and garlic, and lengths of sari material were hung below the windows. These, combined with the multitudes of temples and the brightly-dressed Nepalese, made the streets incredibly colorful, and even the sight of a dead rat in the middle of one street did nothing to dampen our spirits.

"You know, I must be getting hardened," I observed. "If I ever saw a dead rat on the streets of San Francisco I'd be horrified, but here it is just something to walk around. It's funny how you get accustomed to things."

"Let's go to the 'Tantric Yin Yang' for lunch," Ed suggested, when our skipped breakfast made us aware of our empty stomachs. "That's supposed to be quite an interesting place, started by a Texan who was living here a few years ago. It's a hangout for hippies, but it sounds like it would be kind of fun."

109

We found it without trouble; it *was* an interesting place. From a central sunken stage, platforms on different levels rose up the walls almost to the ceiling. Dark red carpeting covered these platforms, creating "couches" for lounging, complete with velvet cushions and carved wooden low tables. Pierced brass Indian lamps hung from the ceiling, strategically located over each "couch." "Hare Krishna" paintings hung on the raffia-covered walls. It was a highly unusual restaurant, to say the least. The food was good: a mixture of Indian and Chinese cooking that seemed to be the fashion in Nepal. We decided to return after dark one night to check out the action.

In mid-afternoon, great clouds gathered overhead and a few drops signaled that it was time to return to the hotel, for we had forgotten umbrellas. (*Damn* those twenty-one flights!)

We were to meet Mama and Sue at their hotel, the swankiest one in town, just before dinner. They had arrived on the afternoon plane from Delhi and we expected that they would be installed in their room by the time we got there. We dressed up in our best and set out by rickshaw in the rain. After a long drive, we pulled up to an imposing gate and our driver got out and stood aside for us to dismount.

"Would you please take us up to the front door?"

"I am sorry, madam, but I cannot. Only taxi can drive up to hotel. I am sorry that you must walk."

The driveway was long and exceedingly wet, and my best sandals were waterlogged by the time we reached the front steps. We entered the deeply carpeted lobby, where several smartly-dressed and -coiffed Americans and Europeans were chatting; we were shown to the room where my mother and Sue were waiting. It was exciting to meet family halfway around the world from our normal milieu, and we talked for a long time before going down to dinner. The dining room was filled with Westerners, which seemed strange to us, who hadn't seen many in the past few weeks. The menu was Continental and very expensive, and the food, when it came, was quite good and elegantly served, and we even had wine—at a stunning price.

"Just for curiosity, let's find out what a room here would cost," I whispered to Ed, as we were leaving. Mama and Sue were on an all-expenses-paid tour, and had no idea how much their luxurious room actually cost. Ed went over to the desk and talked to the clerk, then rejoined us.

"Sixty dollars U.S."

"Good heavens, that is almost ten times what our hotel is costing us! Do you think it is ten times as good?"

110

"Of course not. But they do have an elevator."

Fortunately, the rain had stopped briefly when we started our long walk to the outer gate, followed by Mama and Sue. Our faithful rickshaw driver was waiting for us there. We had looked around for other taxis at the door and had seen none, nor were there any outside the gate. Our driver left to find another rickshaw while we waited.

"What do people do when they want to go into town if they are staying at this hotel?" I wondered.

"Are you kidding? Do you think any of those people will ever go out on the streets? Hell, they'll take a deluxe bus to the tourist attractions, eat all their meals in the hotel, and talk only to other Americans or Europeans. And they'll spend a fortune. And then they'll go home and think that they've seen Nepal."

"But they'll have a nice hotel room," my mother pointed out, laughing. "How is yours?"

"Actually, Ma, I love it!" I said. "But I doubt that you'll want to climb twenty-one flights of stairs to see it."

"You might be surprised," she said. "Tomorrow you must take us up there."

Our driver came back, followed by another rickshaw, and we started toward old Kathmandu. On our way to the Tantric Yin Yang, we passed a temple out of which came the sound of voices singing. We stopped and went in to watch and to listen to the strange instruments and vocal harmonies. It was pleasant in the warmth of the temple after the damp chill of the night. The dim candlelight wavered on the gold and silver of the sanctuary, and the heat of the candles intensified the odor of flowers and incense. As always I was impressed with the *holiness* of the temples. "Surely God must be here, just as he is in a Christian church," I thought, not for the first time.

The Tantric Yin Yang was filled both with young travellers and truly exotic hippies. American "psychedelic" music was playing on the stereo which had been set up on the sunken stage, and the air was heavy with incense and marijuana smoke. We had tea while reclining at one of the carved tables on a dais halfway up the wall.

"This is even more exotic than the temple," my mother giggled as she watched a group of imaginatively dressed "freaks" dancing on the stage. Sue was wide-eyed as she watched the action around us, and we all enjoyed what amounted to an unusual 'floor show.'

It was late when we finally returned to our room after dropping off Mama and Sue, and the stairs seemed a frightful obstacle, but at last we emerged from the elevator house onto the roof just as the moon broke out of the clouds and illuminated the jumble of crazy roofs below us.

"God, this is a great place, isn't it?" we said, before we went inside for the night.

In the morning, the sun was brilliant in a clear sky—it was a pattern we were beginning to recognize: during the monsoon months, clear mornings were followed by gathering clouds in mid-afternoon, and rain by dusk. It generally rained almost all night, clearing up just before dawn.

We went out onto the roof and gasped. The glittering peaks of the Himalayas stretched out across the northern horizon, diamond bright in a pale blue sky. I had thought that the steep slopes surrounding Kathmandu were the Himalayas themselves, but they had been the merest foothills. These mountains were magnificent, breathtaking . . . they seemed to hum in the sharp morning air, a ghostly, vibrant chorus, just out of range of the ear. The Roof of the World . . .

We had arranged for a taxi and driver for the day, sharing expenses with Mother and Sue, and found him waiting at the curb when we got to the street. He was as handsome as a matinee idol, with the great, dark eyes of the Nepalese, and a slim, athletic grace. His name was Bushkar.

"First we must pick up the rest of our group at their hotel," said Ed, "but we are not sure where we should go after that. Do you know of any festivals or weekly markets today?"

"Yes," said Bushkar, "there is a 'blood sacrifice' at the Kali Ghat this morning. Would you like to go?"

Would we! This was a chance not to be missed. Blood sacrifices were not held often, even in Calcutta, and we hadn't even been aware that there was a Kali Ghat in Nepal.

After picking up Mother and Sue, we started up the narrow road that wound through the mountains to the west of Kathmandu. The view was beautiful as we climbed; little terraced rice paddies stepped down the mountain, separated by copses of pine, and the valley below stretched away in the sunlight, emerald and forest green shading to lavender in the distance. As the road flattened at the top of the ridge, we were able to see the Himalayas again, sparkling icily in the northern sky, and we stopped the car and got out for a better view.

A pretty little girl-urchin with a dirty face appeared behind the car, followed by her herd of four goats. She smiled shyly and held out her hand.

"Rupee? Pen?" We couldn't find any pens (we were forever leaving them in our luggage) but finally Mama dredged up some small coins and gave her a couple. Instantly two small boys appeared, holding out their hands, and then several older girls. We managed to find a few more coins, but then gave up when children appeared from everywhere like seagulls, running over the fields, climbing fences, and surrounding us ten deep, crying "Rupees, rupees!" in their shrill voices. We fought our way into the taxi, and Bushkar slowly forced the car through the crowd, horn blaring. As we fled, they stood there in the middle of the road, with hands still stretched out, and stragglers still arriving over the fields. There must have been fifty or more by the time we rounded a bend and left them all behind.

The Kali Ghat was located in a narrow valley which had a limpid stream along one side. Bushkar led us to the open-air temple, which was beautifully situated against the hillside. Gilded ornamental beams arched in to a central pediment suspended over a cut-stone floor. A roofed-over altar was in the rear; ten or so stone effigies of Hindu gods, each in its niche, were ranged along the left side as we faced the altar. The effigies were sprinkled with brilliant red flowers, and splashes of red further decorated them over their surfaces—it was a moment or two before we realized that the splashes were blood.

As we watched, the "killer" cut a chicken's throat and passed it, kicking and flapping, over the effigies so the blood ran onto them. A couple of lean yellow dogs followed the killer as he worked, licking up the blood as fast as it ran over the floor. I shuddered, and then I remembered a scene from my childhood: my grandfather used to kill chickens for the table in exactly the same way. I remembered my childish horror at the flapping, and the blood, and my grandmother coming out to take me into the house, for I wasn't supposed to have been where I could see the slaughter. This memory made me feel better right away, especially when the Brahman priest explained that the chickens would be cooked and eaten by the worshippers after the service. Somehow, the horror lay in *ritual* slaughter. It could be put in perspective simply by remembering that most of us eat slaughtered animals. And we all had to admit that it was certainly an interesting spectacle. As we turned to leave, we almost ran into a couple of middle-aged American ladies who, like us, had hired a taxi to bring them to the blood sacrifice.

"We have morbid tastes, don't we, dearie?" said one gaily, addressing herself to me. "The temple is kind of a cheerful place for such goings-on,

113

isn't it? It's really pretty, with the gold and the flowers. Sure makes something to tell the folks about back home!"

Our next stop was the Swayambhu Temple on "Hippie Hill," just outside of Kathmandu. Our taxi parked at the base of the hill where a large hippie colony was located, and we noticed that their houses looked like any other Nepalese settlement—the same colorful saris were draped over windowsills, and the houses had the "raffish" air that one associates with the Nepalese. Only their long, light-colored hair distinguished the hippies from their neighbors.

We started up a long flight of shallow stairs shaded by a solid canopy of trees which protected us from the sun. The forest was full of large grey monkeys, which begged for candies and made threatening gestures when none were forthcoming. One big male even threw a clod of dirt—or possibly monkey droppings—at us, but his aim was poor. Halfway up the slope on a stone platform, looking like a Hollywood creation, sat an impossibly handsome holy man in the full lotus position. His long white beard and mustache and his white, wavy hair made a nimbus of silver in the sun, and a fresh lei of jasmine blossoms lay on his saffron robe. His hands were turned upward, resting on his knees, and a saintly expression rested upon his perfect features. He was exquisite; no wonder a large pile of rupees covered the cloth beside him. Our rupee joined the stack after he graciously allowed us to take his picture.

At the top of the steep little hill was the temple of Swayambhu, which possessed a really dramatic stupa with the great all-seeing eyes of Buddha painted on all four sides. The dome supporting this gold-topped tower was all crusted and runnelled with the dried milk of centuries of offerings, forming a surface like concrete and several inches thick. Around the base of the dome were hundreds and hundreds of big prayer wheels, most in motion from the propelling of many hands, for this is a major pilgrimage site. It was an amazing picture: the flags flying in the breeze, the people of many races, the glittering gold finial atop the stupa, the marvelously alive all-seeing eyes, and the prayer wheels spinning, spinning. Entranced, we wandered around, drinking in the wonderful sights, and spinning the prayer wheels, which is supposed to be done in a clockwise direction.

We stopped to watch a priest consulting an oracle, who in her normal state appeared to be an ordinary village woman. She put herself into a trance by singing, quite naturally at first, and then, rocking slightly as she sat cross-legged, she got more and more emotional as her voice rose in pitch. She opened her eyes wide and stared at the candle before her, and then quite suddenly went into the trance. In this rigid and unseeing state she was the oracle. The priest questioned her gently, listening intently to her replies, which were given in a peculiarly intense singsong.

At last we dragged ourselves away and returned to Kathmandu in our air conditioned taxi. The day was then very hot, and Ed remarked that what he wanted more than anything in the world was an ice-cold beer.

"Sir, allow me to buy real Nepalese beer for you and your family," said Bushkar, turning down a narrow side-street.

"Thank you," said Ed, naturally, but with a tinge of trepidation in his voice.

Our driver stopped the car and led us through a low stone doorway into a tiny area that was very dark. When our eyes became accustomed to the gloom, we made out a low-ceilinged room of stone with three tiny tables along one side. Bushkar motioned us to one of them and held out the child-sized chairs for Mama, Sue and me. The table was greasy and covered with spilled beer, and the walls were black with the grime of what could have been centuries. A little idol with a face like a gargoyle occupied a niche in the wall next to our table. Flies crawled around on the table and on the fat stomach of the idol, and a few circled in the center of the room. A pretty young woman in a filthy apron came out to greet us and take our order. Her three little tots, as pretty as Japanese children, but grey with dirt, hung onto her skirts.

In an agony of apprehension, I sneaked looks at Mama and Sue, for they were definitely not used to this sort of thing, and I was terrified that they might rise from the table and flee. But no: Mama serenely seated herself (careful, however, not to touch the table, I noticed), ordered a Limca, and smiled charmingly at the pretty owner. Sue had a delicate line of sweat on her upper lip, but she smiled bravely and also ordered a Limca. Ed and I ordered the rice beer, to Bushkar's evident pleasure.

The beer, when it came, looked poisonous, and probably was. It was pale and frothy, served in a bowl that certainly never had seen soap. I steeled myself and drank.

"It is very good, Bushkar," I said, truthfully, and drank it all. So did Ed.

"I dare say one sip would have been as lethal as a bowlful," I said to Ed later, "so I figured I might as well drink the whole thing. And I wouldn't have hurt Bushkar's feelings for anything. It was so sweet of him to buy us a drink."

When we had finished, and were back in the taxi, I surreptitiously handed Ed a double dose of Pepto Bismol and took the same myself. We

115

were none the worse for our little adventure, and I was certainly proud of my family. They had risen to the occasion like troupers.

The four of us toiled up the steps to Star Suite #58, where our penthouse was duly admired by the visitors. I took them into the yellow-tiled bath to show them our resident geckos, but the little lizards were missing.

"I wonder where they are hiding," I said. "They are usually active this time of day. We can hear them chirping at night—it's a comforting sound, for I know the little darlings are busy eating mosquitoes. It positively lulls me to sleep."

The next morning, when I mentioned our missing pets to the old cleaner who came to scrub out the tub and toilet, he waggled his head proudly.

"I kill. Lady no like animal in bath. All gone now."

"No!" I couldn't repress my cry of horror, nor the tears that stung my eyes.

His pleased smile faded to a look of hurt bewilderment, and I could have bitten my tongue. I patted his thin old arm and said, "It's okay. Don't worry about it. I just kind of liked the little things."

"Sorry, mem." He shook his head and shuffled into the bathroom, the picture of misery.

"I don't know which I feel worse about," I said to Ed, as we circled down the flights of stairs, "the lizards, or hurting the old man's feelings. If he had to kill something, I wish it had been those two huge cockroaches who live in the drain, but they are probably too quick for him. They've sure been too quick for me! I'll really miss my little geckos."

When we emerged from the dark hall into the sunshine of the smaller of the two courtyards, we came upon an old man sprinkling colored rice powder on the stone flooring in beautiful and intricate patterns. To one side was a long, low table with an assortment of brass dishes and bowls upon it, and a pile of flowers and candles at one end. We stopped to ask the man what it was all about, but he spoke no English, and after watching for a while, we left, as it was getting late and we had to meet Mama and Sue for their last day in Nepal.

This time Bushkar took us to Patan where the Tibetan refugees' camp was located on a harsh, open plain. The mud houses looked most unprepossessing, but, according to Bushkar and others, the Tibetans have done well for themselves in Nepal. Their principal income was derived from the sale of hand-knotted wool carpets in the Chinese style, and the camp was a popular tourist stop. The carpets could be purchased in any

116

of the Tibetan shops in Kathmandu or Patan, but in the camp one could watch the carpets being made.

We entered the long buildings where the sheep's wool was being carded, dyed, spun, and finally hand knotted at large wooden frames. Red-cheeked Tibetan women, a few men, and one pretty twelve-year-old girl were sitting cross-legged at the frames, their backs ramrod straight, their hands flying. They were singing and laughing as they worked—the happiest group of workers I have ever seen. Outside the buildings were the dye vats—huge copper pots sunk in cement with hot fires under them, boiling the yarn. Workers with colorfully splashed clothing stirred the steaming vats, and one who was evidently tired and taking a break was stretched out on the sloping roof in the sun, sound asleep. The dyes used these days are colorfast, unlike the old vegetable dyes that faded with use, and the carpets are reputed to be extremely durable.

Our next stop was Pashupatinath, one of the holiest of Hindu shrines, on the banks of the Bagmati River, which runs into the Ganges. The temple honors Lord Siva and has a gold-leaf roof which is very beautiful. Unfortunately, and to our great disappointment, we were not allowed into the temple at all, for it is forbidden to non-Hindus.

Returning to our car, we passed the leprosarium, which we had not noticed on the way down. Two hundred lepers lived there, attended by dedicated doctors who have managed either to cure or arrest the disease in the resident patients. They remain at the leprosarium probably because they feel more comfortable there than in the world outside, where they are still shunned. Several lepers sat on the long verandah of the building closest to the road; they looked almost like anyone else, except that several were missing cheeks or noses. I looked down at my well-fed, well-clothed body, and felt faintly guilty for being healthy and strong, somehow reproached by those thin, brown figures on the verandah who followed our progress with their large eyes.

We went back to Kathmandu to the Kumar Kumari house to see the Living Goddess of Nepal. She is the latest in a long line of little girls, chosen by seers and astrologers when they are only four or five years old, and taken from their parents to live in solitary splendor in the Kumari House, where they are worshipped as goddesses. When the little things reach puberty, they are turned out into the street; they are no longer holy, for their blood has defiled them. Their lot is a hard one, for no man will marry an ex-Living Goddess; it is supposed to be bad luck!

We paid two rupees each to an attendant, and the little girl was carried to her balcony, yawned, and stared down at us. She was only six or seven,

117

poor little mite, and a virtual prisoner. She wasn't even allowed to walk, lest she stumble and hurt herself, for no blood must escape her body. I was struck by her look of profound boredom, and my mood, already pale blue as an aftermath of the lizards and the leprosarium, became a deep indigo.

Returning to the Panorama Hotel first, so that Ed and I could change our clothes for dinner, we all entered the little courtyard on our way to the room. It was transformed: a priest was performing the rites that began the "full moon festival," sitting on the colored rice flour designs that we had seen in the morning. He was wearing a golden crown and a gorgeous robe, and he rang a bell with his left hand as he sprinkled various grains and other food with his right into a small fire burning in a bronze container before him. A tiny female attendant held an umbrella over his head to shield him from the sun, and another scurried around, handing him first one thing and then another. Tall tapers of incense burned on either side of him, and Nepalese rope incense, called *dhoop*, smoldered in dishes upon the low table, lending its woody fragrance to the air. A little stone stupa in the courtyard was covered with flowers and candles. This cheerful scene acted like a tonic on our spirits, and soon we were smiling and looking forward to the last evening together with my family.

We left their hotel early, for Mama and Sue had to catch the first plane to Delhi. Ours, to Benares, or as the Indians call it, Varanasi, didn't leave until much later.

When we emerged from the hotel, it was raining hard, and to our dismay (for we had forgotten), there was no taxi, no pedicab, not even a hanger-on waiting for us. I looked at Ed and he shrugged.

"I guess we walk," he said, putting words into action.

Within a couple of blocks our feet were soaked, although our umbrellas kept the upper parts of our bodies reasonably dry. The rain was warm, and the air was sweet. It was still early when we crossed into old Kathmandu, and Ed suddenly said, "Want to walk some more? We're already wet, but it's not cold and it's too early to go back to the hotel. I feel like having a walk. We've been riding around too much lately."

We turned down a previously untrodden street which headed in the direction of Durbar Square, and after a block or two we noticed a large building flanked by a courtyard which, though unlighted itself, reflected light which streamed from windows just outside our view. Curiously we entered the courtyard, turned the corner, and beheld a strange sight: the building before us seemed to be a cross between a temple and a hospital, where people were sleeping amongst various idols in a room that was well-lit inside and open to the courtyard, but separated from it by a wire mesh. Quite a few people, although none of them seemed to be tourists, were standing around in the courtyard, peering into the room. We asked a bystander if he could tell us what the building was, but his English was so heavily accented, and his voice so faint in the thundering rain, that we could not understand him. Another bystander with better English could not or would not tell us anything about the mysterious building, but he did translate for us the text that was painted on one of the walls. I have reproduced the story here as nearly as I can remember it.

"A rich man spent all his money in riotous living until all he had left was a bowl of rice. He put the rice out in front of him and went to sleep, whereupon some birds ate it all. Before they flew away, the grains of rice they had eaten became gold, which they shitted all over the ground in front of the sleeping man. When he awoke, he was richer than ever. Just then, the ogre-god Garuda jumped in front of him and was going to eat him. The rich man was very intelligent, and he said,

" 'Don't eat me, for once you have, I'll be gone and you'll have nothing. Let me live and I'll buy all the bad little children from their parents (who will be glad to be rid of them anyway) and you can eat them!'

"So Garuda agreed, and that is what happens to bad children in Nepal."

Still chuckling over the story, we found the exit and stepped out into the dark and rainy street. I was in the lead, and I turned to continue in the direction of the square, when I ran right into a huge bull who had been standing there silently in the dark. Choking back a shriek, I backed wildly into Ed, treading heavily on his feet.

After a breathless second or two, during which the bull sniffed gently at my face, his heavy nose ring banging me on the chin, I realized that he was a gentle creature, and lost my fear.

"Nice boy," I said, patting him gingerly on his forehead, "nice boy." We carefully tiptoed around his huge bulk, and continued down the narrow street, while the rain poured off our umbrellas in cascades, and we waded through lukewarm puddles two and three inches deep. We tried to continue in the same direction, but after a while we thought we were probably lost.

"It's been such a mysterious and strange night that I wouldn't be surprised if we wound up in the Emerald City of Oz," I remarked to Ed. "I don't think we'll ever find our hotel."

119

But we did. We turned down a narrow lane which curved around in a new direction, and just when we thought we might have to go back, the lights of Durbar Square appeared at the end of the lane. From there we rickshawed home.

We squished up the twenty-one flights for the last time, and in our room I removed my once-best sandals, which were soaked with malodorous mud. I carried them between thumb and forefinger over to the wastebasket and dropped them in. Then I scrubbed my feet with soap and hot water in a bucket and dumped the dirty water into the toilet before getting into the bathtub. There were no towels on the racks, no toilet paper in the holder, and the room boy had forgotten to put the pillowcases on the pillows after he stripped them, but a call to the desk produced them in less than half an hour, via an apologetic desk clerk whom we had awakened for the second time. We crawled into our beds and I was just drifting off when I heard Ed chuckle.

"I was thinking about that bull," he said.

CHAPTER 11

BENARES •

The River

We were sitting in Kathmandu Airport in the late afternoon, waiting to board our plane for Benares, when the wave of nausea washed over me sickeningly. "Oh, God," I thought. "I knew it would happen sooner or later." By the time the plane left the runway I knew I was in for a bad time.

"I'm feeling sick," I moaned.

"Really, honey?" Ed looked concerned. "Where is the Pepto Bismol?"

"In my train case. But I don't know if I could chew one up and swallow it. I don't like the taste and right now I'm not sure I could get it down."

"Sure you can. I'll get you a coke and you can take them like aspirin." He hailed a stewardess.

When the coke arrived, I tried to swallow the large pink tablet.

"It's too big," I gagged. "Maybe I could break it up." I broke two of them into several pieces each and managed to get them down. Then I put my head back against the seat and let misery have its way with me. After fifteen minutes, Ed made me take two more, and then two more after that just before we landed.

"The doctor said to take lots," he insisted. "You are going to take them every little while until you feel better."

By the time the taxi had brought us to our hotel, I had severe stomach cramps. I stumbled down the long outside corridor to our room in a daze, and crawled into bed without benefit of bath. My implacable husband forced Pepto Bismol down me whether I wanted it or not, and I was too miserable to refuse. After a while I fell into a doze between cramps and trips to the bathroom, and after a couple of hours, I did actually get to sleep. When I awakened at eight o'clock the next morning, I was completely free of either cramps or nausea—just weak and wrung out.

"How do you feel?" said Ed, entering from the bathroom.

"I can't believe it. I feel okay."

"Are you well enough to get up?"

"I think so. I don't feel like hiking up a mountain, but I bet I could ride around on a rickshaw."

"There are no mountains in Benares," Ed said, "so haul yourself out of that sack and let's go. What about breakfast?"

"I'm not hungry, but I'll have some tea. In fact, I'd *love* some tea. You know, I really can't believe that I feel so well. That stuff really works! How many did I take, anyway?"

"A whole boxful, plus two from another box."

"My God."

"Well, the doctor *said* to take lots."

"I wonder if it was that clubhouse sandwich I had for lunch that made me sick."

"That could be. You know we are supposed to stick to cooked food only, and Nepal is a hell of a septic place."

"Yes, but I've been eating tomatoes all along."

"You're lucky you didn't get something before this."

"Yes, dear." Meekly.

"*I* don't eat uncooked food."

"You did too. You had salads at Mahabalipuram!"

"That's true. But I think we'd better swear off the dangerous stuff. I was really worried about you last night."

"I know, dear. I promise to be good from now on." Mentally I vowed to be more careful. It was just that I *wanted* things like sandwiches and salads.

That day we took it easy, cruising the streets of Benares and noticing the differences between it and other cities. We crossed the bridge over the Ganges and gaped at the temples and "waiting-to-die" houses that sit atop long and steep flights of stairs descending into the river. They line only one bank, the west one, while the opposite bank is lined only with trees and backed with fields, for there was a legend that the east bank at that point on the river was an unlucky place. I had seen many photographs of the Ganges at Benares, with the crowds on the steps and the crowded buildings above, but had never realized that this development was on one side of the river only. It seemed a strange dichotomy, lopsided and odd, and I had to mentally shake myself to get rid of my preconceived ideas.

Benares, though rather primitive and backward, was vibrant with an atmosphere of almost hectic joy; a palpable feeling of ecstatic anticipation. The proportion of elderly people was very high, and they thronged the streets, along with younger people of every caste and color, most of them with expressions of sublime happiness on their faces. Benares is filled with temples, and lines of beggars sit at the entrances. Most of these beggars are either very old or badly crippled, and a whole row of them is a pitiful sight. After a little thought, we realized why there were so many old people and cripples. They had come to Benares to die. The "waiting-to-die" houses edge the Ganges above the burning ghats, while the holy kites of India circle, circle overhead.

Not all the inhabitants of the holy city are old, however. We saw what passes for a school bus there: a rickshaw modified so that there were two parallel benches about five feet long behind the driver. Ten children were squeezed together on the benches, all dressed in their school uniforms and carrying their brass tiered lunch buckets. They were well-scrubbed, well-fed, and they smiled and waved to us as we passed.

We stopped at some of the places of interest, such as the Monkey Temple, where Hanuman, the Monkey God, protects his little brethren. We removed our shoes, of course, and got our feet even dirtier than at the Calcutta Kali Ghat, for monkeys are not the cleanest of creatures. They sat all around the temple grounds, grooming themselves and each other, picking fleas out of each others' fur, shitting, feeding their babies, and fornicating in bland disregard of onlookers. Ed was trying to take the picture of one large male who had turned his back on us, and he made the mistake of making rude noises at it. The monkey bared his teeth and rushed at Ed threateningly, thoroughly startling both of us. Then he deliberately turned his back on Ed again.

"Little bastard knows he's safe," growled Ed. "Look at him. He's as arrogant as a king."

Our next stop was a silk factory. Beautiful lengths of silk were spread out on the grass in front of the building, probably drying in the sun after the final washing, we guessed. We dismounted from our rickshaws just as a cow came ambling along, heading in the direction of the silk-covered lawn. Immediately a little woman who had been sitting on the front steps leaped to her feet and swiftly gathered up the silks. The cow trod amiably over the lawn while the woman waited, her arms piled high with shining colors, and when the cow had passed, she spread out the bright silks again.

We went inside where we were allowed to watch the laborious process of hand-looming silk with real gold thread, which is nothing more than incredibly thin gold wire wrapped around a silk thread. Jacquard cards punched with the design in code somehow lift the warp (or is it woof?) threads so that the weaver can wind the bobbins of gold or silk around each group of lifted threads, then throw the main shuttle along, catching it at the other side. It was a slow process—we watched for a long time while the weaver worked, and he completed only a few rows, less than one eighth of an inch in length.

When we left, we stopped to watch a *paan wallah* knackily rolling up delicious-looking paan in his stall which was next door to the silk factory. A couple we had noticed at the factory also came out, and stopped to chat. He was pasty white, plump and bald, a Canadian from Toronto, and she was a beautiful Tibetan girl. I asked him if he had tried paan.

"No, I haven't tried it yet," he said nervously.

"How long have you been here?" I asked, thinking in terms of days from the look of him.

"Six years," he replied.

Six years! He looked like he'd been under glass for the entire time! Ed and I, both of fair complexion, were already mahogany brown from just normal moving around out of doors. Where on earth had he spent his time? We edged away, and made our departure as soon as we politely could.

"It takes all kinds," said Ed. "What a wimp. But did you notice her? She was gorgeous."

That evening we decided to go to the local "Kwality" restaurant, part of a well-known chain, famous for its ice cream.

"I crave ice cream and maybe fruit," I said, "but I've lost my appetite for anything else."

The service was leisurely, and we had the opportunity to observe the rest of the customers. Seated next to us was a table of, I believe, Yugoslavs. They were a jolly group, and did they eat! One young man, curly-haired and mustachioed, had a large platter of chicken cooked with rice, a dish of meat rolls with vegetables and potatoes, then a big plate of lamb curry, a huge slab of naan, and then he ordered, and finished, a large platter of chow mein. And he was thin. By that time we were finished and had paid our check, and we had to leave, but I was wishing we could have stayed. I was certain he'd have dessert after that, and I wanted to see if he could finish it.

We set our alarm for four o'clock in the morning, for I had decided to go into the Ganges with the pilgrims.

"Are you sure you don't want to go?" I asked Ed for the third time.

"Absolutely positive. I saw that water today and I'm not interested."

In the morning I put on a dress of thick, opaque cotton and no underwear, for I knew that the water was very muddy. It felt strange, to say the least, to be so under-clothed as we set out in the dark by rickshaw. As we drew near to the river, the first light of grey dawn faintly touched the dark streets, and the sleepers on the sidewalks started to rise from their ground cloths. Others were still sleeping in their string beds, washing, or brushing their teeth with twigs. The cows, pigs, and goats were also just waking up, and the quiet was shattered by the lonesome sound of cocks crowing. The city wore an expectant air, and a steady stream of people had started to move in the direction of the river.

We left our rickshaw when we had got as close to the river as possible, and walked down a long double line of beggars before we reached the ghats. On a platform at the foot of the high and wide set of stone steps leading into the water, a Brahman priest was seated in the lotus position under a large umbrella which later would shield him from the sun. Pilgrims from all over India waded into the water carrying little lamps which they set afloat when they reached waist-deep. Then they ecstatically ducked under the water, poured it over their heads, and swished it around in their mouths. Some drank it. Mothers poured the water over their babies' heads, and dunked the plump, bare little bodies in the holy river. All looked as happy as humans can look when they have reached their heart's desire. Across the river, the dawn was just turning the sky pale grey behind the line of trees along the water's edge.

I went down the steps and started to wade into the water, when the priest called to me and I returned to him. He silently handed me a little boat made out of a single large banyan leaf with red flowers and a tiny oil lamp in it. I thanked him with my hands pressed together in the Indian fashion (*namaste*), and waded in. The water was lukewarm, and very thick and opaque. Lines of greasy black ashes drifted by from the burning ghats. Fifteen or twenty feet out in the current, a white dog floated past, its feet sticking up grotesquely. I hesitated for a moment at that, and then steeled myself. I hadn't come all this way to be defeated by the corpse of a dog, and I knew I'd hate myself later on if I didn't complete my adventure. I waded in until I was up to my chest, and set my little lamp on the waters. It glimmered and danced away downstream and I watched as it joined the other tiny flames that had been set upon the river by the worshippers. I ducked in until the water covered my shoulders, and just then the rim of the golden sun began to show above the trees. I slowly started back up the underwater steps toward shore.

When I emerged, dripping with muddy water, the priest beckoned again, and I received a dark red tilak mark on my forehead. I wrung the water from the hem of my dress and joined Ed, who had recorded the scene on his camera.

"I'm really glad I did it," I said excitedly to Ed. "Did you see the dog?"

"Yep. I knew it wouldn't stop you."

"Aren't you sorry you didn't go in?"

"Nope."

I dried myself off as well as I could, and then we walked upstream several blocks to where the riverside temples and ghats began. Several wooden rowboats were pulled up on the sand beyond the last of the steps into the water, and as we approached, the nearest two boatmen ran up to us, eager to take us out on the river. They were nearly black from the sun; one wore a pink checked sarong, or *lungi*, wrapped around his waist, and the other was in khaki shorts. The muscles of their backs and arms were like cords.

We climbed into the boat and I settled myself carefully on the narrow wooden seat, mindful that I was wearing no underwear. I shivered a little in my damp dress, noticing that already it was dry across my chest, though the hem still dripped muddy water into the even muddier water that sloshed around in the bottom of the boat. As the boatmen pushed off, we slid alongside a young man who stood waist deep in the stream, panning the water for bits of gold or gems from the corpses that had been burnt at the nearest burning ghat. He shrank away from the boat as it passed, because he was an Untouchable, and didn't want to give offense.

The sun was above the trees on the opposite bank now, and flooded the temples and the pilgrims and the umbrellas sheltering the Brahman priests with rich, golden light. Many small boats crowded close to shore, bobbing in the little waves created by all those people. On the ghats (platforms) which thrust out into the river from the steps, bodies burned on heaps of faggots, and the smoke drifted slowly downstream with the current. The smoke smelled painfully of burning flesh, reminding me of a pork roast I had once burnt in too hot an oven. Kites wheeled overhead, spiraling in ever-increasing circles, waiting for a morsel to wash ashore, I guess. A widow in a brand new white sari sat mournfully at the side of her husband's pyre. My sober thoughts were soon dispelled, however, by the happy people who crowded into the river, pouring its holy water over themselves and their children, weeping with joy. Bells were ringing, some of the people were chanting and singing, prayers were being shouted to the skies. It was beautiful and joyous, sad and ugly, colorful, noisy, and rapturous. It was certainly one of the great sights of the world.

At the bridge which marked the end of the ghats, we turned back upstream in a wide sweep, hugging the shore along the edge of the steps in the back eddies where the current wasn't so strong. In places, we were forced to move out to where the current was swift, and here the boatmen would grab the side of a ghat or another boat and "walk" the boat laboriously upstream. This put us right in the middle of the action, so to speak, and our boatmen were kept busy avoiding the worshippers. It also afforded us a close-up view of the shore, and certain pictures flash back vividly: an old holy man in a yellow loin-cloth, his long white beard curling over his chest and his Brahman thread over his shoulder, sitting in a trance just at the edge of the water, cross-legged in the slanting golden sun; an ascetic doing his yoga exercises against an apricot wall; a young mother in a green and gold sari, perhaps her best, pouring water over her little baby's face, the drops glittering as they left her long, dark fingers.

All too soon we reached the landing place, and paid off our boatmen after they dragged the heavy boat up onto the sand. We walked rather stiffly up the stairs and hailed a conveniently hovering rickshaw to return to the hotel, where I stripped off my muddy dress and climbed into a hot tub, to soap off the residue of the holy Ganges, though I carefully avoided scrubbing the tilak mark off my forehead. Then I washed my dress in the same water, leaving a good layer of silt on the bottom of the tub. It was pleasant to be clean and dry again. I went to the mirror to put on lipstick and was disappointed to see that my carefully preserved tilak mark was flaking off my forehead in chunks, so I washed the residue off as well, leaving me without a souvenir of my morning's adventures.

We just wandered for the rest of the day, mostly shopping in the various emporiums by rickshaw, making use of a curious custom in Benares. The rickshaw drivers are happy to take tourists on shopping tours without charge, for they receive a percentage of the "take" from the emporiums. The percentage must be a substantial one in Benares, for while the custom is common throughout the major tourist areas in India, only in Benares did it substitute for the fare.

We went to bed earlier than usual that night, for we were to catch the early train to Agra in the morning, and we were becoming accustomed to nine or ten hours' sleep.

In the station the following morning, we were disappointed to learn that our express train to Agra had been cancelled, and that we would

127

have to take the local slow train which wasn't to leave until eleven. Fortunately, we each had an engrossing book to read, so we looked for a good place to sit. Because of the cancelled train, I suppose, the platform and even the crosswalks over the tracks were crowded with "sleepers," and all the platform seats were taken. Upon investigation, we found that there were first class waiting rooms, which for some reason were divided by sex, so we retired to our respective lounges to wait out the hours.

When at last the time came to board the train, I emerged from my comfortable corner and hurried across the crosswalk above the track, noticing that nearly all the sleepers had left, and only one old man remained. His stringy old legs sprawled out of his diaper-like loin-cloth, where, unbelievably, dark moisture oozed. A horrified glance at his eyes confirmed that he was, indeed, dead, and my knees turned to water. It was a minute or two before I regained my composure and moved away, across the tracks and down to the train where Ed was waiting.

"Poor old soul," I said to Ed later when my constricted throat allowed me to speak, "I guess we Americans see death so seldom that it seems unnatural to us. In my whole life I'd only seen two corpses before we came to India, and those only at funerals, all made up to look like they were asleep. It seems so shocking to see someone like the old man, freshly dead and uncared for. And yet, death happens every day, and to everyone sooner or later. I guess he didn't have a home to sleep in, poor old man. There's one consolation though—he was the luckiest of Hindus—he died in Benares."

The train finally left at noon, and slowly chugged along through the fertile Gangetic Plain. It was like a green parkland all under cultivation, with large trees dotting the fields and sheltering the little villages, limiting vistas to a few hundred feet. The village houses were made of mud, but with sturdy tile roofs, and each hamlet had its muddy tank, often with a water buffalo or two wallowing contentedly, submerged to the nostrils. And we saw camels again, the first we'd seen since we had left Rajasthan. A pair of them stalked haughtily along the path running alongside the train tracks, carrying sacks of something heavy slung on each side of their humps. A child ran behind them, swinging a willow switch in the air. Behind the camels and the child, across a broad field, five women were slowly walking homeward, carrying brass water pots on their heads. Each had one hand raised to steady her burden, and they swayed gracefully as they walked, their bright saris fluttering behind them. They looked like butterflies in the slanting golden sunshine.

128

At dusk we were treated to a flaming sunset which lit the thunderheads to the west with crimson and purple, fading overhead to a surrealistic green before it deepened behind us into royal blue.

When we pulled into Agra Station at dawn, we could see in the distance the Taj Mahal like a baroque pearl floating above the plain.

CHAPTER 12

Precious Stone

It was still grey dawn when we emerged from Agra Station and found a three-wheeler to take us to the hotel we had chosen from our book. As we pulled into the driveway, it was obvious from the start that this hotel had seen better days. Although our book had said that it was situated in a charming garden, the mildewed buildings stood in an overgrown, weed-filled lawn with untrimmed borders. It had such an uncared-for look that at first we thought the place might be deserted. But no: an elderly porter came out of a side door adjoining the main double-doors of the central portion of the building, grabbed our bags and led the way through the side door into a makeshift lobby.

"We have reservations," said Ed, looking around with a what-am-I-doing-here expression. "The name is Knott."

"Yes, sir," beamed the man behind the desk, "please register here."

"Let's look at the room first," I said nervously.

"Can we see the room, please?"

"Certainly, sir."

He led the way to a hot, musty-smelling, dark little cubicle with dingy walls and dirty curtains. I opened the bathroom door—it smelled even mustier than the bedroom, and nothing was clean.

"It is terribly hot in here," I said; "where is the air conditioner?"

"So sorry, Madam, but the central air conditioner was stolen last December."

"Stolen?"

"Yes, madam."

"This room will not do," I said firmly. "What other room do you have? If there is no air conditioning we will need a fan."

"So sorry, madam, but other rooms are all taken."

"When will one become vacant?"

"Maybe tomorrow, madam, maybe the day after."

"I'm sorry, but we will not stay in this room. It is much too hot."

"Perhaps I can get you one later today. Perhaps in an hour. The people maybe are leaving soon."

"May we see the other room now?"

Obsequiously he led the way back toward the lobby.

"Where is the dining room?"

"So sorry, madam, but there is no dining room."

"Our book says there is a large dining room in the center of the hotel."

"So sorry, but we have rented the dining room to the bank."

Sure enough, over the double doors that we had noticed on arrival was a large sign, "Bank of India." The manager led us around to the back portion of the hotel, which looked out into the "cantonment," a park-like area which had been the center of British military life during the days of the Raj. He opened a screen-door and then another door into a large, pleasant room furnished in the fashion of the 'thirties, with a window seat and a slow overhead fan. The room was obviously unoccupied. I looked into the bathroom; it was none too clean but not really filthy. "I can scrub out the tub with my shampoo," I thought.

I looked at Ed questioningly. He nodded.

"This will be fine," he said. "When did you say we can move in?"

"Just a few minutes, sir."

We followed him back to the lobby and registered. Without further ado the old porter took our bags to the new room.

"Why wouldn't he say right away that he had another room?" I asked.

"I bet he was just trying to rent those front rooms because they are hard to fill," he said. "He's an oily son-of-a-bitch, isn't he?"

"I'm sure glad he had this one, since we've paid for one night in advance," I observed.

After a bath and a nap, we walked around the weed-filled garden and took a look at the pool (which had been one of the reasons we chose this particular hotel over others listed in the book). The water in the pool was a dark and opaque green. A sign on the peeling wall above it announced that the water was supplied from a spring and the pool was drained and filled twice a week.

"Yech. It looks like it's been sitting there festering for a month."

"And I was looking forward to having a swim," I mourned.

"What'll it be today?" asked Ed. "There's the Taj Mahal, and the Red Fort."

"Let's start with the Red Fort, and save the Taj for tomorrow morning.

Let's see if we can get in at dawn, and then we can go back tomorrow night. The moon will be at its fullest then."

We went out the gate and looked around for a couple of rickshaws, and when none came by immediately, we started to walk in the direction of the Red Fort. We hadn't gone more than a block or two when the rickshaw I needed pulled up, and after securing another for Ed, we haggled the price down to a reasonable sum and climbed aboard. From our breezy perches we had a great view of Agra, which is an attractive city of broad parks and properly busy Indian bazaars. Most of the large hotels, the Taj Mahal, and the Red Fort are in the parklike cantonment, so we were soon at the gate of the Fort. We paid off our drivers and told them not to wait, and then we headed through the stone gate. We walked along the top of the pink sandstone outer wall and admired the view of the city first, and then "did" the inner buildings, which were of whitest marble. With Fodor's guide-book in hand, we beat off would-be guides and explored passageways, stairways, and roofs to our hearts' content, only turning back from certain passageways when the bat smell became unbearable. We even climbed upon the battlements and saw where defenders once poured boiling oil upon attackers.

We saved the lovely marble palace and last living quarters of Shah Jehan until the end. You can see the Taj in the distance from there, just on the bend of the river Jumna, rising out of the river mists. In my imagination, I could see Shah Jehan dying, a prisoner of his own son Aurangzeb, straining for a last look at the monument to his dead beloved. We went out at last, still lost in thought, to find our drivers waiting patiently for us just outside the gate.

On the way back to the hotel, the drivers suggested that we visit a marble factory, where we watched artisans delicately inlaying semi-precious stones into crystalline white marble. So cleverly were the stones fitted into the marble that the joints were nearly impossible to see. I pitied the workmen, hunched over their exquisite work hour after hour and year after year. No wonder such handwork has disappeared from the Western world. The prices in the little factory were astronomical, and we left without buying anything.

Our drivers swallowed their disappointment and took us back to the hotel, where they tried to make up for the loss of a commission by attempting to overcharge us for the ride.

"But sir, we waited at the fort for three hours . . ."

"No one asked you to. We paid you four rupees each for the ride to the fort, and so we will pay you another four rupees back to the hotel."

"But sir, waiting-time is two rupees an hour . . ."

"No."

With tears in their eyes, they finally accepted the four rupees each, and then brightened a little when Ed added another rupee for a tip. They climbed on their rickshaws and rode away, dispirited.

Ed grinned. "Poor guys, they expected a ten per cent commission on one of those three-hundred-dollar tables. You can't blame them for being disappointed."

We went into the hotel, to find that all the lights were out and the fans didn't work.

"What a lousy place," said Ed, wrathfully. "I'm going down to see the manager."

"Maybe the power is out for the whole town," I ventured.

"I don't think so."

He came back looking grim. "The power is out just in the hotel, and the manager doesn't know when it will be fixed. It's hotter than hell here and I think we ought to move."

"That's okay with me. I really don't like this place anyway."

The manager professed to be very sorry to see us go, but declined to return our deposit. "So sorry."

"Where to, honey?" asked Ed.

"Let's be swanky and go to the Shiraz. It has a pool and what I really want is a swim. Can we afford it? It's a lot more expensive than most of our accommodations."

"We'll put it on the card."

And so we arrived at the high-ceilinged marble lobby of the Clark's Shiraz, one of the two best hotels in Agra.

"A double room? Of course." A snap of the fingers and two bellboys raced up to take our suitcases. Our room had a fine view of Agra and the Red Fort. Below us, set into an emerald-green sweep of velvet lawn, was a turquoise pool. I sat down on the soft bed and sighed.

"This is living."

"Yeah, but if we did this all the time, we couldn't afford to travel all summer. Besides, if we did this all the time, we wouldn't appreciate it so much. Anyway, we wouldn't *want* to stay in a Western-style hotel all the time, would we?"

"No. Not really. But as long as we're here, let's have a swim before dinner."

The alarm clock went off annoyingly next to my ear. I reached over to shut it off but couldn't reach it (we had cleverly placed it just out of reach

133

so I wouldn't be able to turn it off) and at last I woke up groggily and staggered to the window. I drew the drapes and peered outside. It was pitch dark. For a minute I was bewildered; it seemed like the middle of the night. Then I remembered. It *was* the middle of the night: four o'clock. Time to get up and get out to the Taj Mahal to see it by the first light of dawn. The manager at the desk had suggested using rickshaws to go to the Taj; there would be two waiting for us at the front door at four-thirty.

"Wake up, Ed!" I switched on the light and threw my pillow at him as he lay comatose.

"You're mad."

"Come *on*! We'll be late!"

Grumpily he groped his way to the bathroom. "Why don't we just forget about it and go back to bed?"

Our footsteps echoed on the marble floor of the dimly-lit and deserted lobby as we made our way to the front door. Outside, our rickshaw drivers were nowhere in sight.

"Good. Let's go back to bed."

"Oh, come on." I dragged him down the driveway, sure that the rickshaws would be nearby. As we approached the gate, two shadows glided across the street and pulled up alongside us under the street light. Two dark faces grinned, and two slightly-built men dismounted to help us up onto the high seats.

"Sir, my name is Johnny," said Ed's driver, fluently, "and my friend is named Niaz, but he doesn't speak English. He is very strong though."

Niaz smiled shyly at me, showing beautiful white teeth in a very dark mustachioed face. He thrust down on the pedals, and soon we were flying swiftly along the night-black streets.

The trees along the roadside were just barely visible, being only a shade darker than the midnight blue sky. The road was lit by starshine, for the moon had set long ago, and the street lights were few and far between. Niaz was silent, and the only sound was the swish of tires on pavement. The air was soft and slightly cool, and smelled of dew and flowers. I held onto the seat with both hands and let myself fall into a dreamlike enjoyment of the night and the adventure. We continued for a long way like that, with Ed and Johnny far behind, until we came to a narrow street between rows of buildings, and then we stopped at the top of a dark stairway. Niaz motioned me to sit still while we waited for Ed and Johnny to catch up. Then Ed and I, with Johnny as our guide, started down the steps, leaving Niaz to guard the rickshaws. We crossed a wide

134

plaza paved with stones, and noticed that the stars were beginning to fade. A huge black mass rose before us, which Johnny said was the gate to the Taj Mahal, but it wasn't open yet.

"Wait here," he said, and disappeared.

We stood there in the dark of the immense plaza until at last two figures approached. One was Johnny, leading a local guide who said he knew where we could go to see the Taj at first light, for the gates were not to be opened until six o'clock.

"Go with him," said Johnny. "I will be waiting for you when you come back."

Our new guide led us back the way we had come for a short distance along a stone wall, until we reached an arched doorway. By the light of our guide's tiny flashlight we climbed a rubble-filled stairway to a terraced garden. Then we crossed the garden, and entered the portico of what seemed to be some kind of a mosque or tomb. We ducked into a very low doorway into the tomb, and climbed a set of narrow, curving stone stairs; the light from the flashlight bobbed around behind us, coming or going as we crossed in front of it. It was eerie, climbing those steep and narrow steps in the dark, and my senses were unnaturally sharpened to the sounds of our footsteps and those of the guide. It wasn't far to the top of the staircase, where we had to bend double to get through an opening onto the flat roof which surrounded the dome of the tomb. Pillars and a low railing edged the roof, and here our guide deposited us and stood with his hand out expectantly. Ed finally gave him seven rupees after a little haggling, which satisfied him, for he saluted us in thanks and withdrew.

We settled down to wait for dawn, which seemed to be near, for the stars had faded away and a certain pale light was growing in the east. Footsteps warned us that we weren't going to be alone, and the guide reappeared with three young travelers, who greeted us quietly in British and Australian accents. They had slept by the gate all night waiting for it to open (and we hadn't even noticed them). They had a difficult time finding enough money between them for a tip, and the guide finally had to settle for only four rupees after asking for ten. After a little while, back he came with two French couples, but these refused to tip him at all. He finally left empty-handed, but only after a protracted argument. I thought it was a shame that they refused to pay for his service to them, but they were completely blasé about it, and chatted noisily among themselves as if they had been alone.

We had an unobstructed view of the black mass of the Taj over the

135

high wall that surrounds it. Slowly the dark silhouette lightened and became paler as the sky turned from midnight blue to gunmetal and then, almost suddenly, the sky was suffused with coral pink light, and the Taj glowed like a pearl in its setting of rigid dark gardens. I watched breathlessly as it seemed to expand like a bubble, becoming paler as the rosy tints gently became bluer. Finally the pink was gone, and it became ghostly white, floating there like thistledown in the dawn. Beside me, the faint click of the camera told me that Ed was capturing all the loveliness for future enjoyment, but I was thankful that it was he, and not I, who had to take the pictures.

Below us in the garden, Johnny was waving and beckoning to us, so we gathered ourselves together and ducked into the cramped stairway. In a moment or two we were crossing the garden surrounding the tomb and soon we were at the front gate of the Taj. We were the first through the big arched gate when it opened.

I had been prepared to be bored by the Taj Mahal. I had seen so many pictures of it that it had become almost a cliché in my mind, linked with India as the changing of the guard at Buckingham Palace is linked in one's mind with England.

"It's just a building," I had thought, "just a building and probably a little run down. Of course we must see it, but I'm sure it will be disappointing." So I had thought.

It was bewitching. Not "just a building," but a vision, a dream. It didn't look as if it had been put together out of blocks of marble, but rather that it was insubstantial, and would vanish like a bubble if one should touch it.

We walked quietly toward it alongside the long pool which approaches the Taj from the front. Halfway to the Taj Mahal there is a raised square pool which reflects the whole building if it is viewed from a certain spot. We climbed the steps to the level of the pool and stood there for a while, admiring the unrippled reflection.

"It's deep enough," said Ed suddenly.

"Deep enough? Oh, of course. You mean that woman we met who said that the reflecting pool wasn't deep enough for Richard Halliburton to swim in. She must have missed seeing this and thought he meant the long narrow pool leading up to the Taj. That one is only about six inches deep. But this one is at least three feet deep. Oh, I'm so glad, because I always loved that chapter in his book when he described how he stayed behind after the gate was locked at night and went swimming in the moonlight, alone with the spirits of Shah Jehan and Mumtaz Mahal."

Although we had entered the gate with a little clutch of other people, we seemed to be completely alone. Our half-dozen companions had disappeared into the vast grounds or inside the building.

As we watched, the sun came up and gilded the domes and minarets with light, and the shadowy gardens suddenly were bright with color. We walked hand in hand to the platform, where we found an attendant waiting to take our shoes, or give us shoe coverings if we preferred. We opted to leave our shoes and padded up the steep stairway to the base of the Taj.

The white marble facade was covered with exquisitely inlaid precious stones in floral patterns, and we began our exploration by walking completely around the huge building, admiring them. Around the immense entranceway on each side, verses of the Koran are set in black stone. The sculptor was so cunning that he enlarged the words progressively from bottom to top so that they can easily be read from ground level.

We entered the tomb from the front door and stood for a moment in awe, for it is enormous. The dome soars up well over a hundred feet above the floor, and the sarcophagi and surrounding marble partitions are proportionate in size. We were most interested in the sarcophagi: the tombs, as we thought, of Shah Jehan and his beloved wife, Mumtaz Mahal. They were of snowy marble with the finest inlay work we had yet seen. A single candle burned at the foot of the tomb of Mumtaz, and a small lei of jasmine had been placed there for her. I had a tightness in my throat as I looked at her tomb, for I, like most people, was familiar with the story of the Taj Mahal, and the great love that the emperor Shah Jehan had for his favorite wife.

At the beginning, a canopy of pearls had covered the two tombs, and the doors leading into the tomb were of solid silver, but these are long gone, along with the rubies and sapphires that originally sparkled in the inlay work. All that remains are jade, lapis, and carnelian against the satiny white marble, but they are sufficiently lovely to fill the senses.

The pierced marble partitions that surround the tombs are particularly beautiful. The delicate lacework shines with an amber glow where literally millions of hands have caressed it. This in no way spoils the appearance, but only attests to the love that the Indian people have for the Taj Mahal.

When at last we left the grounds and went through the gate into the outside world, I turned to Ed.

"Please can we come back this afternoon and see it in a different light?"

"Again? We're coming back tonight after dark to see it by moonlight."

"I know, but, Ed, as long as we're here, let's see it every way we can. We may never get back to India again . . ." A cold chill ran down my back as I said that, and I knew then that I couldn't possibly stay away from India.

"Sure, honey." Ed shrugged and smiled good-naturedly. "If you want to."

Again, I thanked God for my husband, as I had a thousand times before. I wondered how many men would as cheerfully go along with the whims that resulted from their wives' wanderlust. And he always seemed to enjoy it all as much as I did. I squeezed his hand as we approached our rickshaws and our sleeping drivers.

We returned to the hotel for breakfast and a nap, and were out with our drivers again before noon, for we wanted to see the gold market before returning to the Taj Mahal in the late afternoon. We were accompanied by another couple from the hotel, who wanted to go to the gold bazaar with us. We started back with Ed and Johnny's rickshaw in the lead, and the rickshaw bearing the other couple bringing up the rear. Their driver was old, and he had difficulty keeping up, due partly to his age, and partly to the double load. I noticed that Niaz kept looking back over his shoulder to check their progress, and when we got halfway up a long hill, he suddenly stopped, chocked some rocks behind the wheels of our rickshaw, and ran back to help the old man. I watched him as he pushed the rickshaw from behind while the old man pedalled, until they reached the top, then Niaz ran back down the hill to get me and pedalled all the way up to the top again. He was drenched with sweat from the exertion, but refused to let me dismount to lighten his load; indeed, he was vehement in his refusal to let me walk. I was touched by the goodness of this man, and by his stubborn pride. After we had left the gold market and were within a couple of miles of the hotel, Ed's rickshaw developed a flat tire and could go no further. Niaz motioned Ed to join me on our rickshaw, and he took the crippled rickshaw and allowed Johnny to take us back. The double load was no problem, for the road from that point was flat as a board.

"How old is Niaz?" I asked Johnny. "Is he married?"

"He is about twenty-seven," he answered, "and he has wife and little daughter. 'Love wife.' He cannot afford proper wedding, so he cannot marry her."

I digested this information. I was surprised that Niaz was so young; he looked much older. Then I thought of another question.

"Do you both own your rickshaws?" Johnny laughed. "Oh, no, missus. A rickshaw costs much money. We are poor. The hotel owns our rickshaws, we pay much rent and so cannot save any money to buy rickshaw. I live with my mother and father. My father is retired army soldier, so I have easy life. But Niaz has nothing but muscle, no family to help him. He must work very hard to get money for wife and little daughter. Niaz is very good man, very good friend."

Our second visit to the Taj was as different from the first as night from day. We just stood there gaping from the top of the steps. Thousands of people milled around the grounds, taking pictures, talking, gazing at the Taj. The platform of the reflecting pool was a solid mass of people, and the lawns were dotted with families having picnic snacks. The appearance of the Taj itself was also changed. The late afternoon sun poured molten gold over the *other* side of the domes and minarets, and the shadows were dark blue and sharp. The Taj looked much more solid than it had before; it had lost its ethereal quality and had become vivid and distinct. It was as gorgeous as ever, though, and the milling crowds added excitement and color, owing to the brilliant saris worn by the Indian women. Not surprisingly, many Europeans and Americans were there too, for tour buses make the daily trip from Delhi to Agra and return.

We pushed our way up to the platform, left our shoes alongside hundreds of others, and entered the Taj. Inside it was hot and stuffy, so we made a quick tour around and returned to the entrance, where we discovered a stairway we had overlooked that morning. We went down the very steep stairs to find the actual tombs of Shah Jehan and Mumtaz Mahal deep beneath the floor of the sanctuary. The sarcophagi upstairs under the dome had been empty facsimiles. Oddly enough, it was even hotter and stuffier down in the real tomb than it had been upstairs, so we hastily climbed the steps back into the fresh air.

As we reached the top, we passed an Iranian family coming in—a handsome husband, very pretty wife, and several small children. The reason I noticed them particularly was that the young wife was wearing a poplin raincoat over her long dress, buttoned up to her chin. She had a thick scarf wrapped around her head and neck, and clumped along in heavy leather boots covered with cotton shoe covers. She had a line of perspiration on her upper lip, for the temperature must have been nearly one hundred degrees Fahrenheit, and the sun was like a laser beam.

"Of course, the husband is wearing a cotton shirt and pants, and the kids certainly are not overdressed," I muttered sourly to Ed.

139

We walked around to the back of the Taj, and this time we went to the edge of the platform and looked out over the Jumna River. (In the morning we had been so interested in the building itself that we had forgotten to look at the view.) Below us in the shallows wallowed dozens of water buffalo, looking like fat black slugs in the water. They snorted wetly and noisily—obviously in their element, enjoying themselves. Little boys swam near them, laughing and splashing. Beyond the river, flat grassland stretched out before us, shimmering in the heat.

"Wow it's hot!" said Ed. "Let's go back to the hotel and have a swim."

At nine o'clock, we set out for the third and last time to the Taj Mahal through the warm, dark streets. Traces of dung smoke lingered in the air from the cooking fires, and we passed people carrying oil lamps as we sped silently along. I kept looking up at the sky, hoping to see the stars, but clouds and mist obscured them, and there was no sign of the moon.

When we reached the arcade area near the Taj, lights and noise greeted us—a wedding was taking place! The little square was brightly lit by about ten men who upon their heads carried pyramids of gas lanterns supported by wooden frameworks. People dressed in their colorful best crowded around the groom, who sat solemnly on his horse, his face covered with a curtain of jasmine. The horse's beautiful spangled and mirrored cape sparkled in the brilliant light. A brass band was playing loud Indian music, and the instruments gleamed like gold. The bride was sitting in a car with her attendants, hiding her face in a red and gold sari. People were pushing money in to her through the open window of the car, and we joined them, adding our ten-rupee note to the others. She peeked at me and smiled, then ducked her head and covered her face again. People held out sweets to us, which we accepted and ate to their delighted laughter. Then the crowd started to move away from the arcade, and several people tried to push us along with them, but we had other fish to fry, so we reluctantly refused their invitation. We waved them out of sight, and then we were able to follow their progress for quite a while by the noise and the lights which were reflected by the buildings in the distance.

"I wish we could have gone with them," I sighed, "but I want to see the Taj by moonlight even more."

We purchased tickets for the third time, and entered the dark gateway. The Taj sat as we had seen it that morning, a shapeless black mass against the midnight blue of the sky.

140

"No moon tonight," croaked an old man at my elbow, Cassandra-like.

We walked down to the reflecting pool, where a handful of others had gathered. A Japanese man was setting up his tripod despite the clouds that threatened to hide the moon for the rest of the evening. A gaggle of Indian youths chattered together behind us, and a little clutch of young German travelers slouched morosely off to one side. We sat on the warm marble with our feet dangling over the edge of the dais and prayed.

All at once the moon popped in and out of the clouds, gleaming fitfully, and then as we watched, it drifted into a black cloud and disappeared. Ed and I walked up to the base of the Taj Mahal and back along the fountain pool, just to get away from the chatter of the boys and our disappointment. After we had returned to the others we discussed leaving. However, we were reluctant to give up completely, so we thought we'd give it just a little longer. In answer to our prayers, the moon ventured out timidly, then sailed up into clear sky, illuminating the Taj Mahal with magical, brilliant light.

It was transformed. The inlay work of precious stones, which had been nearly invisible by the light of early morning and unremarkable at a distance under the shimmering sunlight of afternoon, leapt into prominence by moonlight. The Taj Mahal looked for all the world as if it were made of lace.

Silence fell on our little group at last. Even the Japanese man stood, camera forgotten, gazing at the most beautiful building in the world by moonlight. Then the cameras came out and everyone but the Indian youths and I busied themselves with tripods and exposure meters, and muttered guesses as to how many seconds to give a time exposure.

Ed took several pictures at varying exposures, and then we packed up the paraphernalia and walked back to the Taj Mahal beside the long pool for the last time. Fireflies winked in the shrubbery, and a frog croaked suddenly nearby. We located him at once, a round, fat fellow in the middle of the path ahead of us. He croaked once more and then leaped, suddenly graceful, into the still waters of the pool, where he swam powerfully away from us. The gate at the base of the platform was closed and locked, barring us from the Taj itself. We touched the warm marble and then walked back towards the entrance gate, looking back every now and again to fill our eyes with magic.

"Well, you can't say we skipped over it lightly," said Ed, chuckling, as we passed out through the gate.

"It was wonderful, wasn't it? Aren't you glad we saw it in so many ways? And it was different every time. Oh, thank God the moon came out."

We got back "home" a little after midnight, feeling as weary as Niaz and Johnny looked as they turned their rickshaws toward their homes. It had been a long day, and we had only one more before we had to leave Agra.

We woke up with the alarm at seven-thirty the next morning and lay in bed for a while, lazy after the full day before. I ordered tea on the house phone. "Please may we have ready-made chai and toast sent to room 204?"

"Chai?"

"Yes. Ready-made chai. Milk tea."

"Okay, okay."

After a half hour's wait (utilized to take my bath—I hadn't been in India for six weeks for nothing), there was a knock on the door. The turbanned waiter entered, bearing the usual silver tray covered with a white cloth. He set it down on the low table and uncovered it with a flourish.

I removed the lid from the teapot, which revealed clear tea.

"We wanted ready-made chai. Milk tea."

"Eh?" The eyes squeezed shut as if in pain, the head waggled from side to side.

"Milk tea."

Silence.

"Please take the teapot back and bring us chai. Ready-made chai. Milk tea."

He took the pot and went out, still shaking his head. We ate our buttered toast and jam while we waited. In a relatively short time, he reappeared with the teapot.

"Milk tea?"

"Yes, madam."

This ritual was enacted every morning in every large hotel in which we stayed in India. The waiters, kitchen staff, and bellboys seemed unable to comprehend that Westerners might enjoy the traditional Indian tea. They brought us black tea no matter how often we repeated that we wanted "ready-made chai. Milk tea." We could only suppose that *no* Westerner had ever before ordered milk tea in India. It was readily available anywhere in the street and in Indian restaurants, but never—to Westerners—in the larger hotels. And it didn't matter if we had room service or whether we went down to breakfast. We had to send back a pot of black tea every time.

We had decided to spend the morning going to Fatehpur Sikri, leaving the afternoon in which to prowl the shops, which Agra had in abundance to lure the tourist. We had to take a taxi instead of rickshaws, for Fatehpur Sikri was located several miles outside of Agra; we ordered one at the hotel desk.

As we pulled away from the portico, we could see Niaz and Johnny waiting along with other rickshaw drivers. We waved to them as we passed, for we didn't want them to waste the morning waiting for us, but we felt vaguely guilty as their eyes followed us down the street, even though we had told them of our plans.

At Fatehpur Sikri we were immediately besieged by hawkers when we got out of the taxi. We pushed through them and bought our tickets, only to be besieged by would-be guides when we walked through the gate.

"No guide. No. No guide."

"No, goddammit, I said NO!" Ed snarled, as a portly little man tried to attach himself to us for the third time. He fell back a little but followed us for a long time before he finally gave up and returned to the gate to await other game.

"Persistent little beggars, aren't they?"

"Yes, and I *hate* guides of any kind, but particularly when I can hardly understand them. Remember that old burglar at Mount Abu?" I giggled in remembrance. Ed shot me a dirty look.

"It *was* funny, honey, you must admit. At least, it was funny to me."

The city, built by India's first great emperor, Akbar, was fashioned of bright red sandstone; a sandstone so hard and dense that the carvings which cover it are as sharp and clear now, and as beautiful, as they were on the day they were completed. The buildings were exquisite, surrounded by lawns and trees which were of a peculiarly intense green, contrasting with the red of the buildings. There was a square central tank of thick green water, and a large courtyard that contained the harem quarters for Akbar's wives. It was not hard to imagine him wooing one of his concubines on the balconies and terraces of the beautiful building. We climbed up onto the roof of the audience hall, and from there we could see the first of the tour buses arrive from Delhi, bringing the crowds with it. We climbed down again and crossed the open space (fighting off the hawkers who descended on us like vultures and clung to us like limpets) between Fatehpur and Sikri.

Sikri contains the famous Victory Gate which Akbar built to celebrate the consolidation of his empire, and the beautiful little mosque of white marble which is one of the wonders of the Indian world. Inside this perfect little building, an imam (priest) sells silk threads to visitors, which

143

they then tie to the pierced marble screen that surrounds the sanctuary. It is said that if you make a wish when you tie your thread, it will come true. As I tied mine onto the satiny marble, I wished with all my heart that I might come back to India.

Outside the Victory Gate was the large well that contained the water supply for the ill-fated city. Youths and men were diving from the sides of the well into the bright green algae-thickened water about fifty feet below—for a price.

A little boy of about ten with a big grin and hair plastered wetly to his forehead accosted us. "Ten rupees, I dive. Okay?" We shook our heads and turned to go.

"Oh, mister, please? I dive. Only ten rupees. Six. How about four? Two?"

He was sure cute, and I was weakening. Ed hauled me away by the arm.

"He might break his neck. Don't encourage him."

"You're right, honey. Gosh, he is so cute. Can I give him a couple of rupees for not diving?"

Ed laughed. "Oh hell, why not." He pulled out two rupees and we went back to where the kid was standing, still looking hopeful.

"No dive. But here's two rupees," I smiled at him and he grinned back, unbelieving. He grabbed the two rupees and ran, whooping and leaping in long bounds down the hill.

"You sure made his day," laughed Ed. "Come on, let's go have lunch."

We had the taxi driver drop us off at the Kwality downtown, and dismissed him. Then we went into the cool, dark, pleasant little restaurant and ate ice cream and mangoes for lunch. When we emerged and looked around for a conveyance, two rickshaws pulled up alongside us.

"Niaz! Johnny! How did you know we were here?"

"We say to ourselves, 'They are hungry, they must eat lunch.' So we come looking for you."

We climbed up onto the familiar seats and set out toward the shopping district.

"You want inlaid marble? I know good store, Subhash Emporium. Prices not too high."

Johnny was right; it was a good store. We made a number of purchases there and emerged to find Johnny and Niaz wearing broad smiles. "We get good commission," Johnny explained. "All shops pay commission to rickshaw drivers who bring customers to buy."

144

"That's wonderful, Johnny." We were happy to see them so happy.

The day went quickly, and when we returned to the hotel we took pictures of Niaz and Johnny before saying goodbye to them.

"We'll send you a copy," we promised, "in care of the hotel."

"What time do you leave?" asked Johnny.

"Six o'clock. We have to go by taxi because of the suitcases. Goodbye. I hope we'll see you again before too long."

Ed pulled out his money pouch and handed Johnny a one-hundred-rupee note. "It's for both of you, half and half," he said. "You've been the best drivers we've ever had. Thanks."

We waved to them as they drove off, and went inside.

"It's only about ten dollars," he said, somewhat shamefacedly, "and they've been great."

The next morning we were standing in a wet grey dawn waiting for our taxi on the front step, when two rickshaws came up the driveway.

"This is present for you," said Johnny, while Niaz smiled and nodded, and then they handed me a large, shining brass milk pan.

"So you won't forget us."

I clutched my beautiful pan and we shook hands all around.

"We'll come back," I said, through my tears.

The taxi appeared and we climbed in. The last I saw of them was their arms, still waving as we drove out of sight.

CHAPTER 13

Backwards into Delhi

We climbed aboard our chair car, which was the first we had seen since Jaipur. It was the "Taj Express," a famous train that takes tourists from Delhi to Agra and back. We were early, so we had our choice of seats.

"Where shall I put this?" I asked Ed, indicating my heavy milk pan. "I can't carry it along with my suitcase and train case."

"Jesus Christ. Isn't there room in your suitcase?"

"No. It's too bulky. I wouldn't be able to close it. Don't you have room in yours?" I asked in pleading tones.

"Jesus Christ," he muttered again. He put his suitcase on the seat, opened it, and surveyed the neat rolls of clothing sandwiched between purchases we had made. He picked up the heavy brass lamp we had bought in Rajasthan and weighed it in his hand, scowling. Then he looked at the brass pan and shook his head.

"It won't fit."

"Yes it will. Look, honey. Just take out this stuff"—here I started to remove things from the center of the suitcase—"and put the pan in the bottom, pack things around the edge"—I continued, following my own directions—"and fill up the pan with the items we took out."

"That pan weighs at least five pounds," he said in lugubrious tones. "Pretty soon I won't be able to get my suitcase off the ground. And I sure as HELL won't be able to get it up here!" He heaved it with difficulty up onto the overhead rack and surveyed it. It hung over the edge by at least eight inches.

"It will kill somebody if it falls off that rack," he said gloomily, "probably me, because I'll be sitting right under it."

Soon other passengers arrived, and in due course the train jerked and started to back up. I watched the passing railroad yards, waiting for the shunt and the stop before it started up again going the right way. The train slowly gathered speed, and soon we were rattling along backwards through the countryside.

"It's going backwards," I observed somewhat redundantly.

"I noticed that," said Ed, chuckling. "I think they probably start this train in Delhi with the coach facing the right way going down to Agra. When it returns, they just run in another engine facing in the other direction, and drag the whole thing back to Delhi. Saves them from turning the whole train around."

And so it was that we rolled the whole distance backwards into Delhi.

When we arrived, Ed called the Five Star Guest House, but unfortunately they were full, for we had forgotten to let them know that we had a single night's stopover in Delhi before going on to Amritsar. He looked at me questioningly.

"What'll we do now? Shall we stay at the other hotel? The one we stayed in first?"

"Let's look in the book and see what else there is. I'd like to stay near Connaught Circus and go to that bazaar we heard about." We found a seat in the big, crowded station and rummaged through our belongings until we found our book.

"How about this one, Bunny? Nirula's Hotel right in Connaught Circus. It is supposed to have a great salad bar and an ice cream parlor. It's not too expensive either."

Outside, a rickshaw pulled up and a muscular youth with a round, smiling face descended.

"Where do you go?"

"Nirula's. But we need two rickshaws."

"Oh, no, sir. I am very strong. No need for two. Please madam. I will help you up. Sir, please. Two rickshaws very expensive. I have room for luggage also."

In no time we had been cajoled onto the seat, which really was wide enough for the two of us, and the suitcases were squeezed in at our feet. Our driver gave us a wide grin and swung onto the seat.

"My name is Chindra," he said in amazingly good English. "I would like to be your driver while you are in Delhi. Are you staying very long?"

We liked him right away, and we liked the way he powered us along, seeming not to notice the double load plus luggage. It was quite a long way to Connaught Circus, and part way there we had to go through an underpass that had a long uphill grade. Ed immediately got off, and Chindra flashed him a grateful smile, but would not let Ed help push the rickshaw.

147

"Thank you, sir, I do not need help to push. The lady is not so heavy."

When we reached the hotel we suddenly remembered that we hadn't bargained in advance for the fare.

"How much?" asked Ed.

"Five rupees."

With a bemused expression, Ed pulled out some bills. He peeled off a five, and then a two, and offered them to Chindra.

"Too much, sir. Only five rupees. I want to be your driver all the time. Okay? When I shall pick you up?"

"Later this afternoon we have to go to the Indian Air Lines office. How about three o'clock?"

"No problem," said Chindra, waggling his head happily. He rode off, turning to wave to us as he went.

"Only five rupees! I expected him to ask for fifteen, considering the double load plus the luggage. In fact I wouldn't have been surprised if he'd asked for twenty."

We went to Nirula's salad bar for lunch, and guiltily loaded our plates with forbidden delicacies. All the tables were taken, so we found seats at the bar, where we enjoyed the food and listened to the soft rock music playing over the sound system. Presently two "freaks" sat down next to me, and I couldn't keep my fascinated eyes off them. They were both tall and emaciated, one reddish blond and one brown-haired. The darker one wore his curly, wiry hair in a "fright wig" sticking out in all directions, and he had huge curly "muttonchops" and a ferocious-looking mustache. He wore a tight, holey striped T-shirt like an Apache dancer, and faded, threadbare bell-bottomed jeans. The blond had his waving tresses in a waist-length pony-tail, long, curling sideburns, and he sported wire-rimmed granny glasses. He wore an embroidered Indian shirt and faded purple pants with drawstrings at the ankles. They were both barefoot, both pale and very clean, and both cheerful. They greeted Ed and me with big smiles and introduced themselves.

"Hey, man, I'm Jake an' this is my pal Zooey. We're from New York. What're you two doin' in India?"

They talked like Cheech and Chong, and I loved them from the start—they were funny, kind, and eccentric, and they kept us laughing for an hour with their stories.

"Yeah, man, we came to India because we had some friends, like, an' they said there were some, like, groovy opium dens in Calcutta. Man, they was right. We can't remember how many we went to, man! We can't remember much about Calcutta at all!" Zooey emitted a high cackle.

"But we got malaria in Calcutta," said Jake. "Spent like two months in the hospital. We just got out last week. Man, we was sick. Our mothers wouldn't recognize us now."

They had been youthful hippies together in the late 'sixties, tramping around Asia, visiting all the places where they could get cheap drugs, and having a high old time. But after a couple of years they had gone home, broke and sick, and together they had found jobs in the Post Office, where they had worked ever since. The wanderlust had lured them back again, and they were planning to revisit some of their old haunts.

"I wish my mother could see you, like travelling around India without a tour group," said Zooey. "She thinks anyone who would come to a place like India must be nuts, man. She don't understand me. When I get home I'm goin' to tell her I met this nice lady and man her age who travel like us, man. But she'll, like, never believe it."

We finally tore ourselves away, laughing, after wishing them well.

"I hope they don't kill themselves with an overdose or something," I said to Ed, soberly, when we were out on the sunny sidewalk. "They seemed to have no sense of self-preservation at all. But I liked them so much."

We were running a little short of money, so we took ourselves to the American Express office to cash a check. It was a stuffy little room at the top of a long, steep flight of stairs and there were long lines at each of the two windows. (This was in contrast to the large, modern, air-conditioned office on the other side of the landing, which contained the American Express Travel services. There, several languid clerks waited behind polished desks, and the two or three customers were seated in large easy chairs while they were being helped.) In the crowded little cashiers' office most of the customers were bearded and youthful travelers, and they all seemed to have troubles of one kind or another. They were also mostly European, to our surprise. European or not, they all carried American Express Travelers checks, and half of them seemed to have lost them. We waited endlessly while they quarreled with the cashiers, pleading and threatening by turns, and using up the minutes as if there had been no long impatient lines behind them. The men were a colorful if not a clean lot; many of them made Jake and Zooey look conservatively dressed by comparison. I watched as a filthy youth with long, curling hair and gold earrings, who was no more than eighteen or nineteen years old, worked a wad of worn notes of various denominations out of an ancient leather pouch. He wanted to exchange them for American dollars. His British girl friend won the prize that day for eye-catching costumes: she was

149

dressed in a long sequinned black wool evening gown that clung hopefully to her skinny breasts, with a white turban, white sox, white-strapped high-heeled shoes, and black shorty string gloves.

A dispirited man of about thirty-five in front of us was from Germany. He was very short, blond, and dirty, dressed only in a pair of filthy black pants held up with a frayed rope. His eyes were sunk into his head, and his voice was hardly more than a whisper while he told us that he had been in India for sixteen years.

"I vant to go home," he croaked, "but I haff not heard from mein mutter und fatter. I write zem but zo far zhey haff not write back. I need money zo I can go home. I sink I die priddy zoon if I stay here." He looked at us pitifully, but we couldn't help him. Neither could the cashier, who listened to him dutifully while he described his troubles and then sent him hopelessly back to the post office to wait for the letter that perhaps would never come.

After two long hours it was our turn, and, mercifully, we were able to get our business transacted quickly and to get out of there, away from the depressing stories and the fetid air produced by too many dirty bodies in too small a space. We were a few minutes late getting back to the hotel, where Chindra was waiting for us on the sidewalk.

Along the way to the airline office, Chindra asked us the usual questions—how old we were, whether we had children, how much money we made, and suchlike. When Ed went inside I sat in the rickshaw and asked Chindra a few of my own.

"Are you married?"

"No, Missus, not yet. But I am getting married in two months."

"You are? Congratulations, Chindra. Have you known her long?"

"Oh, *no*. I have never seen her. It would not be proper for a Hindu boy to see a girl before they are married."

I hesitated before asking him an even more personal question, but curiosity overcame delicacy.

"Chindra, do you think you will be happy with the wife you have never seen?"

"Oh, *yes*! My mummy"—I stifled a giggle at this—"wants me to be happy. She would not choose wife for me that I don't like."

"You are looking forward to your wedding, then?"

"Of course. It will be a very fine affair. We will have a fine dinner with many sweets, and all our friends and families will come. I am very happy. I have bought two rickshaws so I can support wife. I rent one to other man; soon I will have three. Then I can afford many children."

After Ed rejoined us in the rickshaw we stopped at a copper market which extended down several blocks of a narrow street lined on both sides with stalls where copper and brass items were made and sold. Handmade brass milk containers were the number-one item, judging by the quantity of them for sale, and they were beautiful—about twelve inches tall and ten inches in diameter, with weighted round bottoms and flared rims, and cunningly made with copper seams and copper rivets. The lovingly polished brass and copper gleamed on all sides, tempting me. I weakened immediately, covetously eyeing one milk can in particular, one with big copper rivets just below the rim.

"Honey . . . ?"

"You're kidding!"

"Oh, please, Ed. I really want one, they are so beautiful, and they're so cheap. See, this one is only about fourteen dollars . . ."

I could see him waver. A bargain is one thing Ed cannot resist.

"Please, honey."

"How the hell are we going to carry it?"

"You'll think of something. You always do. How about if we were to buy one of those string bags to carry it in?"

"I guess that would . . . no. I must be nuts to even think of it! We've still got nearly four weeks to go, and we'll be taking buses from here on."

"Well, on the buses the luggage just goes on the top, we won't have to carry it much."

"Fourteen dollars. Oh, all right." He sighed. "I'm nuts. I swear I am." He pulled out the money and paid for my goody, making the proprietor of the stall smile from ear to ear. I suspect that the price was somewhat higher than he would have asked of an Indian customer, but we didn't mind. It was still cheap. We stowed it in a little box beneath our seat in the rickshaw.

The Palika Bazaar under the park in the middle of Connaught Circus was our next stop. Here was displayed everything made in India, from coir and shell items from Kerala to saris from every province; and not only that, but most things seemed to be cheaper there than they were in the places from which they had come. I bought a wonderful sari from Orissa which was of heavy silk with a border of tie-dyed threads. The proprietor of the small official stall of the Government of Orissa explained that the silk threads used in the border were tie-dyed in bundles first, and *then* were handwoven to produce the design. This procedure is so difficult that it is used in only two places in the world: in India, and one tiny town in Japan. There were dozens of saris of all colors in the place, but the one I wanted was in the window display. It was a deep pumpkin color with a black, white and burgundy border, and I had fallen in love with it.

"But madam," the proprietor said, almost tearfully, "we have many saris like that one. Here, here, and here."

"But that's the only one of that color."

"Okay-okay, no problem," he said sighing, shaking his head resignedly as he climbed into the window to retrieve my prize. He took about fifty pins out of it, shook the dust away, and showed me how to fold it properly.

"This is lifetime sari," he said proudly. "See, very heavy silk. You give to your daughter someday."

I clutched my treasure as we left, noticing that Ed seemed very cheerful for a change. Usually when I bought something he was rather grim.

"You're sweet, honey, not to mind that I bought that sari."

"It's okay, Bunny. *You* get to carry it. There's plenty of room in your suitcase for that. What I hate is when you buy something that weighs fourteen pounds and is too big for your suitcase!"

"Tomorrow we must catch the early train to Kalka," said Ed, when Chindra dropped us off at the hotel. "Can you pick us up at five-thirty?"

"No problem, sir," said Chindra. When the whisper of his tires had died away in the distance, I turned to Ed.

"Honey, what can we give him for a wedding present?"

"Geez, I don't know. That would be nice, Bunny. He hasn't accepted a tip. Of course, I'll give him a nice tip tomorrow."

"Yes, but we should give him something for the wedding. I know! Our thermos bottle. We've hardly used it because the water purification tablets make water taste so awful, and anyway, tea and pop are always available. That thermos wasn't so expensive for us, but seven dollars U.S. is a lot of rupees. I think he'd like it."

"Sure, that sounds like a good idea. Anyway, it isn't going be hot where we're going, so we won't need it."

At the train station the next day, Ed gave Chindra an extra twenty rupees and the thermos which I had wrapped in plain paper.

"It's for your wedding, Chindra," I said. "Open it."

"Thank you. It is the best wedding present of all," he said sincerely, and his pleased smile followed us into the station.

Nearly all the cars were air conditioned, and our tickets were only good for first class non-A/C. We walked almost the length of the train before we found the non-air-conditioned first class sleeper car with our name on it. The compartment was modern, light, and cleaner than usual. Like Indians, we dragged out our "sheets" (the dress lengths of printed cotton from Madras) and spread them on the seat on our side of the compartment, blew up our inflatable pillows (purchased in Udaipur), took off our shoes and made ourselves comfortable. Presently our compartment mate entered and made himself similarly at home, tucking his bare feet off to one side in an un-Indian-like manner.

"Good afternoon," he said very pleasantly, "I am Gurdial Dhaliwal."

He was a Sikh, a professor at Azmer University; a dapper dresser, fluent in English, and a very nice guy. We were leaving Hindu India and entering the Punjab, where Sikhs are in the majority, and Mr. Dhaliwal was the first we had met.

Sikhs are taller than most Hindus, well-muscled, well-fleshed, and the men have an arrogant bearing. Practicing male Sikhs wear turbans and do not cut the hair of either head or chin; however, long beards are out of fashion, so they often twist their beards into hair-net chin straps and tuck them up into their turbans. They wear western-style trousers and shirts, and tend to wear polished shoes and dark sox instead of the sandals usually worn by Hindus. The women favor knee-length tunics over trousers instead of saris, and toss long scarves rather rakishly over their shoulders.

The Punjab is a rich agricultural region, but it is flat and dull, and the day was hotter than a steel mill in August. There wasn't a cloud to be seen, and the sun blazed down in a sky of molten brass. Our windows were open, and the wind brought with it a load of dirt that got in our hair and our eyes. The seats became covered with a layer of brown dust, and so did we, as I discovered when I looked in the rest room mirror. I gave myself a quick sponge on my face, hands and arms, and returned to my seat, where I tried to get interested in a diagramless crossword, but I was too hot and uncomfortable to concentrate. Our companion slept, and we sat in an agony of boredom, dozing off and on, as the interminable hours passed.

As we were nearing Chandighar, the capitol of the Punjab, Mr. Dhaliwal woke up and asked Ed if he would like to learn how to wind a turban. He took off his dusty pink turban and brought out a clean length of pale blue material. We saw that his oiled hair was gathered into a topknot on his head and ringed with a steel band. He started to wind the material around his head carefully, creasing it and pinning the folds with shiny straight pins as he went along, giving the material a twist both in front and in the rear. He used at least a couple of dozen pins before he was through.

153

"Do you have to do that fresh every day?" asked Ed, admiring the professional-looking finished product.

In answer, Mr. Dhaliwal doffed his turban like a hat and made a little bow. "We only re-do when it is wrinkled, or when it becomes dirty," he explained. "I am meeting important official in Chandighar and want to look like a gentleman. Or like I came in air-conditioned carriage." He chuckled.

He brought out a package of bidis and offered them to us. We refused and he lit up, and then brought out a flask of whiskey.

"You do not smoke, I see," he said, "but perhaps you will join me in a drink?"

We were glad that we could accept, and the bottle was passed around. Mr. Dhaliwal tipped his head back and simply poured a slug of whiskey into his mouth without touching his lips to the rim. We had seen other Indians doing the same thing when they drank from the public water dispensers, but we had been unable to duplicate the feat, so we rummaged through our train case for cups. We spent what was left of the trip in easy conversation until our companion left us at Chandighar.

I was belatedly putting the cups away in my train case just as we reached Kalka, when I happened to glance in the mirrored lid. My sweat had turned into little black rivulets which had wandered down my neck, and the area under my nose was noticeably darker than the rest of my face. I had a large smudge on one cheek where I had wiped off sweat with the back of my hand. I looked awful. Much worse than Ed, who didn't perspire as much as I did. I ruefully followed him down the passageway, wishing it had occurred to me to take out a package of tissues, which I had thoughtlessly left in my big suitcase.

Outside on the curb, I put down my luggage and without thinking, wiped my sweating face on my arm, inadvertently smearing it with moist black dirt. Then I laughed and shrugged.

"Do I look as bad as I think I do?"

"Worse. Your face is smeared with black on one side. What did you do to it?"

"Oh, shut up."

At Kalka Railway Station I gave myself a quick sponge in the ladies' room before we changed to a most unusual train to take us up the mountain to Simla. Actually, it wasn't a train at all, in the usual sense of a train being a series of cars drawn by an engine; it was just a single car, and what a tiny one! Not more than fifteen or sixteen feet long and only about seven feet tall, it sat smugly on the track in its trim blue and silver

154

paint. It contained four bench seats which filled the car from one side to the other, each reachable by its own door, and a short front seat next to the driver. We climbed into the first bench seat behind the driver, delighted for two reasons: we had never seen anything like it, and were looking forward to the trip, and secondly, we had an unobstructed view of the track ahead as well as the view through the side windows. Luggage was a problem, because there was no overhead rack, no luggage area, and no room under the seats. Ed looked around and then shrugged and stacked them on the seat next to us.

We settled ourselves and waited for the onslaught of passengers, hoping we wouldn't be forced eventually to sit on top of our suitcases, but only a handful of passengers got on. We set off for Simla with a total of five persons. The three people behind us, each of whom had snagged a comfortably upholstered bench all to himself, immediately went to sleep.

Scenically, the trip was not unlike the well-remembered toy train ride to Ootacamund, but this had other charms: one hundred and three tunnels of handcut stone, each neatly numbered above the archway of the entrance. We chugged along the narrow-gauge track, brushing against wildflowers on both sides of the little car. As we climbed into the mountains, the terrain became steeper and steeper, and the little car went slower and slower, affording us views of charming mountain towns clinging to the slopes. Often we passed hardy peasants tilling the tiny terraces alongside the tracks. These people were short and wiry, with weatherbeaten faces that seemed to have a Mongolian cast overlaying their Indian features. They grinned and waved as we passed, leaning on their tools as they stopped to watch the train go by. As we climbed, craggy firs and deodar cedars edged the mountains against the darkening sky.

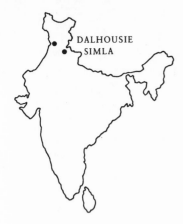

DALHOUSIE
SIMLA

CHAPTER 14

Wild Goose Chase

It was long past dark when we pulled into the pretty little railway station in Simla. We had made no reservations, but as usual we had a hotel in mind. We knew that the monsoon season was off-season in Simla, so we weren't afraid that the hotels would be full. As soon as we pulled in, two porters came aboard, grabbed our suitcases, and thrust tokens into our hands. When we descended from the train, two other porters wrestled the baggage away from the first two, and a shouting and shoving match ensued. I got tired of it in about thirty seconds, and picked up my suitcase, which they had left standing on the platform, forgotten in the melee. Ed followed my example and we trudged up the hill to a taxi stand dragging our suitcases behind us.

There, asleep in a great cocoon of a sleeping bag inside his taxi, lay a skinny, timid-looking youth with a little pencil mustache. Roused, he staggered out and looked bewildered when Ed and I asked him to take us to the Woodville Palace Hotel. It became obvious after a few minutes of futile shouting and gesticulation that he knew not a word of the universal tongue. Ed went back down the hill and returned with a porter, who explained what we wanted to the little man. We piled suitcases on top and inside, and climbed in.

Alternately pumping the gas pedal and the brake, he set off, making little runs along the street until he spotted the headlights of a car a block away, then he would lurch into the ditch to await the passing vehicle. Stalling frequently, we made our perilous way interminably on and on, around Simla's steep hills, long past the point at which I had decided that we were lost forever. Nearly half an hour later and an estimated ten miles farther, we lurched and shuddered up a steep hill to a great, dark stone mansion. There was not a light to be seen anywhere. Ed got out and reconnoitred, finally finding a sign that said that this was, indeed, the Woodville Hotel. It was, unbelievably, closed in August.

Cursing Fodor's, which had neglected to mention this little detail, we used all our wiles, plus the services of three different policemen met along the way, to try to communicate to our driver that we wanted to go to the Clark's Oberoi Hotel (the biggest and supposedly the best in town), which we thought that even he could find.

"*Clarke's! The Mall!*" I screamed in his ear, for the fifth time.

"Gabble, fibble, gibble," he replied, his large eyes swimming. "Addle waddle."

I could have strangled him. I lapsed, defeated, into the silence of despair, while our taxi alternately crept and lurched through the dark and now deserted streets. At last we found ourselves back at the railway station, where a helpful porter somehow communicated our desires to the driver and volunteered to go with us and carry our bags up the hill.

(Hill? Carry them up the hill?)

Gradually, on being taken to the place, we were made to understand that the taxi *could not use the road up to the hotel.*

"Jesus what a place," muttered Ed under his breath as he paid off our wretched driver, who no doubt returned in relief to the cosy nest from which we had pried him.

The porter balanced our two heavy suitcases on his back and started up the hill. We carried our smaller cases and packages. *Steep*, my God, and about half a mile in length, the road zigzagged it's way up the mountainside. Because of the unaccustomed altitude and the fact that we were already tired, we were exhausted halfway up, and my grunts and gasps accompanied every step of our weary way. It was humiliating to realize that I, with my light load of one little case plus a package, trailed the porter by at least a hundred yards by the time we reached the top, and he was carrying two enormous suitcases, one of which I could barely lift off the ground! Just before midnight, we staggered into the lobby of Clarke's Hotel, and secured our room. After bathing away the filth and the sweat, we crawled into our beds and instantly lost consciousness.

We awoke in the morning surprised to find that the room was pitch dark.

"What time is it?" I asked, for the travel alarm clock was on Ed's night table.

"Ye gods, it's nearly nine! How come it's so dark?"

The mystery was explained when we pulled the curtains back from the "windows." They looked out onto a dimly-lighted hall—we had an inside room. I was indignant.

157

"For the price we are paying for this we ought to have a window. Let's look for another hotel, preferably one that's within our budget."

We were also eager to see Simla in the daylight, so we hurried into our clothes and went outside. Out on the mall it was a beautiful sunny morning. The birds were singing, the deodar (cedar) trees which grew all around spread their spicy fragrance, and monkeys scampered about by the hundreds, eating the chapattis put out for them by householders and restaurant patrons. The air was crisp and bracing, and the sun poured over the steep streets, which were really too narrow to be anything but footpaths. No wheeled vehicles plied these streets; everything in Simla was carried on the backs of porters who shuffled along bent double under their burdens. (Did this help to explain why we'd had so much trouble the night before? It was an embarrassing idea; I suppressed it.) We saw men carrying sofas, telephone poles, and sacks of cement on their backs. When a load was too heavy for one man, ropes were attached, and the object (in one case a wire spool weighing hundreds of pounds) was dragged along by several coolies. We noticed lots of schoolchildren, for Simla has many private schools left over from the days of the Raj. In their uniforms of pleated skirts and shorts, ties, and white shirts, the kids could have been English children except for the color of their skins. They all wore sweaters and most of the girls had their beautiful hair plaited in braids that hung below their waists. They were obviously from well-to-do families, for the private schools of Simla are the finest in India, and the tuitions are high.

We were on the lookout for a good hotel as we walked along, revelling in the cool air, but not having much luck finding what we were looking for. We tried the old Grand Hotel, a legendary British hotel with beautiful half-timbering and leaded-glass windows, but it had been converted into a "holiday home" for government employees only. Another lovely building that attracted us proved to be a government building with a large sign in front forbidding any photographs! We eventually learned that it had once been the British Governor's mansion. An hour's search got us nowhere, and our stomachs began to protest, for we had eaten nothing but a few cookies since breakfast the day before.

A largish stall with the name "Tara" over the entrance stood at a crossroad near the beautiful government building, and we entered it gratefully. A large man with green eyes was frying *alu parathas* on the griddle just inside the entrance, and we ordered three of them (one apiece and one to share). We chose a tiny table inside, right by an open window

158

that overlooked the back side of the steep town and the Himalayas beyond, and waited in a pool of sunshine for our food. We wolfed the parathas, which were the best we had ever eaten. Accompanied by rich, sweet chai and ice-cold apple juice, they made a breakfast to remember.

With renewed vigor we resumed our search, and at the very top of the "mall" we finally found our hotel. It was a brand-new tall building just behind the old British Manse: the Hotel Mayur. When we saw the room, we nearly despaired, for it looked to be beyond our means. It was just too modern and posh to be a budget hotel. Without hope, I asked the price. "Only two hundred rupees plus eight per cent luxury tax," said the manager, and then he added "with a fifty per cent reduction in the off-season".

"We'll take it," we said simultaneously, and followed him down to the lobby to register and to collect a couple of porters to carry our bags up from Clarke's. We knew we'd never be able to carry them up those hills by ourselves.

It was noon by the time we had got settled; too late to do any serious sightseeing. We walked the streets, gawking at the mountain views, feeding the monkeys, shopping in the bazaars. We stood at the edge of the mall and surveyed the town. Just below us stood a large stone building that looked familiar.

"Bunny, isn't that the Woodville Palace Hotel down there?" Ed started to laugh. "The poor guy had to go all around the base of the mountain—it looks like it's about twenty miles from here—just to get to that hotel by the back way, when it's so close to the center of town. No wonder he was so confused."

I felt my face getting hot as I guiltily remembered how I had shouted at the poor taxi-driver.

"Those porters in the station were quarreling over our baggage because they were planning to carry it on foot to our hotel, and for a big fee. And our taxi probably was waiting for a fare back down the mountain, when we came along, ruining his day. Poor guy. But why the hell didn't our books mention that Simla had no automobile roads?"

"Because *India on $15 and $20 a Day* hasn't got a section on Simla, and I guess we didn't look carefully enough at the others." Mentally I vowed never again to get excited and yell when dealing with service people. Sometimes they knew things that we didn't! We stopped in at the Tourist Bureau and booked an all-day tour for the following day, and ended the afternoon in one of the coffee houses for which Simla is moderately famous. We were surprised to find after dinner that we were

159

sleepy at nine o'clock, as usual, even though we had drunk several cups of excellent coffee rather late in the day.

The next morning we stopped in at Tara for breakfast and then proceeded to the Tourist Bureau for our tour. While waiting for the bus, we made the acquaintance of several young travelers: Eric and Ian from England, a sturdy, freckled American girl called Happy, an Anglo-Indian girl from London named Marion, and her husband, a handsome red-headed New Zealander, whose name we never learned.

The bus, when it eventually arrived, was beautifully clean and comfortable; we climbed aboard without having to scramble for a seat. The windows were transparent, without the usual public-bus layer of dirt. We started off over the narrow, precipitous road, just charging along, taking all curves, and there were many of them, at breakneck speed! Settling deeper into my downright luxurious seat, I quit "driving the bus" after about ten minutes, and just enjoyed the scenery. I figured that if this was to be my last ride, I'd enjoy it to the hilt. What a way to go! So we tore along, the mountainside falling away inches from my left hand, down thousands—*literally* thousands—of feet, great cedars and fir trees shading the road, the Himalayas stretching away ridge upon ridge in the distance. Beautiful wildflowers grew everywhere there—ones I'd never seen before, such as a pretty blue flower with thin, rose-veined petals, and a lovely cerise blossom shaped like a buttercup, with leaves like a strawberry. On our first stop we saw our first yaks, great fat black long-haired beasts with wicked little eyes and long horns. Despite their fierce appearance, they docilely allowed tourists to climb on their broad backs and be photographed for a two-rupee fee. Nearby was a cold-drinks stall, and we walked over to get a Ginger Squash for me. The proprietor filled a glass one-third full of ginger syrup and started to add—ack—*water* to it.

"No, please. No water!" I cried, just in time.

Looking at me quizzically, he shrugged and filled the glass all the way to the top with ginger syrup. "Crazy foreigners," his expression said. I could hardly blame him.

The syrup was strong and sweet-spicy, and we shared a few sips before discreetly pouring it out behind a bush in a convenient depression in the earth. Ants were already starting to home in before we had finished pouring.

Chail, our longest stop, was once a palace but was now a hotel, set in velvety lawns and colorful flower beds. Except for the magnificent views of the Himalayas all around, we could have been in England or in

Victoria, British Columbia. The building itself was an early nineteenth century manor of grey stone with mullioned windows and many chimneys, and the ground floor rooms, at least, were high-ceilinged and gracious. In one of them, a stately dining room with bay windows and crystal chandeliers, we had our lunch.

We chose an enormous table near one of the sunny windows, for the room was chilly in the thin mountain air. We were joined by all the young travelers and immediately began to share experiences with each other after the manner of globe-trotters. Eric and Ian were lone roamers; each had been to India several times before for long visits, moving south in the winter and north in the summer. Marion and her silent Kiwi said little, but were evidently enjoying themselves.

"Me muvver was born 'ere," she said, in a soft cockney accent that contrasted oddly with her dark, half-Indian beauty. "Wen me 'usband an' me got married, we fought we'd cum 'n see me Mum's country. I luv it."

"How do you like India?" I asked Happy.

"India's hard to like," she said. "All the *poverty*, and it's so grubby!"

"Where have you been?"

"I flew into Bombay, and spent a couple of days there, but it was so hot and dirty, and all those beggars . . . I just went to the airport and got a plane to New Delhi and came up here to Simla. Then I'm going to go on to Kulu and Manali, up in the mountains. I hate India."

"You should give it more of a try," I said. "We didn't like Bombay either, but the towns in Rajasthan and on the coasts are just wonderful. I think you'd like them."

She shook her head. "Not me. You know, what I hated in Old Delhi were all the cows. Ugh!" She shuddered. "All those rotten cows, acting like they owned everything, eating all the food that should have been for people! If it was up to me they'd kill the cows to feed the people, so they wouldn't be starving."

"I don't think anyone is starving . . ." I began, gently.

"Oh, come off it. Everyone knows that people are starving in India. Look at Mother Teresa—people are just dying like flies in Calcutta . . ."

I glanced at Eric, who shrugged and cast his eyes heavenward.

". . . and I saw some beggars in New Delhi with their ragged little kids. It was disgusting, and those fat cows walking around. They ought to kill them, that's what they should do!"

"Those cows all belong to ordinary families—they're not just wild, you know," I said, "and the milk they give is the only complete protein these

161

people have, because Hindus are mostly vegetarian. If you killed all the cows, the milk would be gone too, wouldn't it? And then what would they do? That's why the Hindu priests made the cow sacred back in the early days—so the people wouldn't kill the cows during a famine. Once they're gone, they're gone, and then the people really would starve to death. Even the cow dung is precious; it is the only fuel the poor people of India have."

"Oh, that's just propaganda from the Indian government. I don't believe it. They just don't want to buy oil from the Arabs! Anyway I hate India! This is more like it, though. I like it here."

"This is India too."

She paused at that, a little bewildered. Then she said defensively, "Well, I like it here anyway."

"Just like home, eh?" I knew it was no use to try to reason with her. Like lots of other people's, her preconceived notions went too deep.

In a way, it is really no wonder that people think the worst; India seems to have a bad press. It is rare to see anything encouraging about India in print. Most people assume that people are starving to death in great numbers; actually, India's last bad famine was over twenty years ago, and *we* hadn't seen any starvation. Even in the slums, people looked reasonably healthy, and in the countryside they certainly seemed to be sturdy.

We finished our lunch, still friends with the little American girl, due to Ed's skill at smoothing ruffled feathers. I tend to get somewhat shrill in an argument, and Ed often must undo the damage when I am through offending my opponent.

Our last stop after a long, scenic trip through the mountains was the Khari Bungalow on the Simla-Kalka road, where we had chai and apple juice. A storm was brewing in the north. Towering charcoal clouds gathered and raced toward us like elephants in a stampede, swallowing the previously sun-gilded mountainsides one by one as they came. The rain came with them and soon was spattering on the windows of the bungalow where a moment before sun had poured in on our tea-table. Exciting peals of thunder shook the building again and again as the storm passed overhead. As we waited for it to subside somewhat, we gave our new friends our home address and told them to stop in to see us anytime. Then we all promised to keep in touch, even though we knew that we would probably never see or hear from any of them again. We climbed in the bus for the last short ride back to Simla.

By the time the bus dropped us off near the Tourist Bureau, the rain had stopped and we climbed the long hill up to the Mayur Hotel, part of the way under giant trees that dripped so that the path was a shallow stream under foot, and my hair was soaked. We were damp and chilly by the time we entered our room and took off our soggy shoes.

"How about a drink of brandy?" asked Ed, reaching for the pint bottle we had bought the previous day after a drought that had lasted since Agra. He held it up critically against the light, for the level had *risen* and the contents were much lighter in color than they should have been.

"Son-of-a-bitch! Someone has drunk some and watered it so we wouldn't know." He poured some into a tooth-glass and eyed it glumly.

"I don't suppose we should drink it," I ventured. "The water he used was undoubtedly tap water. What do you think? Do you think the brandy would kill the germs?"

"It looks to me as if he drank about three-quarters of it, it's so pale! What's left probably wouldn't have the strength to kill anything. Oh, damn it all anyway! I was looking forward to a drink."

After prowling around restlessly for a while, he sighed and put his shoes and socks back on.

"I'm going out for more. Be back in a few minutes."

While he was gone I dried my hair and propped myself up in bed with the covers pulled over my legs, and busied myself with my diary. Outside the window, a setting sun shone redly beneath the heavy clouds, silhouetting the firs and the British mansions along the mall, and a single monkey prowled the roof of the manse just below our window, looking for bread crumbs tossed there from the hotel kitchen. Soon it would be dinner-time. I sighed with happiness and snuggled into my covers.

"I wonder what they're doing in California," I thought, pityingly.

We awoke to a clear blue dawn, amidst the din of birdsong. The air was chill and strongly pine-flavored, and the steep streets were already full of coolies, shuffling under their loads, and flocks of schoolchildren, shivering in their navy sweaters. On the horizon the Himalayas were an icy saw-toothed line, diamond bright. We had a date with a bus at eight o'clock, but there was time to have a quick breakfast first. We got into our clothes, turned our suitcases over to a couple of porters with instructions to meet us at the bus depot, and hurried down to Tara for the last time.

"Three alu parathas, please," we said to the green-eyed proprietor, just as we had the previous two mornings, and sat down at our usual sunny table.

When we were finished and were paying the tiny amount that he asked,

I said, "We won't be seeing you again because we're leaving Simla today for Dalhousie. We've sure enjoyed your breakfasts!"

"No charge for you, madam," he said, shaking his head, and handed back the money.

We tried to protest, but he was adamant. We thanked him and then tried to get him to let us take his picture. Again he shook his head and turned his back as we took a picture of his little restaurant-stall. When we put the camera away, he came outside and waved goodbye.

Dalhousie was much farther from Simla than it looked on our map. The road down from Simla was narrow, winding, and scenic. Our Hindu driver was fast, my God; on that road and under those conditions, he just boiled along, dodging trucks, kids and cows, and taking sharp curves at dangerous speeds, tires screeching. He was certainly expert, throwing that steering wheel around and letting it spin back, his corded muscles straining his tee-shirt and the sweat dampening his back despite the cool morning. I half expected every minute to be my last, but those thoughts threatened to spoil my enjoyment, so I put them out of my mind, as I had the day before. No use worrying. The beautiful mountain scenery raced by as we lurched from side to side around the curves. A river sparkled far below, and suddenly I was exhilarated by the pace, by the morning, by the scenery and the sunshine. I reached for Ed's hand and he grinned at me.

"Quite a ride, huh?"

Near a nameless little town not far from Kangra we stopped and pulled off the road. The driver held a whispered conference with his helper, and the latter started off down the road toward town. We sat for a while while the sun got hotter (we were down to only a couple thousand feet above sea-level) and the flies buzzed against the window. The driver got out, found a shady spot, sat down and dozed off. Several of the passengers did the same, but we found it was actually cooler in the bus, so we stayed in our seats. The minutes passed, and finally an hour had evaporated in the still air. At last Ed got off and woke up the driver. I watched as they talked for a while; finally he got back in and sat down.

"Well?"

"He sent his aide into town to take a bus to Kangra to buy a new fan belt. He said the fan belt would cost fifteen rupees and he was not authorized to spend that much in the town, and that's why the helper had to go to Kangra and get one from the bus service depot there."

"God. You could have given him the fifteen rupees. That's only a dollar fifty."

"Yeah. If I'd known, I would have. Anything to get going. But it shouldn't be too much longer—Kangra is only about fifteen or twenty miles away."

We sat for another thirty-five minutes dozing in the heat before the helper returned, but then we were on our way again in no time, bouncing along the pretty green rolling countryside. Kangra is the traditional center of Indian miniature paintings, and I had been regretting that we hadn't the time to stop off and see the city; but when we got there, it was a dusty, unattractive place.

A horde of passengers descended on the bus at Kangra, and squeezed themselves and their boxes and baggage into the aisle and into every nook and cranny of the vehicle. They hung from the ceiling straps and the poles that guarded every seat, and pressed against Ed who was in the aisle seat so that he was forced against me by the sheer weight of their numbers. They were friendly and smiling, but in such close quarters we were in no mood to make friends; all we could do was smile back and endure. We travelled like that for a long time until we came to another large town, where the bus emptied like magic. We raced forward and flung ourselves into the front window seat, where we were protected from the crowds, before the bus could fill up again with a new batch of passengers.

We travelled through a lovely lake district in Himachal Pradesh: hilly, broken country with lots of trees, very green and lush. Cane-fields extended down to the shores of several pretty blue lakes, one of which we crossed on a low bridge. I was looking out the open window into the path of the sun on the lake, when I saw a corpse floating quite near the bridge, face up in the sparkling water. Its bloated limbs and belly made it look like a rubber baby doll, and it bobbed gently as it slowly rotated upon the lake.

At Pathankot we acquired a new driver, a Sikh. He was expert, and much more careful than our previous madman. I was thankful for that, because the road, as it approached Dalhousie, became narrow and steep, and it was long after dark when we finally arrived.

CHAPTER 15

Strange Encounter

We had chosen a hotel which was supposed to be close to the bus stop. When the bus dropped us off, bag and baggage, on a dark and lonely corner, we looked around for some sort of indication as to where the hotel might be located.

"Where did I put that damned flashlight?" muttered Ed as he rummaged through his suitcase. He finally found it in his over-the-shoulder bag and we walked around the area, shining its weak beam all around us, but finding only trees at first.

"There it is!"

"Grand View Hotel" the sign said, and pointed up a steep and narrow footpath that led straight up the hill. Ed pocketed the flashlight before we picked up our suitcases and the large box containing the milk can, because his hands were full. We started up the trail. It was dark, for the new moon was a silver shaving, and its feeble light barely showed us the way. The footpath was pebbly, and about half its length was in shallow steps.

"I hope it's not too far," I said, gasping, after we had gone a few hundred feet. My right hand was already stiff from carrying my heavy suitcase, so I set it down, moved my train case from one hand to the other, and picked it up again in my left hand. Only a few feet farther along we came to the hotel, which was situated on a terrace from where the mountain fell away steeply down to our left. By the faint light of the moon we walked along the hotel front, until we came to a small lobby whose welcoming lights streamed out onto the flagged terrace.

A middle-aged man in white pyjamas registered us with surprising efficiency and exquisite courtesy, then he came around the counter and picked up our suitcases, which he carried as he preceded us to the room (really a suite). He seemed to be the manager, the bellboy and general factotum all rolled into one, and I mentally dubbed him the "Major Domo."

"I bring you charcoal, very cold tonight, you will need a fire," he said; "five rupees extra, bedding also five rupees."

I explored our premises while we waited for the Major Domo to return. We entered onto a sun-porch with big windows which was furnished with overstuffed chairs upholstered in chintz and a low green wicker table, a little wobbly due to the unevenness of the floor. The bedroom was next, with a tiny fireplace on the far wall next to the bed. Beyond this chamber was a large dressing room, and the bathroom opened off that. All the rooms had been painted and repainted; they were now a rather gloomy blue. There were faded flower-printed curtains as well as doors between all the rooms. The entire apartment dated from about 1925 and had not been touched, except for painting, since; even the light fixtures and switchplates dated from that era. It was a little run down, chilly, and decidedly damp, but somehow it managed to be homey and cozy at the same time. The actual temperature must have been somewhere in the upper fifties, and sinking.

When the Major Domo returned he lit a fire in the bedroom and made the bed, then informed us that he had ordered buckets of hot water for our baths.

"I hope you will be very comfortable," he said, and when we thanked him he waggled his head, in that endearing gesture to be found only in India.

When he had gone I turned down the newly-made bed, and discovered that the sheets were so damp that they started to steam along the edge nearest the fire. The blankets weren't exactly dry either, so I pulled them off the bed, and draped the top sheet over two chairs which we pulled up to one side of the fireplace. The bottom sheet, we hoped, would dry from the increased heat in the bedroom.

"I wonder what happened to the hot water we were supposed to get," said Ed.

"I suppose they had to heat it. It's not very late . . ."

"It's after ten, and it'll be another hour before we're through with our baths."

"Good thing. Otherwise the sheets wouldn't have time to dry. Have we got lots of charcoal?"

"Lots. It doesn't take much charcoal to make a hot fire."

I wandered into the bathroom, where I discovered four large, steaming buckets of hot water awaiting us. Only then did I realize that the "bath boy" had crept in and gone out through a little back door that I hadn't even noticed was there.

"Glad I wasn't undressing at the time," I thought, and firmly shot the bolt to make sure he didn't come in again.

By the time we had finished with our hot dipper baths the sheets had dried tolerably, and we crawled into bed. We lay awake for a while, watching the glowing coals, and then drifted off to sleep for the first time in our lives in a room warmly lit by the flickering reflections of a fire.

We woke late in the morning, and took our time getting up.

"Let's not do much today," I said. "I've got a lot of laundry to do, and we've *got* to dry that bedding. Last night I was steamed like a lobster!"

We opened the windows and doors to a flood of sunshine, and went outside. The Himalayas loomed there right in front of us, their snowy crests wreathed in mists. We walked to the edge of the terrace and looked down, down, into a deep valley that fell away thousands of feet below and then rose on the other side to soaring heights. A big bird wheeled in the distance, but otherwise there wasn't a sign of life, and the silence was absolute. The air was sweet with the incense of the cedar trees, and roses and carnations bloomed along the white picket fence that kept us from falling down the mountainside. We turned to look at the hotel, which we had only dimly noticed the night before. It had the quaint facade of a gingerbread chalet in the Victorian style. The appearance and atmosphere were pure British, and there was nothing there to suggest India . . . nothing, until one turned around and bumped into the Himalayas.

We ordered tea and toast to be served in our sunporch-sitting room, and then after breakfast we got to work. I stripped the bed and took the sheets and blankets out to the terrace, where I draped them over the fence in the sun. "There," I thought, "that will dry them out once and for all." Then I did my laundry and my hair, and while I was sitting there at the mirror, rolling the last curler up, Ed came in and said, "Come outside and see this."

I followed him out to see a very large, long-haired black-and-white monkey sitting on our blankets on the fence, dreamily staring out into the valley.

Ed whispered, "Don't scare him, Bunny. I want to get a picture." He fussed with the camera and managed to get two pictures before the monkey noticed us.

With a shriek, it leaped two feet into the air and then raced along the fence, baring its teeth at us and shaking its fists in the air before disappearing into the trees at the far end of the terrace.

"Good heavens, we really scared him!"

Just how much we had really scared him became apparent when I started to gather up the bedding. He had urinated on the blanket!

Ruefully I took it to the Major Domo and explained what had happened.

"No problem, madam," he said soothingly. He produced a clean blanket and started to enter our room to replace it on the bed.

"That's okay," I said, "never mind making the bed. I'll take it." It was damp—as damp or damper than the bedding had been the previous night. I didn't dare drape it over the fence outside, for I thought the monkey might come back, so I hung it over a couple of chairs in the dressing room.

"We'll have another fire tonight," I said to Ed, "and dry it then, along with the mattress. The rest of this stuff is really dry now. I don't want to be steamed again tonight."

In the mid-afternoon we went out for a walk. Dalhousie had been a hill station in the days of the British Raj, although not as famous as Simla or Ootacamund. A sleepy little town, it is sprinkled sparingly over half a dozen steep and heavily wooded hills. The roads are only footpaths, for, as in Simla, wheeled vehicles are not allowed past a certain point. Unlike Simla, fame, politics and tourists have passed it by, and it is now peopled by prosperous retired Indians from the plains, hill tribe people who carry on their traditional occupations, Tibetan refugees, and service people who provide for the others. The pretty homes of vanished Englishmen, now occupied by well-to-do Indians, peek through the trees and the mist which drifts in toward evening.

At Ghandi-chowk, the mid-town bazaar, we saw half a dozen wiry short men with Mongolian features gallop into town and tether their horses at the end of the square. The horses were as small, stocky, and tough-looking as the men, and they snorted and stamped, blowing steam from their nostrils while they were being secured to the rail. The men headed for the barber stalls which stood on one side of the bazaar, where for a pittance they would be barbered, shaved with a straight razor, their ears cleaned, and their nose and ear hair clipped.

"I'm going to get shaved by an Indian barber one of these days," said Ed. I heard someone say once that it's a great experience to be shaved with a straight razor."

We had dinner in the dining room, and then, full of contentment and good food, we retired to our room, built a roaring fire, and dried our bedding before crawling in. We were asleep by nine, long before the fire died down. We had decided to go to Chamba, "The Gateway to the Himalayas," in the morning.

At six o'clock we ordered bed tea and then walked in a leisurely fashion to the apparently deserted bus station, only to see the quiet square erupt with people just as the bus arrived. We rushed to the door hopelessly trailing the crowd, too late to get a seat. By the time we struggled aboard, the seats and even the aisles were filled to overflowing with local people, their bags, packages, boxes and children piled haphazardly everywhere. I found three square inches of seat corner halfway down the aisle, but soon found that I could not stay there because my ample rump needed a lot more space than that. I tried standing up, but the ceiling was too low. Ed was sitting on the engine cover in the front next to the driver, and there seemed to be more room up there, so finally I climbed and shoved and pushed my way to the front and sat down on some baggage between him and the single seat next to the window. At first I was riding backwards, and I could see very little, but soon the driver stopped and he and his helper got out to fix a flat tire. While they were outside, a dour-looking man came up to the front and indicated that I should get off his suitcase (I guess he was afraid I would crush it), leaving me without a seat. Ed moved over as much as he could and I perched next to him, but as soon as the driver returned, he ordered me off the engine cover, because with me on it he didn't have a clear view of the road. The young man in the single seat next to the window put a net bag stuffed with cloth onto the dour man's suitcase and patted it invitingly. What the hell! I had nowhere else to sit. Turning my back on the reproachful eyes of the dour man, I resettled myself facing the front windshield, and from my new perch, squeezed between the nice young man and the hot engine housing, enjoyed the trip to Chamba for all it was worth.

The view was wonderful! The road was one of the most spectacular I've ever seen: precipitous and perilous, barely ten feet wide and unpaved, it threaded its way along the sheer mountainside with the river Riva far down to our left. We careened along, while I kept my nose to the windshield, bracing myself with both hands, on that roller-coaster ride. Terraced rice paddies faced us on the opposite side, and huge ponderosa pines lined the road on our right. There was no traffic. Thank God. Goodness knows what we'd have done if we had met a car on one of those hairpin turns which the driver so confidently took at top speed!

Behind me, a woman started to sing, and soon all the passengers were singing Hindu songs, swaying to the motion of the bus, smiling with their beautiful teeth. How I wished I could have joined them, but of course I contented myself with listening and enjoying with all my might. In this festive spirit, we travelled the forty-six kilometers or two and a half hours to Chamba, not counting the forty-minute stop to fix the tire.

The road to Chamba entered the town over a new bridge which augmented but did not replace the medieval stone bridge that had straddled the Riva for a hundred years. The town itself mostly clings to the steep mountainside except for the grassy maidan which is on a flat place just above the river. There are a few lovely stone buildings and two or three ancient Nagara-type Hindu temples in Chamba besides the university for which it is famous.

We followed a steep stony street straight up the mountainside toward a famous shrine. Small donkeys passed us carrying loads of cement; their masters simply loaded them up at the bottom of the hill, gave them a smack on their round rumps, and up they went without any guidance at all, to the building site at the top of the hill. There they were unloaded and sent back to the bottom with another smack. They were fat, attractive little beasts, and only occasionally strayed to one side or the other to snatch a mouthful of grass on their way. Then they would cock their heads insouciantly, as if to say, "Sure, we work, but we have our fun too!"

Nearing the top, ahead and around a curve, we heard a loud rumbling noise as if a runaway wagon were bearing down on us. Alarmed, we leaped to one side as a strange contrivance, like a toboggan, without wheels, came bumping and slithering down the steep incline. Five or six little boys and half a dozen milk cans were aboard it, and four big boys, one at each corner, guided it with ropes as it careened along. The little guys were whooping with glee; they were having as much fun as kids on a sled in the snow.

After we had climbed the steep street for about a dozen blocks, we reached a level spot and sat down on a bench facing a green and pretty little park. Above us on the mountainside the shrine sat smugly, still a goodly climb away.

"How about it? Do you want to keep on going?" Ed asked.

I gazed up at the hill. "I don't know. Do you want to?"

"Nah. I'm getting hungry. Let's go find a nice restaurant and have lunch."

When we arrived back at the maidan we stopped to watch students playing soccer on the grass. It was a hot day in the bottom of the valley,

171

with the sun beating down, and it was high noon; but the young players looked as cool as cucumbers in their white slacks and shirts. A fat yellow dog chased the ball as it was kicked back and forth, barely avoiding the speeding feet, his long pink tongue hanging wetly from his mouth, as he twisted and turned with the ball. Somehow he avoided disaster, but finally got too tired to continue, and limped over to our side, out of breath and gasping. He flopped down on the edge of the grass and watched avidly until the ball came too close, then the silly creature heaved himself up and attacked it again.

We had lunch overlooking the furious Riva. Then Ed stood up.

"We'd better see about the bus back to Dalhousie."

At the station we tried to buy tickets inside, but the wicket was still closed after half an hour's wait, so we gave up. Ed asked several people when the bus was due to leave, but most didn't understand him, and the rest said "I don't know." No one knew the bus number either, so we ended up outside, waiting for the bus to arrive, so that we might ask the driver these vital questions.

A couple with a little boy who had been on the same bus came over to us and introduced themselves.

"My name is Mira Kumar, and this is my husband Ramesh," said the beautiful woman. "Please, share my umbrella. It is so hot in the sun. Our bus is not due for nearly an hour."

We chatted while we waited, which helped to pass the time, although I was quite uncomfortable under her prolonged and hungry stare. She never took her eyes off me, and seemed to drink in every detail of my face, hair, and makeup, as well as my dress; even my sandalled feet did not escape her gaze. I was relieved when the bus arrived at last, one hour and ten minutes late.

In the general melee that followed the arrival of the bus, I was fully occupied in gaining the door before being trampled by the crowd, and I found myself inside almost before I knew it, the third through the door. I threw myself full length upon the first double seat and waited for Ed in a prone position, not daring to sit up until he was safely beside me, lest someone grab the empty seat. When he finally appeared he was visibly shaken.

"Bunny, I just saved a woman's life. She was right next to me while we were running for the bus, before it had stopped, and either she tripped or she was pushed, and fell right underneath, in front of the wheel! I just scooped her up by the back of her dress, without even thinking! She was as light as a feather, just a tiny little skinny old lady. I'm still shaking!"

172

Mira and Ramesh and their little boy had also managed to get a seat on the bus before it was jammed to capacity, but I was glad to see that they were far in the rear. The crowd was less jovial than they had been on the trip out, and most slept all the way home, including me. The luxury of having a seat, and the warm sun pouring in the window after our long wait in the station induced drowsiness which was impossible to combat, and I sank into the delicious sleep that only a moving vehicle can provide.

At the Dalhousie corner, Mira caught us before we could make our escape, and invited us to dinner that evening.

"There is a very nice restaurant in town, the Amritsar. We would be happy if you would come with us. Can you meet us there at eight o'clock?"

I could think of no graceful way to decline, so we accepted, still feeling uncomfortable.

When we arrived at the Amritsar, Mira and Ramesh were already there, with their little boy, Vickash, and with them were Mira's sister and brother-in-law, who had *their* little boy. We all crowded around the largest table, and Ramesh ordered dinner. The food was delicious, but we were distracted by Vickash, who continually climbed under the table and up on his parents' chairs, fought with the other little boy, and whined. Mira kept up a constant stream of endearments and entreaties:

"Oh, my darling, do not do that, please. Oh, my sweetest, you must not pull that dish off the table. My dearest, please don't scratch Narain, that's a good boy. Oh, you are mother's darling," while poor Ramesh tried futilely to resettle the brat in his chair.

When the waiter approached the table after we had finished, Ed got up to intercept him, intending to grab the check. I saw them talking quietly, and then Ed returned to his seat next to me. While the others were busy trying to drag the loudly shrieking Vickash away from the open window out of which he had been trying to climb, I took the opportunity to pluck at Ed's sleeve.

"How much was dinner?" I whispered.

"Nothing. Ramesh had already paid for it."

"He DID?"

When Vickash had been safety settled on Ramesh's lap, Mira leaned across the table.

"Please accept my bracelet. You must take it, please," she said, and pressed the bracelet she had been wearing into my hand. It was a pretty thing: "jewels" of red and blue glass set in polished brass. Frantically I

173

reviewed in my mind the contents of my purse, certain that I had nothing to give her except possibly a ball-point pen.

As if she had read my mind, she said, "Please, I would like to have your lipstick. It is such a beautiful color."

Gladly I fished it out and handed it to her. "It's lucky that I have enough of the other tube to see me through the rest of the trip," I thought. (I am of the generation that would as soon be seen in public without my clothes as without lipstick.)

"How long are you staying in Dalhousie?" I asked.

"We are supposed to leave tomorrow morning," she said in a sorrowful voice. "I want to stay here, but Ramesh wants to go to Kulu and Manali." She looked balefully at her husband. "He does not consider what *I* want, only what he himself wants. You will be staying here?"

Incautiously I answered, "We were going to leave tomorrow afternoon, but we like it here so much that we may stay for another day before we leave for Kashmir."

Later, after we had said our thank-yous and our goodbyes, and were picking our way by flashlight along the dark footpath toward the Grand View, I said to Ed, "You know, I was sure they would stick us with the check. I really feel kind of guilty, the way I felt about them. She made me feel so uneasy . . ."

"Hey, *I* thought they were going to ask us some enormous favor, like 'By the way, could you give us one thousand dollars U.S.?' or 'If you don't mind, would you please take Vickash back to America with you?' " said Ed, laughing. "I was even more suspicious than you were."

"Well, it just goes to show how mistaken you can be," I said. "It was just the way she *looked* at me, I guess . . ."

Suffused with goodwill and kindly feelings, we decided to stay on in Dalhousie for one more day. We still had a couple of days worth of "slack time" left, and there were some walks that we had not taken. Why not?

In the morning we wanted something more than bed tea and were eating in the dining room, when I noticed people approaching us, silhouetted against the window. To my horror, as they neared our table, I recognized the Kumars. Mira pulled out a chair at our table and sat down while Ramesh nervously stood behind her, shifting from one foot to the other.

"We have decided to stay in Dalhousie also," she began, her beautiful eyes boring into mine, "and then we are going to Kashmir with you. We can all share a houseboat! Ramesh agrees that Kashmir is *much* better than Kulu and Manali."

174

My whirling mind searched for avenues of escape.

"Yes, but . . . uhh . . ." I trailed off. I couldn't think of a thing to say. My appetite deserted me, and I could only toy with my food. I glanced at Ed. He was stoically eating, not looking at anyone.

Somehow we got through breakfast, and rose from the table. Suddenly I had an inspiration.

"We haven't had our morning baths yet," I lied. "Please excuse us."

"Oh. You should have had them before breakfast. Now we must wait . . ." Mira began, but she was interrupted by Ramesh.

"My dear, they want to have their baths. We will see them later, perhaps." He took her arm firmly and started to lead her away as we gained the safety of our room.

"Honestly, honey, I feel hypnotized, like she is a snake and I'm a nervous little bird," I said. "I think she is a little crazy. I really believe that Ramesh thinks so too. He is terribly embarrassed for her."

"Well, here we are in our room," said Ed. "Now what?" He peered through the window. "Take a look."

I peeked out through the curtains. Mira and Vickash were sitting in the wicker chairs which the Major Domo had put out on the terrace for us. Mira looked as though she was prepared to wait all day if necessary.

While I stood there, trying to think what to do, Ed had gone into the bathroom. Then he returned, smiling conspiratorially.

"Come on. Let's get out of here."

I had forgotten the back door which was used by the "bath boy" to bring our hot water in. We let ourselves out, giggling and feeling ridiculous.

"We may be adults, but I feel like I did as a schoolchild, sneaking into the forbidden area behind the curtain in the auditorium. Isn't this crazy?" I whispered, still giggling.

"Shut up. She'll hear you."

We didn't dare to try to join the main path toward the bus stop, as we would certainly have been seen, so we turned in the opposite direction, toward the end of the terrace, still hidden by the hotel buildings. There, fortunately, an overgrown path led up the hill through the forest behind the hotel and we followed it until it joined a paved footpath. We had no idea where it led, but we turned in the direction away from the hotel. Our hearts were light, for it looked like we had succeeded in shaking our unwanted friends.

"What are we going to do now?" I asked. "We'll have to get out of here without her seeing us. I think we should leave today, as originally planned, don't you? The bus leaves at four, and there isn't another one to Pathankot until mid-morning tomorrow. We can stay overnight there or in Jammu and take the early bus to Kashmir. We'd be on our way long before they'd reach there. I suppose it would be easier in a way to just tell her that we don't want them to come with us, but I know she'd make a scene, and I hate scenes. And it would hurt Ramesh, after he's been so nice to us."

Our path led eventually to Ghandi Chowk, and Ed suddenly said, "Hey. I didn't shave this morning in all the excitement. I'm going to get shaved by that barber—the old bald one who looks as if he'd been here since the British Raj—he's probably the most expert of the lot."

In the barber's stall the old man whipped out a scalding hot towel, draped it around Ed's face, and stropped the razor professionally. Then he lathered Ed's cheeks and chin with suds a couple of inches deep. Delicately and dramatically he drew the gleaming razor down the jawbone, causing Ed to flinch visibly. As the barber worked, the vanishing lather revealed a decidedly pained expression on the face undergoing treatment. At last the old barber wiped Ed's face with the hot towel and sprinkled him with cologne. A couple of rupees changed hands, and Ed joined me on the sidewalk.

"Well, how was it?"

"Look," he said in an aggrieved tone, and held his cheek out for me to see. It was covered with little red spots. "He beheaded every follicle on my face! So much for the superior shave you're supposed to get from a barber."

I felt his chin. "It's nice and smooth, though," I said soothingly, "and you smell divine."

We continued down the main street past the Amritsar, where we had eaten the night before. We hadn't seen this part of town in daylight, and we wanted to see as much as possible before we left. We noticed a sign in the garden of what appeared to be a hotel, and went closer. The sign read:

AROMA 'N CLAIRE'S Hotel.
This is back. Front is exquisite!

We were amused and curious, so there was nothing to do but go around the block to see the front. We agreed that maybe the hotel with the odd name wasn't exactly exquisite, but it was certainly attractive, and we decided to have lunch there. Prudently we ordered hardboiled eggs and extra bread and apples to take with us on our bus trip, and stowed them in our string bag.

176

By the time we returned to the Grand View, we were confident that Mira would no longer be waiting in front of our room, so we took the main "road" and stepped along briskly in an ordinary manner. Suddenly Ed took my arm and put his finger to his lips. He nodded in the direction of a small guesthouse that I hadn't noticed before, nestled in the trees at the bottom of the hill next to the bus stop. We could just see it through the bushes that lined the road. Mira had pulled a chair outside the room and was sitting there on the lawn near the open door, watching the path to the Grand View Hotel, which was open to her view for half its length.

Quietly we retraced our steps until we found a pathway that led toward the hotel from the back. After a few minute's walk, we saw that we were on the same path we had taken that morning, and quickly found the overgrown trail down to the rear of the hotel. Once safely in our room again, we repacked our toilet articles and were ready to go. A glance at Ed's watch told us that our bus to Jammu would arrive in less than half an hour, just enough time to pay our bill and go down to the station.

We never saw the Kumars again; when we arrived at the station, the guesthouse lawn was empty and the door to their room was closed. We boarded the bus without incident, securing excellent seats near the front window, and soon were on our way.

"I wish all this hadn't happened," I said mournfully, "I feel so bad that we had to avoid them like that. I didn't *want* to hurt their feelings . . ."

"Bunny, there was nothing else to do. She would have stuck to us like glue, and she made us uncomfortable. Forget it."

This little speech cheered me up, and I settled myself into my seat to enjoy the ride. The mountain scenery was lovely, and it had been dark when we had arrived three days before, so we hadn't seen it. As usual, as we descended in altitude, the temperature gradually rose. The terrain changed from wet coniferous forest, much like that of British Columbia, to semi-arid farmland that resembled California's Sierra foothills.

We arrived in Pathankot after dark. Ed asked someone in the nearly deserted station whether there was a bus to take us further on to Jammu, as we wanted to catch the eight o'clock bus from Jammu to Kashmir in the morning.

"No bus tonight. Only five o'clock train to Jammu in the morning."

"Okay. We'll take the train then."

"But where are we going to stay tonight?" I asked Ed. "The book says there isn't a decent hotel in Pathankot."

As if in answer to my question, a hotel tout appeared suddenly, holding out a card, which I accepted and peered at under the dim light from the station window.

"Air Line Hotel," I read aloud. "New building, deluxe rooms with modern baths attached. All amenities. Air Conditioned. Near the railway station."

Ed shrugged. "Sounds okay. We might as well try it—we don't know of any others, and it's getting late. I hope it isn't too expensive."

A rickshaw pulled up providentially, and I climbed aboard. Ed looked around for another and soon we were rolling down the dark and dusty main street of Pathankot with our suitcases and the boxed milk can balanced at our feet.

We pulled up at a brightly-lit building right on the street: the kind of place that lurks in every city center in the world, where prostitutes ply their trade, and pale, stubbly men lean against the wall; the kind of place that one instinctively turns away from. Sighing, I climbed down from the high seat. Sooner or later, I had known, we were bound to run into a place like that, and the time had arrived.

"Maybe we'd better have the rickshaws wait . . .." began Ed, but his voice trailed off. There *were* no other hotels. He looked at me to see how I was taking it, with the slightly worried sideways look that a husband of long standing gives his wife when he knows that she is going to *just hate* something.

"It's okay," I said. "I knew it was going to be awful. We'll just have to grin and bear it."

We picked up our suitcases and went through the front door into a small, dim central courtyard paved with flagstones. I looked around for scurrying rats, but my suspicious eyes saw only litter in the dark corners. A brightly-lit office adjoined the courtyard, and from this a slight man emerged.

"Have you got an air conditioned double?" Ed's voice sounded dubious.

The little man assured us that he had an air conditioned "deluxe double," " . . . only eighty rupees."

He took Ed's heavy suitcase and led the way up the stairs. Rather sourly, I handed my suitcase to Ed and then followed the two of them up the winding staircase for three flights. Behind us came both our rickshaw drivers, obviously making sure they would get their cut. The manager opened a dirty door and we stepped into the room, which had smudged walls, torn drapes partly covering filthy windows, a dark bathroom to the left of the door. The manager turned on a large and noisy "swamp cooler" that sat in front of the window. It wheezed and clanked, but it seemed to be in working condition.

I put my overnight case on the scarred dresser and stripped the blanket off the king-sized bed, revealing a decidedly wrinkled and rather grey-looking sheet and sad, stained pillows.

"These sheets"—a misnomer since there was only one—"are not clean," I said firmly but, I hoped, pleasantly. "Please may we have clean ones, and clean pillowcases too."

"No problem, madam. That will be eighty rupees."

"In advance?"

"Yes."

I had a sudden inspiration. "We will pay you when you bring clean sheets and pillowcases." His face fell. He shuffled his feet uncertainly and then left.

Ed's rickshaw driver poked his head in the open door.

"You need rickshaw in morning, sir?"

"Yes, we do. We want to go to the train station at four-thirty. Okay?"

"Okay, okay. Two rickshaws?"

"Yes. You'll be here for sure? Out in front?"

"Yes, yes. Ten rupees each for early."

"Ten each? Oh, all right."

The drivers left, pleased smiles on their faces.

Ed surveyed the room rather grimly. "Jesus Christ, what a dump, Bunny. Do you think you'll be able to sleep?"

"Sure, I've got my sleeping pills. As long as we get clean sheets it'll be all right. What's the bathroom like? I really need a bath. It's so damn hot here compared to Dalhousie."

As I spoke I went into the bathroom and turned on the light. It was a mistake. The walls were filthy, and the floor was indescribable, with dirt an inch thick in the corners. Cockroaches scuttled into the drains and behind the toilet. The toilet seat was broken, and even its black paint could not disguise the crust of shit that lined the inside edge. It smelled of urine and worse. I recoiled and shut the door. Then, sighing, I opened it again and went inside. I had peed in places just as bad, and on this trip, too. Crouching a couple of inches above the horrid seat, I relieved myself, and washed my hands under running water in the cracked basin.

"I wish I were a man, if only for a few minutes," I remarked to Ed when I went back into the bedroom. "You're lucky. You can use that toilet without getting too close to it."

The manager re-entered the room with a fresh sheet, and began to

179

remake the bed. The new sheet was clean, and I breathed a sigh of relief—too soon. After smoothing the blanket over the bed, he plumped up the pillows and turned to me, smiling blandly.

"Where are the clean pillowcases?" I asked him.

The smile left his face and he spread out his hands.

"So sorry, laundry didn't bring clean pillowcases," he said nervously.

"We must have clean ones. See, these are very dirty." I pointed out various damp-looking stains and several dark hairs on each pillow.

Shaking his head over the difficulties of dealing with demanding female ferenghis, he left the room again.

"Do you feel like going out to eat?" asked Ed.

"Not really. I'm tired and I'd just as soon eat the stuff we brought. We've got bread and hardboiled eggs, don't we?"

"Yeah, and apples. They're in here somewhere," he said as he rummaged around in his shoulder bag.

We ate sitting on the bed on the clean sheet, in front of the noisy swamp cooler.

"I should be miserable," I thought as I munched my apple, "but I'm not. If anyone had told me I'd have to sleep in a place like this and eat leftover bread and eggs insted of a proper dinner, I'd have been horrified. But here I am and I'm perfectly happy, if not comfortable." I grinned at Ed and he grinned at me.

"I wonder if he'll come back," he said, referring to the manager.

"Oh, he'll be back. We haven't paid him," I giggled.

The manager appeared in the open doorway.

"So sorry, no pillowcases. But I brought clean sheet for pillows." He shook out the sheet and then folded it in half and tucked it around the pillows.

"That's fine," I said. Ed paid him, and he left. We locked the door behind him, thankful that it had a sturdy bolt in addition to the usual lock.

I got my well-used length of material out of my suitcase and spread it over the bed, on top of the clean sheet. I washed my face, neck and arms with "Wet Ones," took a sleeping pill with what was left of a bottle of club soda from Ed's bottomless shoulder bag, and laid down on the bed, still wearing my favorite sundress. Ed undressed down to his underwear and turned out the single naked lightbulb that hung from the ceiling. The garish electric lights outside cast strange shadows on the walls, and the whine of a mosquito competed with the "swamp cooler."

"What an awful place," I thought, and then I was asleep.

180

It was long before dawn when we stumbled outside, dragging our suitcases and carrying the big box with the milk can. Ed's rickshaw driver was there but not mine. (I suppose he had decided that even ten rupees wasn't enough to get up at four-thirty for.) We shared one rickshaw with some of our paraphernalia stowed at our feet and some balanced behind our seat, resting on the collapsed canopy. The streets were dark and deserted until we approached the railway station, where crowds of people waited for the early morning train to Jammu.

The trip, in a first class sleeper providentially available, was fast and pleasant. At least I thought it was—I slept the whole way.

CHAPTER 16

The Lake

The bus to Kashmir was a "special" bus, with reserved seats. Because it was going to be a long day, Ed purchased three seats for the two of us, so that we would have adequate room for comfort. When we boarded, we found that the dull-looking man who had sold Ed the tickets had given us two seats in the three-seat row plus one across the aisle, completely defeating the purpose. Ed immediately got out to see the station master about it. He returned looking grim.

"He said just to use the three seats together," he said, "but he refused to alter the ticket. You know what will happen: someone will claim that seat, and we'll be out of luck. I argued, but he just ignored me and started to talk to someone else. He just didn't want to stick his neck out by changing that ticket."

"Give it to me," I said.

Swiftly, I changed the number of the unwanted seat to the number of the window seat that we needed, and sat back to await developments. Soon a young man approached and said that we had his seat.

"I'm sorry," I said sweetly, "but the clerk made a mistake, and the station master said that these were our seats. The one across the aisle is yours." And I showed him the altered ticket. He accepted the unwelcome news, as I was sure he would; to most people, the *written* word is law!

Ed eyed me admiringly. "I've got to hand it to you, Bunny, that was brilliant," he whispered. "Where are those 'Wet Ones'? I'll wash the window. The scenery should be great going into Kashmir."

Ed was right; the scenery was great, but the trip was an exhausting one. Halfway to Kashmir, in a beautiful mountain pass, the road was interrupted by an enormous slide. Buses and trucks were stopped for a long way before and after the slide; we came to a halt at the end of a line of at least one hundred vehicles. We could see the entire road ahead of us for several miles, and nothing was moving. After sitting in the bus for a while, we got out and sat on the edge of the roadbank overlooking a deep valley. It was a lovely spot, and the day was gratifyingly cool, but we were anxious to get going. The minutes stretched into an hour, then two.

Suddenly the engine of the truck ahead of us started, and the sound of starting engines drifted up and down the line. We quickly climbed aboard as our bus began to move, but after a hundred feet, we came to a halt again. This time the wait was shorter, and then we started to move very slowly forward. The slide was directly ahead of us: a huge mountainside of denuded earth that continually shed stones and sand that slid down its face onto the road below. The road had become a narrow trail of loose, shifting sand and gravel, and vehicles made the perilous crossing at their lowest speed. As it crept past, hugging the bank, every truck or bus dislodged rocks and earth which cascaded down into the valley. Finally it was our turn, and slowly we inched our way along the inside edge, easing over rocks that had come down from the bank above, and trying to stay away from the treacherous outer side. I was amazed at the stoicism of the passengers, who endured the hardships and danger without complaint, but there was a collective sigh of relief and a happy stirring of relaxing bodies when the crossing was completed, and we reached the paved highway again.

The ordeal wasn't quite over yet, though, for we had to slowly pass the glut of oncoming vehicles which had encroached on our side of the road in their eagerness to move ahead. The engine ground as we inched along at a snail's pace for another hour, and then we entered a long tunnel. Inside, diesel fumes blackened the air and choked us, making all the passengers cough and gag. A little boy across the aisle threw up, and the baby behind us started to wail. I searched my bag for a kleenex, but as usual I had left them in my suitcase, and all I could find were Wet Ones. I pressed one to my nose and breathed through it, but the fumes from the moistening solution made me light-headed, and I had to stop. I looked at the towelette; it was charcoal colored where my breath had passed through.

"I think I'm going to faint," I said to Ed. "This is awful; I feel terrible."

"Me too," he said. "It's dangerous to breathe these fumes. I hope we're through before long, or people are going to be very sick."

But it was a long time before we came out into the sweet air. When we did, my eyes were bloodshot and my throat was sore, and I was worried about the poor little baby behind us. It was very quiet and looked as though it was nearly unconscious. It's mother jiggled and crooned to it in an agitated fashion until at last the fresh air revived it, and the color came back to its cheeks.

The rest of the trip was uneventful but for the most part unenjoyable. We both had headaches and were content to just sit passively. All that provided temporary distraction were the road signs the Indian Government had erected along the way. They were something like the old Burma-Shave signs that had once enlivened the roads of America, only these were in a less humorous vein. Marching alongside the highway in series of three or four, they bore such messages as:

Delay the first
Space the second
Stop the third

—advice on birth control—; or

Trees mean water
Water means rice
Rice means life

—the Government is trying to discourage the cutting of trees.

It was late in the afternoon when we rounded a bend, and beheld the Vale of Kashmir spread out before us.

The Himalayas surrounded the valley in ranks of jagged splendor, crowned with gold-tinged clouds. They guarded the serene vale below which swam in the honey-colored light of late afternoon. An azure lake half filled the valley; the rest was a tapestry of golden green that receded into the mists at the foot of Nanga Parbat, the great mountain whose lofty head rose far above its neighbors at the far end.

We forgot our headaches and our scratchy throats as we eagerly leaned out the open window and drank in the scene. Then our descent was swift, and soon we were on the valley floor being carried down a highway of singular beauty, which ran between lines of tall poplars whose long shadows crisscrossed the road in front of us. Fields of crocuses lay on both sides of the road at first, for Kashmir is a center of saffron production. After a while they gave way to rice paddies and truck gardens. We reached the shores of Lake Dal just before dark.

Srinagar, pronounced "Sirrynugger," the capital of Kashmir and its only good-sized town, lay on the lake shore just where the Jhelum River left the lake and meandered through town with its burden of houseboats and river people. The town itself was medieval in appearance, much like Kathmandu, with narrow streets and top-heavy half-timbered brick houses of three or four stories. The bus station was located in a modern section of parks and concrete Government buildings. We were finally deposited, hungry, dirty, and dog-tired, on a broad and park-like avenue, where, mercifully, taxis were waiting at the curb.

We had reserved a houseboat—a "super-deluxe" houseboat called the *New Texas*. A large sign above the brightly lit quay read:

NEHRU PARK WELCOMES YOU. HIRING OF SHIKARAS

FOR SIGHT SCENES OF PARTIES, SHOOTINGS, ETC.

Lined up along the floating wharf were a dozen shikaras: double-ended wooden boats with upcurving prows and sterns, and curtained shelters in the center. Behind the brightly-printed curtains were plump reclining seats, almost beds, with piles of pillows upon them. Each had a sign in the front, according to the whims of its owner: "Good Luckin," said one, and another: "Super Delux," and another: "Hevean King." "New Modl," read yet another.

We walked down the steps to the pier, not knowing quite what to do. I felt that we had just entered a new and strange world, and we were a little bewildered. How were we to reach our houseboat? Across the water, the lights of a hundred houseboats glimmered, but how were we to find ours? The shikaras bobbed at our feet, each one so inviting; each one empty of anyone at all.

"Mr. and Mrs. Knott?" A dark and handsome young man appeared beside us; he had evidently been waiting among a little group of men at the top of the steps. "I didn't know what time you would arrive. The plane from Delhi arrived at two o'clock but you were not on it. I thought you might not be coming . . ."

"And you met the plane and then waited all this time?"

"Well, I didn't want to miss you. My name is Amin. I will take you to the *New Texas*."

Guiltily I remembered that we had nearly put off our arrival until the next day. (All we'd have risked was our deposit. Would he have waited all that day too?)

"We came by bus from Jammu," Ed explained.

Amin grimaced. "Very bad trip. You should have taken a plane."

Quickly our luggage was loaded in the back of the shikara, and a young boy materialized to take charge of the single oar. Amin helped me into the boat and soon we were settled in the couch. He sat in front of and facing us on a jump seat and we were off, gliding across the dark water which gleamed up ahead with the lights from the houseboats. The moon rose over a black mountain; a silver orb in a clear indigo sky.

We pulled up to a houseboat which was decked out with dozens of colored pennants, "To welcome us," Amin said. The houseboat had a

185

front verandah with built-in seats. The woodwork, of fragrant red cedar, was intricately and wonderfully carved over every inch of its surface. The front door had lace curtains which parted to reveal a room of a magnificence for which we were completely unprepared.

The houseboat was large, with two bedrooms in the rear, and contained a dining room as well as a large living room. They were a wonderland of carved wood, oriental rugs, and colored concealed lighting. The bedroom, with its king-sized bed on a dais and peach lace curtains, was an eye-popper.

"It looks like a French house of ill-repute," muttered Ed.

Amin opened the door into a small and surprisingly plain bathroom and gave us towels and soap.

"Dinner will be ready in half an hour," he said. "It is roast lamb. We were not sure what you would like, so we usually have that the first night."

"That sounds wonderful," I said sincerely. I was dying of hunger, for we hadn't had anything substantial since lunch the day before, and nothing but cookies and tea all day today. There was just time for a bath for me and a shower for Ed before dinner.

Later, lying in our enormous bed, warmly comfortable and full of a succulent dinner, I said dreamily, "I feel exactly like Conway did in *Lost Horizon*. After today's gruesome bus trip, it's hard to believe that we've ended up here, in the middle of the *Arabian Nights*. Isn't it a fantastic place, Ed?"

"Snrx-x-x-x-x," snored my romantic husband. "Snrx-x-x-x-x, puh, puh, puh."

* * *

A beautiful and somehow familiar sound woke me at dawn. I lay in the dim room and listened. The lovely sound rose and fell like something I had heard before—of course! It was the muezzin, calling the faithful to prayer: we were in Muslim territory. The houseboat rocked gently; maybe it was the wake of a shikara taking someone to the mosque that caused it. The air smelled heavenly sweet . . . I drifted off to sleep again.

At eight o'clock we were seated at the polished dining room table, eating savory omelettes. Our table waiter was called Majid; he was the brother of Amin, and was also handsome and charming, and like his brother, mustachioed. He dished up steaming portions before we knew we wanted them, and kept the teacups brimming. Amin joined us at the table, and we learned that their father owned the *New Texas* and that the whole family worked there and lived behind the big houseboat in a small

186

one, where grandfather and mother cooked, and little sisters helped to wash up. Perhaps that explained the delightful sense of home that permeated the place. I sighed with pleasure for the fortieth time and buttered myself another piece of toast.

"What shall we do today?"

"You are staying for how many days?" Amin asked.

"Five or six, I think," Ed said. "We don't know much about Kashmir, beyond the obvious tourist spots like the Shalimar Garden. What do you suggest?"

"Let me be your guide," said Amin. "I will charge you reasonable price each for five days all sightseeing around Kashmir." He named an extremely low figure which we felt was more than satisfactory. We accepted with alacrity, and he outlined the day's program: a shikara trip around the lake, a picnic lunch, and a swim in adjoining lake Nageen. I went back to the room and packed my bathing suit and sun-tan lotion into a string bag. Our suitcases were lying open and Ed had uncharacteristically half-unpacked; I called to him.

"The room doesn't lock," I said. "Do you think our stuff is okay to leave around? Maybe we should lock our suitcases before we go."

"Hey Amin," Ed called, "can we just leave our stuff around?"

Amin stuck his head in the door and said, "No need to lock anything. In Kashmir everything is safe. Kashmiri people do not steal. My family assure you that nothing will be missing."

We looked at each other and shrugged. "Okay."

When we went outside, we saw that while we had been eating breakfast, the sky had clouded up and a gentle but persistent rain was falling. Disappointed, I asked Amin if we should call off our boat trip, but he insisted that the rain would not last.

"Soon it will stop. Do not worry, it is warm, and the sun will come out."

We stepped into the waiting shikara and Amin went inside, to reappear with a large basket which he stowed behind our seats. Then he tucked a big tarpaulin over our legs to protect us from drifting raindrops. Our twelve-year-old oarsman, whose name was Ishmael, could not handle a whole day's shikara ride by himself, so he had been joined by another muscular young man for the occasion. They bent to their oars with a will, Ishmael crouching in the Kashmiri fashion at the prow, and the new young man in the rear. Amin took his place behind our seat.

Mist hung heavily just above the trees and dimmed the horizon, and the rain, which had pattered lightly at first, increased its volume and soon water was pouring in streams from the canvas top, soaking the curtains and dampening the tarpaulin. The water was dimpled with raindrops and we were enclosed in a small wet world comprised of our shikara and the lake surrounding us in a fifty-foot circle; the rest of the universe had vanished into the mist. A disembodied hand appeared around our seat back and we saw that it contained a freshly opened beer bottle.

"A beer would be nice," said Amin. "This one for Bunny, next one for Ed coming up."

A beer *was* nice, and before our bottles were empty, the rain had slackened and soon ceased altogether. Tentatively the sun peered through the mist and then blew it away with its hot breath, and the lake surface began to steam. We removed the tarpaulin from our legs and it was folded up and stowed away. The curtains were tied back and our oarsmen found new energy. As we cut swiftly through the now satin-smooth water, the men began to sing a rhythmic Kashmiri song that kept time with their oars.

We slowed as we passed beds of lotus—the luscious pink flowers as large as luncheon plates, their enormous leaves covered with drops of water that looked like moonstones in the sun. I reached out to touch one, and the water drops slid over it like mercury, catching the light as if they were precious jewels.

Near the lotus beds were plots of vegetables; carrots and cauliflower, squash and kohlrabi, green onions and beans. We could almost watch them grow in the hot, steamy sunshine.

"These are floating gardens," said Amin. "Farmer builds a . . ." he searched for the right word ". . . a floor of branches, then pulls up weeds from bottom of lake and piles on top. Then he piles earth on top of that until pretty thick. It floats on top of the water, then he plants vegetables. See those poles? They hold floating gardens still so they won't float away. But sometimes another farmer will steal part of a garden and move it to his garden." He laughed.

"What do they use for fertilizer?" asked Ed. "I've never seen better looking vegetables."

"Stuff from holding tanks in houseboats," said Amin succinctly. "Once a week farmers collect from the houseboats and they put that on vegetables. Very good fertilizer."

This was no shock to us; most third world countries and a lot of European countries do the same. Still, we wondered how the lake stayed so fresh and clean. The water was limpid to the bottom, which we could see clearly ten feet down (in most places, though, the lake is quite shallow—three to six feet seemed average).

"The lake is so clear, Amin," I said. "You'd think it would get dirtier."

"Many springs come up from the bottom of the lake," he explained, "and make the dirty water all run away down the river. The Jhelum is very dirty."

We stopped at a little island covered with nicely maintained gardens and a wooden pavilion that extended over the water. We gazed down into the water at the edge of the pavilion. Dozens of tiny fish swam around in the shifting light beneath the surface. Suddenly they all darted away, and out of the darkness under the platform swam a huge trout, lazily propelling himself into the pool of light that the minnows had vacated.

"Oh, for my fishing gear," sighed Ed. "I wonder how much a fishing license would cost?"

Amin named a staggering figure and the idea died at birth.

He spread a cloth on the grass and proceeded to unload food from his basket for our picnic lunch. He had brought plenty of food and beer, and brewed up a pot of tea on a Primus stove.

We snoozed on the grass for a while after lunch, sleepy from the beer and the unusually large noon-time meal. I was awakened by the tickling on my arm as a large praying mantis daintily picked his way along it. I shooed him away and woke Ed, who was snoring.

"Let's go. I'm dying for a swim."

First, though, Amin took us to the "Mosque of the Hair of the Beard of the Prophet," a handsome new marble building in the modern section of Srinagar. We left the shikara at the dock and walked over to the mosque. I was sure I would be barred from entering, because from the Muslim point of view I am of the lesser sex, but—since I was a foreigner, I guess—there was no objection, and I removed my shoes and followed my Lord-and-Master into the sacred precincts. (Local women must worship in the downstairs section, where no doubt it is dull and stuffy.) The sanctuary was really very impressive, with crystal chandeliers, thick dark red carpets, and a special shrine for the repository of the single hair from the prophet's beard. We dropped a rupee or two in the offering box as we left, for I really was grateful to have been able to enter a mosque at all.

It was only a short boat trip to Nageen Lake, which we entered under a highway bridge that divided it from Lake Dal. Nageen is even cleaner and purer than Dal, and a little deeper. At the far end was the "swimming

189

boat," a big barge with an upper deck for sunbathing, and steps leading into the lake on both sides. At the rear was a changing room, and tea and *gedunk* were available from a little stall on the main deck. Most of the customers (and *all* of the women, every one of whom was wearing a sari though all the men wore bathing suits) sat on folding chairs on the main deck, watching the few men who were actually in the water. I got the impression that most of the people there were tourists from Hindu India. There were a few young local men like Amin; they were the ones who were swimming. Local women were entirely absent. The three of us quickly changed into our suits and were soon in the water, which for temperature, clarity, and sweet freshness has never been equalled in my experience. We spent the hot part of the afternoon alternating between the sundeck on top and the divine water. I noticed that Ishmael and his helper had crossed the lake to a quiet spot where they were swimming also, *sans* suits.

We were rowed away just at the time of day when the sun slants in golden shafts through the trees. I reclined on my pillowed couch, one hand trailing in the cool water, while I watched the river life along the canals and Ed was kept busy taking picture after picture. Weeping willows dipped their elegant branches in the water, sheltering families of ducks. The ducklings followed their fat parents in little flotillas. Children, their plump brown bodies innocent of covering, cavorted in the shallows at the water's edge. A waterfront store, facing the canal, was closed and padlocked—its owner sat on the platform, his feet dangling over the edge, fishing. Other waterfront stores were open, doing a brisk business with shikara owners who did their shopping by boat. The canal grew busier, for it led right through the center of Srinagar, where the top-heavy brick houses leaned over the water, and arched bridges spanned the canal at every block. We came upon a traffic jam of small houseboats and barges, and had to bump and scrape our way past them. Their owners stuck their heads out the windows and grinned at us. Kids ran along the sides of their boats and waved. A naked little boy who was jumping up and down at the edge of a boat landing waited until we were alongside him and then jumped in, splashing me with muddy water. He came up laughing and sputtering and waved happily when I laughed also. Then we went under a final bridge and came out into the calm and sunset lake.

It was dusk when we pulled up to our houseboat, and the lights were shining out of our lace-curtained windows. Majid and Grandfather met us and led us through the dining room, where the table was set for the meal, and into the hall.

"Dinner in 'alf 'our," said Majid.

We were bathed, freshly changed, and starving when we sat down at the table by candlelight (for the power had failed again).

"Cuff for soof" (cup of soup) said Majid in his inimitable accent as he swiftly filled our bowls with a thick, spicy liquid. It was a Kashmiri dinner that night, a succession of wonderfully flavored dishes that we had never tasted before. After dinner we had tea from the family samovar.

"Milik?" asked Majid, solicitously.

(Certain consonants are always separated by vowels in the Kashmiri language. Hence, *milik* and *silik* for milk and silk, *Sirinigar* for Srinagar, and so on.)

We undressed by candlelight and were in bed at eight-thirty. We were asleep by eight-thirty-one.

In the morning after another of Grandfather's omelettes, we set out by taxi for the Royal Spring Garden, the first of the famous gardens built by the Emperors Akbar and Jehangir in the 1600's. Amin had come with us, and he explained that the Royal Spring had the purest and finest water in the world. The garden was approached at lake level and rose in a series of terraces, culminating at the top with a grotto that contained the spring. The water flowed from a pipe for easy drinking. Ed and I looked at each other—we had just climbed up the hillside—we were hot—a drink of water would taste so good. Should we?

What the hell. I put my foot on the stepping-stone located so conveniently under the spout, leaned forward, and drank a deep draft of cold, sweet water—the first I had tasted in over two months. It was wonderful! I drank again.

"Hey, let me have some too."

We took turns until shame made us offer the place to Amin, and then a busload of Indian tourists came in, eager to try the wonderful water, and we retreated.

"I didn't realize how much I missed water," I said wonderingly. "You know, I've never drunk a lot of water at home; I always reach for tea or juice or coffee . . . but now I crave water. Isn't it funny?"

We wandered slowly down the terraces, admiring the well-maintained gardens that glowed with familiar flowers: roses, salvia, pansies—all the flowers beloved by the western world. They did well there in temperate Kashmir, tended by gardeners who might have stepped out of *The Arabian Nights*. One of these approached us and handed me a long-stemmed apricot rose—my favorite color. I accepted it without thinking. Instantly he held out his hand for baksheesh. Ed looked reproachfully at

191

me and pulled out his change, picked out one rupee and handed it to the rascal.

"Ten rupee, ten!" cried the rascal, indignantly refusing the coin.

Quickly I handed him the rose and we walked away before he could change his mind.

"Sorry," I said. "I forgot myself. I'll bet he wishes he'd taken the coin when he had the chance." I looked behind us. The rascal was following sadly, still clutching the rose. When he saw me looking, he increased his pace, but we resolutely ignored him and soon he tired of the game and went back to his weeding. Amin, who had carefully stood aside during this exchange, smiled and pulled at his mustache.

The Shalimar Garden was even lovelier than the Nishad. It had been built by Jehangir, the father of Shah Jehan, for his wife, Nur Jehan, whose name means Light of the World. He must have loved her, for the garden he built for her was simply exquisite.

A black marble pavilion located at the back of the garden was being restored on the inside. The paisley frescoes had been water-damaged and were being replaced by exact copies in the same paints used in the 1600's, which were made from ground jade, lapis, turquoise and henna. Some of the frescoes were still beautiful, and we were glad that we could admire them in their original condition. The pavilion itself was a graceful thing with arched openings overlooking the fountains and the flowers. There were fountains everywhere, and the sound of water combined with the smell of flowers increased our pleasure beyond the merely visual.

We sat on a stone "lily pad" in the middle of a central pool just below a five-foot waterfall, where the sound of water drowned out all other sounds, and where the fine mist drifted around us, cooling our warm faces. Two pretty little girls, about six and seven, dressed in the tunic and trousers most little girls in India wear, were jumping from stepping-stone to stepping-stone just above the falls. They saw us watching them and hopped over to one side, disappearing from view. Then they reappeared at our level, clutching one another and giggling. I beckoned to them and they shyly came to the edge of the pond. I dug out a couple of the sample-size lipsticks that I carry to give to girl-children and handed one to each.

They snatched at them and applied the lipstick with gusto, giggling all the while, and then ran off, gripping their treasures in their little fists, shrieking with childish laughter. We saw them later, lipsticked from nose to chin, in the company of their parents. They waved to us and then buried their faces in their mother's sari in fits of giggles.

When we tired of the gardens, Amin took us back to the houseboat for lunch, and then out we went again to visit a carpet factory. We were shown some of the operations which, as in Nepal, were performed under primitive conditions. The lighting was so bad that I wondered how people could work all day like that, peering at their fine work in semi-darkness. As always, the workers were cheerful at their looms. They did the tedious hand-knotting with an almost casual air, producing carpets exquisite in their intricate designs, and lustrously silky in texture, and no wonder: at four hundred knots to the square inch, they were superior to any carpets we had ever seen. We were taken into the showroom and shown piles of them. The salesman unfolded each one and shook it out, tossing it with a flourish on the floor. I wanted them all and was dying to buy one, but they cost quite a bit and our budget couldn't stretch to accommodate such an expenditure.

"Someday we'll come back and buy one," said Ed.

"Promise?"

"Absolutely."

We fancied a walk after that and left Amin, assuring him we would get back home in time for dinner. We asked him to drop us off at the Government Tourist Emporium, a half-timbered Dickensian reminder of Olde England, and spent a couple of hours at that fascinating store looking at more carpets, shawls, and other crafts produced by Kashmiri workers. The prices were excellent in all categories, although the silk and wool carpets were not quite as fine as those in the factory we had visited. We bought saffron much more cheaply than we had seen it anywhere else in Kashmir, and certainly at a pittance compared to what they ask back home for a thread or two of that most expensive of spices.

As we left, we noticed a high embankment behind the emporium, and climbed it to see what was up there. It was "The Bund," a walk along the embankment of one of the canals through town, and we set off down the paved path. The wide canal below us was muddy and quite still, and it was edged with houseboats that had seen better days, and were ending their careers accommodating youthful travelers and, sometimes, semi-permanent hippie residents. A small group of the latter were sitting yoga-fashion on the upper sundeck of their decrepit houseboat, smoking marijuana or hashish from hookahs. The herby aroma of "grass" or "hash" came wafting up to us. Both boys and girls were colorfully dressed and the boys were very hairy, and I thought them as interesting in their way as the genuine Kashmiri river people were in theirs. Further on was a small Kashmiri houseboat with wide planks leading to shore.

193

On one of the planks a pretty woman was washing her clothes with soap, kneading the pile of sudsy wet cloth upon the plank. On the deck were two old men smoking a two-pipe hookah, but this time the unmistakable aroma of tobacco drifted up to us. Behind them, in the open doorway of the cabin, a young man knotted a carpet upon a loom.

We looked away from the river to the other side of the embankment. A half-timbered cottage behind a charming garden caught our eye, and it wasn't until we noticed people coming and going that we realized that the cottage was actually Grindlay's Bank. The verandah was furnished with cushioned wicker chairs and the garden was sweet with hollyhocks and marigolds. Just beyond it was the post office, another cottage with cream-colored paint and a garden that was even prettier, with roses along the picket fence. The long British reign had produced some surprising anachronisms in India; what amazed us was that they had often been maintained so lovingly by the Indians.

Further along, the pathway became narrower as we left the former British enclave around the Government Tourist Emporium and the canal entered the downtown area of Srinagar. Houseboats became more numerous and even poorer. Shops lined the pathway—shops full of carpets, jewelry, and papier maché showrooms, giving way to grocery shops and barber stalls as we progressed.

At a wide curve in the canal, an old man in the traditional Kashmiri pyjamas was ironing tablecloths with a charcoal iron—a great, heavy contraption that opened up to admit glowing charcoal. The old man had placed a padded board on the coping itself and was doing his ironing there, with the broad view of the canal before him. We stopped to watch, interested in the way he zipped through his ironing and expertly flipped the tablecloths into pleats accordian-fashion as he finished ironing each length. He let us heft the iron —it must have weighed at least ten pounds.

We decided to make our way back to our houseboat, and turned down a side canal which seemed to lead in the right direction. It was a noisome slough, lined with derelict houseboats. The water was thick and greenish-grey, and the odors rising from it were vile. We hurried along, holding our noses.

"Do you suppose that is *eau de toilet?*" I asked.

"No. Actually . . ." An expression of refined discrimination crossed Ed's face. "Actually, I believe it is *Channel Number Two.*" I was shrieking with laughter as we turned off the stinking slough at the first street we came to, causing the numerous pedestrians to stare at the strange ferenghis. The streets were crowded with shoppers picking up last minute ingredients for their dinners. We passed stalls devoted to hot chilies—green and red, large and small; stalls selling boxed tea leaves; stalls selling nothing but different kinds of peas and beans, all colors and sizes, and about thirty different varieties. Rice stalls, in which were barrels filled with different kinds of rice—I counted seventeen—of different degrees of whiteness, and with differing aromas. (India is an olfactory paradise; both of us enjoyed the variety of smells that we encountered in the bazaars—naturally some smells, including that of the slough, were not so pleasant.) There were barber stalls and sari stalls and stalls selling the little baskets lined with fired clay pots which Kashmiris sling under their clothes in the wintertime to keep themselves warm. We wandered along, peering and taking pictures, ourselves as much a curiosity to the local people as they were to us. The afternoon was melting into evening when we realized that the air was getting chilly and dusk was nearly upon us, and we had no idea where we were.

"Do you see a taxi anywhere, Ed?"

"No. I've been watching for a while. I don't think many tourists get into this part of town; probably we should look for a three-wheeler. But I haven't seen one of those either."

We chose a direction and walked rapidly down the narrow street in the gathering dusk, hoping to find a major avenue where we might locate a conveyance. After a few blocks, we found what we were looking for, a wide thoroughfare; and shortly thereafter, a three-wheeler came put-putting along. Within a few minutes we were back at the quay, where we found Ishmael patiently waiting for us in the shikara. Our own home had never welcomed us more warmly than our houseboat did that evening, all lit up and with fresh flowers on the tables. Amin was in the living room, all smiles.

"I was worried about you, thinking you get lost in the town."

The spicy aroma of curries and Majid's greeting from the dining room warned us to hurry. In no time we were seated at the table, candles were lit, and an exquisite dinner was put before us.

"I'm going to be spoiled for the rest of my life, after Kashmir," I said. "How will we ever go back to our workaday world?"

CHAPTER 17

The Mountains

We were scheduled to go on a horseback ride in the morning. I hadn't expected to ride a horse on this trip and my only shoes were sandals. Amin eyed them dubiously when he saw me.

"Those are not good shoes for riding," he said. "Maybe you borrow my boots for today. Besides, it rained last night."

"That's okay, Amin. I'll manage." If I had to walk at all, I thought I'd be glad for my own shoes, even if they were sandals. We let him talk us into borrowing jackets from him and from his father though, for he said it would be cold up on the mountain. We were going to a place called Seven Springs at more than eleven thousand feet elevation.

"I am very sorry I cannot go with you today, but I have arranged that you take taxi of a friend. He will pay horsemen. I have fixed picnic lunch—sorry, not as good as yesterday—here, in this bag." He showed me an enormous bag. "You give to horseman to carry up the mountain." Amin clucked over us worriedly.

"We can take care of ourselves, Amin," I said. "See you tonight."

The road led through many little towns that were unlike any we had seen in India before: brick houses of three or four stories, with corrugated roofs and crudely adzed wooden frames and doors. They looked as if they'd be cold in the winter. The streets were of mud, and they had become morasses after last night's rain.

The people we saw were quite fierce-looking, even the women, who wore distinctive head scarves that covered their foreheads and were tied in the back. They wore trouser outfits that looked something like those of the Sikh women. We saw a few women in *bourkas*—the tent-like cover-alls with cutwork netting for the eyes which are worn in Muslim countries. These "tents" were beautifully made of brown or black material with tucks and pleats, and fancy hand-stitching. I remembered that a male author had enthused about the mysterious come-hither quality that women possess when wearing one; however, to me women wearing the bourka looked like Halloween witches, with their black-shod feet incongruously hanging out below the skirts, and their faces masked.

Here in the countryside, the little girls were as bold and saucy as the little boys, and stared at us with their piercing eyes as we passed. Even the dogs were different—big, heavy-boned and heavy-coated, although they were mangy looking like most Indian dogs.

As we left the valley and started up the mountain, the views became spectacular, and the trees were no longer poplars, willows, and chinars (plane trees), but pines and firs. The firs were of a type we had never seen before, but the pines looked like the ordinary lodgepole and ponderosa pines found in Western America. There was a complete absence of underbrush. We saw peasants gathering up even the tiniest twigs that lay on the ground in their never-ending search for fuel. Even the lower branches of trees were conspicuously lacking. The grass under the trees was cropped as smooth as any park lawn by cattle and goats which grazed their way through the forests, accompanied by sturdy children.

The usual "Burma-Shave" signs erected by the government were seen along the roadsides, including one that made us laugh:

PLEASE DARLING, DO NOT NAG ME

WHILE I AM DRIVING

At Gulmarg, which means "flower meadow," we were handed over into the care of a horseman who was about fifty years old, grizzled of head and spare of build, with splayed feet thrust into run-over plastic shoes without laces. I couldn't see how he could walk in them, for the backs of the shoes were crushed by the old man's heels, and they slapped at each step; but they certainly didn't seem to bother him. He called over a younger man, whose footwear was in exactly the same condition, and two thin ponies so small that I couldn't see how they could possibly carry Ed and me several thousand feet up the mountain. The fifty-year-old was my horseman, and he held out the stirrup with one sinewy hand and proferred the other. I put my foot into the stirrup, which was awfully high off the ground, and dragged myself with difficulty into the saddle. The saddle was very odd, with a decided hump in the middle, and I settled myself into it gingerly, wriggling around to try to find a comfortable position. There was none. Unwisely, I decided that I could make do, and after Ed had climbed aboard his mount, we were off.

"What is my horse's name?" I asked the old man.

"Sunflower," he lisped, through his remaining three tobacco-stained teeth.

197

Ed's horse was "John," but they should have been called "Fairyfoot" and "Windy," because mine continually slipped and stumbled, and Ed's farted at every other step. Fairyfoot must have had a deviant passion for Windy (they were both stallions) for he continually pressed his nose into Windy's skinny tail, affording me whiffs so potent they took my breath away.

The trail led straight up the mountainside through the forest, over rocks and roots, and most of it was greasy and sodden from the rain. About halfway up we forded a broad stream with a bottom strewn with round rocks ranging from the size of oranges to large boulders—difficult going for our poor horses. Our horsemen relentlessly sprang from boulder to boulder, dragging the horses behind them. The poor little beasts followed willy-nilly, slipping and sliding as they stumbled along. I was perched there nervously, watching Fairyfoot's hooves negotiate the rocks, when the worst happened. He stumbled and then fell to his knees, throwing my upper body violently over his head. At that moment Windy farted loudly and odoriferously directly in my face. Fairyfoot scrambled to his feet, lurching my body backwards. I was just straightening up when a wet branch which had been bent by Windy's passing hit me across the face. The combined assault on my person and my senses left me reeling, and it was a while before the muttered curses left my lips and I started to pay attention to the scenery once more.

The horses were hampered not only by the substantial weight of the ferenghis on their backs, but additionally by their masters, who lightened their own weary way by holding onto the tails of their poor little beasts.

"No! Let go of him! Let GO!" I screamed at my horseman, finally, as his additional weight started to drag Fairyfoot back down the mountain at a particularly steep and dangerous spot. He did let go, surprised, and an equally surprised pony shot up the trail as if he'd been goosed.

From then on I made it clear that Fairyfoot was only going to carry me, and the old man had to make it on his own. It didn't seem to bother him; he bounded up that mountain as if he'd been fifteen years old, shoes flapping and his bony old elbows sawing up and down. His shoes gradually filled with rocks and dirt, and I winced each time his sockless feet came down on them, but it seemed to hurt me more than it hurt him, for he was as cheerful as only a man can be who has a rich customer for the day. Ed's horseman, being younger, had depended less on his horse for help, and bounded from rock to rock like a gazelle.

All the way up the long trail, the humpy saddle cut into my coccyx, for though I tried to take the weight on my legs, the angle at which we were climbing forced my suffering tail-bone back into the saddle. I was anything but an experienced rider, having been on a horse only three or four times in my whole life, and I knew nothing about adjusting the stirrups to the length of my legs. The stirrups were so short that my knees were practically around my chin, until finally I realized that they were all wrong and had my horseman lengthen them, but the damage had already been done. By the time we reached Seven Springs, my rear was in a terrible state.

We came over a rise to see the beautiful meadow spread out before us. Behind me my horseman gave Fairyfoot a tremendous smack accompanied by a banshee yell, and suddenly I was flying along at a full gallop. My rear was pounding on the saddle as I hung on like grim death. The ground was a blur beneath the horse's hooves and I wanted to close my eyes, but I was terrified that if I did, I'd lose my balance and bash out my brains on the rocky meadow. I was just deciding that the old man had taken revenge for being deprived of his tow rope and was bent on murdering me, when Ed on his horse drew alongside me, and I realized that I had not been singled out for punishment. Ed's face was grim and his knuckles were as white as mine. After what seemed an eternity, our poor old ponies, gasping and panting, covered with foam, slowed to a trot and then stumbled to a halt, and we slid off them, trembling with fatigue and reaction to the wild ride. We looked back, and there came our horsemen, bounding along with ease and obvious enjoyment.

"Good ride, eh?" croaked the old man. "Sunflower like to run at end of trail. Always run! Hee, hee." He slapped Ed on the shoulder.

"You okay, Bun?" asked Ed. "Jesus, I thought I'd never hold on. I've never galloped on a horse before."

"Neither had I," I said, and laughed shakily. "But my poor rear will never be the same. My saddle is so *awful*! How's yours?"

"Mine's fine. What's the matter with your saddle?"

"It's got a hump in the middle. Take a look at it."

Ed walked over to Fairyfoot and ran his hand over the saddle. "Look at this, Bunny. This saddle is broken right in half underneath! Didn't you notice it before you started?"

"No-o-o. I knew it felt lousy, but I thought it was just too small, or maybe poorly made, or something."

"Jesus. We'll have to do something about it going back. You can't sit on that again."

I sighed with relief; Ed would take care of it. I hadn't the faintest idea what he'd do, but he'd do *something*.

199

"Let's eat."

We looked around for a likely spot to serve as our picnic place. The beautiful meadow stretched out around us, girded with dark firs. Wildflowers starred the lush green grass that was being cropped by dozens of horses. Seven tiny springs bubbled out of the ground in low spots. The water was clear as crystal and cold as ice. Fairyfoot and Windy had each straddled a spring and were sucking up great drafts of water. There was birdsong and the caws of many crows: great big black birds that hopped clumsily amongst the horses.

On our right was a hut, a tea stall, dug into the slope of the hillside. It looked as if a giant had stuck a knife into the hill and pried the sod up, propping it with logs. A crackling fire burned in the back against a hearth with a chimney that stuck up through the sod. Unsanitary-looking dishes were stacked upon a counter of hand-hewn boards. The place contained three small tables and folding chairs which spilled outside into the sunlight.

We chose a table that was half in sunshine, sat down with our bag lunch, and opened it up. It contained half a roast chicken, two boiled potatoes, and two large tomatoes (which we ate), two hardboiled eggs and two cheese sandwiches (which we gave to our horsemen), two large pieces of slightly stale cake (which the crows loved), and two big apples (which Fairyfoot and Windy would eventually enjoy). We bought delicious chai from the stall and I sat there, carefully resting my weight on one hip, dreamily sipping from the chipped and obviously not-too-clean cup, and reflected on the deadening of my sensibilities since the start of this trip. "Would I have drunk from this cup at the beginning?" I asked myself. "Probably not . . ."

I raised my eyes to the view down the meadow. The nearly ever-present clouds had parted, and Nanga Parbat, her icy face a delicate blue-white against the intense blue of the sky, stood there naked, revealed in all her loveliness. I nudged Ed, and we just sat there for a long time, watching. Then she drew her clouds about her again.

We took the apples over to the horses, and the unexpected gift evidently gave Fairyfoot a fit of frisk, for he took off at a run. Gathering up a harem of mares, he thundered off toward the end of the clearing at the head of the pack, to the horror of my horseman. It took him fully half an hour to catch the horse again, and when he did, he beat that poor beast with a stick until I screamed at him to stop. He came back sullenly, shaking his head, probably wondering what on earth he had done to be saddled with such a picky female customer, no matter if she WAS rich.

He hobbled poor Fairyfoot and withdrew to the deepest reaches of the dugout, where he drank tea and sulked.

We took a walk around the perimeter of the meadow and then sat down outside the dugout again for a final cup of tea before leaving. As we sat there, two young Sikh men, smartly dressed in white shirts and pressed trousers, and wearing polished dress shoes, dismounted from their horses and sat down at the next table. They nodded in a friendly fashion to us, and we both said "Good afternoon."

Instantly they invited us to their table and then offered us drinks of neat whisky which we drank from our teacups. They were tourists "doing" Kashmir for the first time, and they were energetically enjoying everything.

"Madame, I have never seen anything to compare with this wonderful scenery," one said in his excellent English. "My wife and I are most certainly having a delightful holiday in Kashmir. I hope that you are also enjoying."

They were so nice, and so friendly. I wished that we could have met their wives, who, as they told us, were waiting down at the hotel in Gulmarg for them. Ed and I took their pictures with our camera, then with their cameras. We posed for their cameras, and then posed again while they took our picture with our camera. We were all fast friends in five minutes.

We dragged ourselves away, finally, sorry to leave our new friends, and even sorrier to have to climb aboard our horses again for the return trip. Our horsemen rounded up Fairyfoot and Windy (even hobbled, Fairyfoot had managed to get quite a distance away).

"You ride John," said Ed. "I'll walk. No honestly, Bunny, I'd rather walk anyway. I'm not used to riding and I need the exercise. Besides, my tail-bone is sore."

So I climbed up on Windy, and though I winced when I sat down, I was happy to find that the saddle was much more comfortable. I'd have been even happier to walk, but my sandals were inadequate for the really rough and muddy trail. We set out with Ed and my horseman in the lead, Windy and I following, trailed by Fairyfoot.

The sounds of his stumbles and falls on the way down the steep trail made my hair stand on end, and I was more than ever thankful I wasn't riding him. When we reached the paved road at the bottom, we walked the rest of the way back to our taxi. We had covered about eighteen kilometers, or over ten miles. I thanked God that we had accepted the loan of jackets from Amin, for the afternoon at that elevation was decidedly chilly, and my sandaled feet were frozen. Every bone in my body ached.

That evening, when I climbed into a mercifully hot bath, I discovered that my inner thighs were black and blue down to and including my knees, and my tail-bone was swollen hard and was hot to the touch. I couldn't sit comfortably for two days, and I was so stiff that every time I got out of a chair, my legs nearly gave way under me; but when all was said and done it had been worth it.

We awoke to raindrops dripping from the eaves and splashing into the lake.

"What's on for today?" I asked Ed. ("Was it worthwhile to get up at all? Maybe I should just roll over and go back to sleep.")

"Some place called Pahalgam." He looked over the rather tattered piece of paper Amin had given us and compared it with our map. "I think it's up here near the Pakistani border. It's quite high too—we'd better borrow those jackets again."

By nine we were on the quay and seated in another taxi. I shifted around gingerly, putting my weight on first one hip and then the other. GOD, my rear was sore!

We turned south toward Jammu along the lovely poplar-lined road again, noticing that walnut, apple, and mulberry trees grew everywhere, reaching their tender green branches up to the gentle rain which was already beginning to slacken. By the time we came to a halt at our first destination, the rain had stopped and there were bright blue gaps in the clouds.

We got out of the taxi and approached a ruined temple—a Hindu temple, dedicated to Vishnu the Preserver. It was laid out like the temples at Mount Abu, with a raised central sanctuary in a large courtyard, with sixty cells surrounding it in a sort of portico. It must have been lovely once, but it had been torn down when Islam came to Kashmir. All that was left were the foundations, with a few remnants of beautiful Hindu carvings to tantalize us.

Our next stop was a holy spring at Islamabad, still a major Hindu shrine. Sadhus, or holy men, were camped in flimsy tents on the grounds, and several of them stood around dreamily, their emaciated frames, wild dreadlocks, and the marks of Siva on their foreheads setting them apart from the sturdy Kashmiris.

The icy-cold springs came boiling out of the hillside behind the shrine and were contained in stone pools. A school of perhaps two hundred enormous fat trout swam lazily in the largest of these, and we wandered over to take a look. Instantly the trout converged toward where we stood, and actually stuck their noses out of the water, begging to be fed. A teen-aged entrepreneur sold us a bag of unleavened bread with which to feed them. The trout churned up the water in their eagerness to get the crumbs, completely ignoring the two holy men who lathered their naked skeletal bodies with soap and then plunged in amongst the fish.

"You'd think the soap would foul up the water and hurt the fish," I said.

"Not with that much water coming into it all the time," said Ed, "I've never seen such a copious spring. I'll bet there is a complete change of water every few minutes . . . Look over there, Bunny. You can't tell those two hippies from the holy men except for the color of their hair."

He was right—they were just as emaciated and every bit as unkempt . . . but not half as clean.

We got back on the road for our run to Pahalgam, which was ninety-six kilometers from Srinagar in a high valley in the mountains.

When we arrived there, we drove through the little town, and took a narrow road up the canyon to a rickety bridge consisting of tiny branches laid crossways over two logs, and with two planks for the wheels of the car laid on top of them. This flimsy contraption spanned a raging mountain river that seemed to gnash its teeth in anticipation of our crossing. I eyed it askance.

"Are we going to drive over that thing?" I asked Amin.

"Yes, we have our picnic on the other side."

"Right on the other side? Right there?"

"Yes."

"I'll walk."

Ed gritted his teeth and squared his jaw in the fashion of fearless males and kept his seat. I got out and leaned in the open window.

"I hope your will is up-to-date."

"Oh shut up."

The car eased onto the creaking bridge and slowly inched its way to the other side. I expected it to give way momentarily, but somehow it held, and the taxi emerged triumphantly on the farther bank.

I picked my way across, amazed that the rickety bridge held even my weight without crashing into the wild water below.

We had our picnic lunch on a little island right in the middle of the foaming, jade green glacial river. I sat on a log, winced, and got up. Then I tried sitting on the ground on a rug that Amin spread for me. That was worse. Finally I folded up the rug and placed it over a hollow place in the log, and eased my suffering rear onto that. Comfortable at last, I ate in the warm sun, and later dozed a little.

"Look at that, Bunny!"

I awoke with a start, and followed Ed's pointing finger.

A herdsman was leading six fat red and white cattle onto the rickety bridge, and the animals were actually following him across, carefully placing their big hooves on the planks intended for car wheels. They crossed the island, and started across an even smaller and more perilous bridge to the other bank.

"Well, now I've seen everything. I wouldn't have believed that *any* animal would have ventured onto those bridges, especially big, heavy steers like those," I said.

"They're braver than you were," chuckled Ed.

"I didn't mind walking," I protested. "I just didn't want to go over in the car."

We decided to walk back into town with Amin, and let the driver pick us up there for the trip back. As soon as we crossed the bridge and started down the road, we met a long line of Indian soldiers marching uphill toward the Pakistani border, which was only a short distance away. They were admirably disciplined and never turned their heads to look at us (although they did slide their eyes around as they passed). Most of them were handsome and youthful, and all were smartly turned out in khaki uniforms that were more or less all alike, but with hats and turbans of various colors and insignia denoting the regiments they belonged to. There were Pathans, Sikhs, Gurkhas, and Rajputs: representatives of the military races and castes of India. Like military men the world round, they were scrubbed and pressed, buffed and polished to a fine sheen. Most wore large and fierce mustaches. I must say that I have never seen a finer looking group of men.

We had just passed the last of several hundred soldiers, when we came upon a gang of men loading timber on a truck. There were seven of them, and they chose a huge log from a pile in a yard alongside the road. They got it started with a big stick which they used as a fulcrum. They chanted as they rolled it uphill until they reached a clear space to the road. Using the stick as a pivot to turn it, they got it out to the road, chanting all the way. To our Western ears the chants sounded romantically musical, although what they were actually saying was probably: "Uphill, let's go, uphill!" or: "Turn it right, turn it!" or something equally prosaic. Once on the road, they rolled it downhill to the truck, which had skids up to the truck bed. After scaling it

204

(measuring it to determine its board feet), up it went onto the truck. They made it look so easy!

As we approached Pahalgam, the skies had clouded up and a gentle rain started to fall, and we ran the last few feet to our taxi, which fortunately was parked in the outskirts of town. I was still a little tired from our strenuous ride of the day before, and I dozed most of the way back, only waking when we stopped for "pee and tea" in another little town along the way. We had our tea under an awning in front of the tea-stall, and watched a plump puppy eating at the freshly killed carcass of a chicken in the middle of the road. He kept dodging trucks and buses until a big one picked up the carcass on its wheel and left only a damp spot, which the puppy mournfully licked.

We got home relatively early, for it was the night of the Kashmiri feast which Amin had promised us, and our last night in Kashmir. Amin invited us to see the preparations for the feast, and incidentally to meet his mother and his smaller brother and little sisters, an invitation we accepted with alacrity. He led us onto a finger of land which extended along one side of the *New Texas* and back to where the small houseboat on which the family lived was tied. We went aboard and ducked our heads to go into the cabin, which was perfectly bare of any furnishing other than the carpet that covered the polished board floor. We sat on it (wincing as we did so), and soon Mother entered, followed by Gulshan, the teen-aged sister; Habib, the little brother; the littlest sister, Famida, who was about seven; and a niece, Purvais, who was a six-year-old giggler. Only Gulshan spoke a little English, as she attended high school.

We were given coffee and pastries. As we ate, Mother pressed an orange ribbon into my hand as a present ("For your hair," Amin translated). Fortunately, I had come prepared for something like this, and I delved into my purse and presented Gulshan with an agate necklace purchased in Agra, and pretty mirrored birds which we'd bought in Jaipur for the two little girls, plus a lipstick for Mother. Habib received one of our remaining ballpoint pens.

After much smiling and nodding, and admiring of gifts, we were led outside where the preparations for the feast were under way. Ten or twelve beautiful stainless steel pans were ranged on the ground against a stone wall, and in front of these sat four men who were preparing the food. Two were chopping vegetables, and two were making *gustaba*, the national dish of Kashmir— pounding mounds of lamb on a wooden slab with huge wooden mallets. They alternated whacks on the slab: "squap-squap! squap-squap!" as the mallets came down on the squishy meat.

205

There was a big outdoor stove on which were huge pans of simmering mixtures that sent rich and spicy aromas to our nostrils.

We returned to our room to get ready for the feast, for nothing but our best clothes would do that night. When we were dressed, we sat on the verandah of our houseboat to watch the lake.

It was late afternoon, my favorite time of the day, and the low sun cast its radiance on the far shore. Beyond was a backdrop of towering black clouds, and flashes of lightning played over them at intervals, too far away for us to hear the thunder. A beautiful little kingfisher sat on a piling in the water about ten feet away, his irridescent blue feathers gleaming in the sun as he leaned intently forward, watching the water. Suddenly he folded his wings back and dived straight in, coming up in an instant with quite a large fish speared on the end of his long, slender beak. He struggled up to his perch and then banged the fish's head on the piling until it ceased to struggle. He tried to swallow it, unsuccessfully, until he noticed us watching. "I hate audiences," he plainly told us, and flew away with the fish still speared on his beak, barely able to stay aloft. We sat there until it was dark, and Amin appeared on the deck of the "feast boat." There was already quite a party aboard, for a group of French tourists were also being entertained, and they greeted us quite pleasantly when we entered and removed our shoes. We had to duck our heads, for the ceiling was low, like the houseboat that Amin's family lived on. Padded muslin covered the entire floor, and there the party sat, propped up against pillows. The windows, which ran the length of the interior, were innocent of glass and admitted the fragrant night air. We found places on the floor against a window and lowered ourselves gingerly, sitting on one hip with our legs curled up on one side.

Barefoot waiters placed starched white cloths in front of us and put out the dishes just as the boat started to move into the middle of the lake. Then the cook came around and deftly ladled food out of the cooking pots, one dish at a time. In order, we were served: rice, lamb curry, lamb ribs, lamb meatballs in spicy red sauce; kofta kebab, looking like cigars; *paneer* (homemade cheese) with a fragrant red sauce, a heavenly chutney of walnuts, a large meaty bone in a mild red sauce, spinach with tiny meatballs, and finally the *pièce de résistance,* the gustaba—swimming in its creamy yoghurt gravy. A feast indeed, ending with spiced tea and salty pastries.

"I hear the food in Ladakh isn't too great," I whispered to Ed after we'd finished and were trying to find comfortable positions for our overstuffed bodies on the floor.

"Good thing. We've gained back every pound we lost over the past few weeks, and then some. I'd be lucky to be able to see my feet after a couple of weeks here."

A boat had pulled alongside and the musicians came aboard. A beautiful, earthy-looking young woman in ordinary Kashmiri dress entered, carrying a pile of clothes over her arm.

She proceeded to put on a gathered skirt of velvet over her clothes, then a silver lamé jacket, and a silver threaded scarf wrapped around her forehead and tied on the side. Thus warmly attired, she began to stamp her feet, keeping time to the music, and then started to sing. Her song became more and more passionate, and she launched into a furious dance, singing at the top of her lungs all the while—wild songs, in which the musicians joined their voices in the chorus. One by one the guests were pulled to their feet and made to dance with her—there were some hilarious performances by a few of the Frenchmen and Ed. After she had worn out all the guests, the musicians leaped to their feet one at a time and joined her in the middle of the floor. I'll never forget it. The dances were wild, with definite sexual overtones, and one handsome young musician leered and grimaced as he gyrated and twitched. That brought down the house, and marked the end of a fascinating evening.

We were returned to the *New Texas* and packed our bags before going to bed. I went to the window after we turned out the lights and looked across the peaceful lake. A faint sheen of moonlight glimmered on the water and the only sound was the gentle slap of wavelets against the houseboat. The air was very sweet.

Tomorrow we were going to Ladakh, and I had been looking forward to it, but just then, I didn't want to leave Kashmir.

Sighing, I sat down heavily on the bed. Ouch! Damn it.

"I don't want to leave, do you?" I whispered to Ed, but he was already asleep.

CHAPTER 18

The Road to Shangri-La

A min insisted on hiring a taxi to the bus station—he said that it was included in the package price, and he rode along with us to see us safely on the bus to Ladakh.

"When you come back from Ladakh, you stay on the *New Texas?*"

"Yes, Amin. We'll be back on Friday by plane. Then we leave for Delhi on Saturday."

We started down the poplar-lined road toward Sonnmarg, high in the mountains and our last stop in Kashmir. Our destination was Leh, the capitol of Ladakh, which lay in a large valley on the Tibetan Plateau, at an elevation of twelve thousand feet.

The driver, a portly Sikh, was an expert at the wheel, but he had a habit of farting, and we soon dubbed him "Windy," like the horse. Every now and then he'd raise a buttock and let fly—then open his door in the vain hope that no one would notice. He could have hired out to the Nazis as a secret weapon, his gas was so poisonous. The passengers pointedly gasped and choked, and opened the windows, but it made no difference. Windy Singh kept right on "singing."

Most of the passengers were Indian tourists or Ladakhis, but there were seven Westerners in addition to ourselves: three American youths, a young German, two Australian girls, and a French doctor.

The weather was cloudy at first, but as we began the long climb into Sonnmarg it became sunny. The bus was stopped by a convoy of army trucks just outside the little mountain village, and we got out and walked into town, knowing that the bus wasn't going anywhere without us. Sonnmarg was quaint, with wooden sidewalks and plenty of little stalls, at one of which we got lunch. We ate at a ramshackle wooden table out on the sidewalk with the Aussie girls and the American boys.

When we had finished, a hawker tried to sell us "musk" which looked like the testicles of some small animal, covered with brownish hair. He put the "musk" in his fist, and then passed his closed fist over the back of my hand, and commanded me to smell my hand. I did so: a strong but pleasant odor had somehow been applied to my skin. He tried to convince Ed and me that the musk smell had passed all the way through his hand onto mine, but we remained unconvinced. He was able to do a brisk business with the other tourists, however, both Western and Indian.

A blast from the horn of the bus brought us back to our seats, and soon we started up the narrow canyon beyond the town. For a long way we followed the beautiful mountain stream that rushed alongside the road, and then the bus slowed down and shifted gears into the lowest ranges. I stuck my head out the window and looked up at the mountainside in front of us. Unbelievingly, I looked again and turned to Ed.

"I think that is the road up ahead. Take a look. You won't believe this."

I got out of the way and Ed stuck his head out of the window.

"Holy smoke!" He grinned. "That's quite a road."

It zigzagged its way up a nearly vertical mountain face, looking like a thread clinging to the mountain. It seemed to go up forever. We could see trucks and buses ever so slowly inching their way up that impossible-looking road, and we knew that soon we would be up there with them. A pleasurable shiver ran down my spine.

We started up the eight-foot-wide, unpaved road just behind a fuel tank truck. Despite the switchbacks, the road was very steep, and fifteen miles per hour was a good average speed. We ground along in low gear, occasionally shifting to second for a minute or two, and then dropping back to low again. The truck ahead was a little slower than ours, and Windy tailgated shamelessly, and blowing his horn every few seconds. The truck driver ignored us completely, and continued to use the exact center of the road, causing Windy to shake his head impatiently and lean on the horn again. Eventually, at a wide spot where the road switched back upon itself, we attempted to pass, but the truck speeded up to retain its lead position. Our driver resumed his position about two feet behind the truck and continued to blow his horn, and at every switchback made an attempt to pass. After a few of these abortive efforts, one of the young travelers in the back lost his nerve and started to shout.

"He's going to kill us all! For God's sake, somebody make him stop!"

Quietly, Ed said, "Take it easy. He's just trying to make the truck move over."

"God! Make him stop!" the boy almost blubbered, but then he hunched into the corner of his seat and subsided, ashamed of his outburst. The rest of us avoided looking at him, trying not to embarrass

209

the boy. The truth was that probably most of the passengers in the bus secretly felt the same but would rather go to their deaths than say so.

At the next switchback, the road was quite broad for a distance, and Windy grabbed his opportunity and was past the truck before the other driver knew it. We all sighed with relief—now we could enjoy the view.

We settled back into our seats as the bus ground its way up the mountain. We were on the right hand side of the bus, and as usual, Ed had let me have the window seat. The scene around us was one of austere beauty. The mountain fell away below—indeed, it fell away about a foot from the right-hand wheels of the bus—into a deep, narrow valley thousands of feet beneath. Steep mountainsides swept down from all sides to the other end of the valley miles away. They were green at their bases, but the tops were brown and bare, dusted with snow at the summits. The extraordinarily clear air made it easy to see for a great distance—Sonnmarg was a tiny collection of dots at the far end of the valley. I looked down the nearly vertical slope below and saw the road, pitifully small and insignificant, with tiny black bugs crawling along it that were trucks and buses like our own.

The Srinagar-Leh road is the only road into Ladakh, and at that is only open during the summer months. It is heavily used, for Ladakh borders on the two countries that India fears: China and Pakistan. She therefore maintains a large contingent of her army in Ladakh, and supplying the base keeps the convoys moving on the Srinagar-Leh road. Access is controlled; after a certain time in the morning, the road is closed to vehicles leaving Sonnmarg, for by then the traffic from Leh starts to arrive, and two-way traffic involves tedious and dangerous backing to turnouts whenever two vehicles meet. It cannot be prevented altogether, however, and this partly accounts for the extreme slowness of the journey.

The western slope of the Himalayas is a wet, green land, covered with firs below treeline and snow above. Yaks, the shaggy black cattle of the high country, and wild mountain goats called ibex graze in the open meadows far above treeline. Glaciers creep down the canyons, and the air is icy in the upper regions except in sunny, sheltered places, even in the middle of summer. We had long since closed our window by the time we started up to the first pass, for clouds occasionally drifted down from the peaks and blotted out the sun.

Gradually the forests and meadows near Sonnmarg had given way to the barrens above treeline when we crossed Zoji-la, the first pass, at 11,696 feet, just after noon. The clouds had disappeared by this time, and a brilliantly blue sky—bluer than any sky I had ever seen—threw into sharp relief the shining snowy peaks around us. We began to see a few people; first a couple of women in heavy woolen clothing, walking along a stony pathway that paralleled the road, and then farther along the path, a group of horsemen on little ponies raced the bus, ki-yi-ing like cowboys in a Western movie. We threw open our window to see them better, and they laughed and waved to us, standing in the stirrups to see *us* better. Herders tended flocks of angora goats, yaks, and donkeys that grazed on the slopes.

We approached the town of Drass, the second coldest inhabited place in the world. It was situated in a broad valley that was green and gold with mustard flowers. The little town consisted of a single row of mud and stone houses along the road, and the bus pulled up to this row of buildings and stopped.

We piled out of the bus and followed the crowd into the nearest building, a primitive restaurant named "Tea Stall Cold Land." Rickety tables and short benches stood on the dirt floor, and we chose one near a window, for the room was quite dark. We ordered chai and drank it thirstily. It was particularly delicious, which we attributed to the yak milk it was made with. We emerged into the sunlight, blinking while our eyes became accustomed to the brightness, and nearly ran into the pair of young Americans from the bus.

"How was the chai?" they asked.

"Great."

"No kidding? We thought it might be the salty butter tea we'd heard about."

The legendary butter tea reputedly is drunk all through the high Himalayas, and I must admit that it didn't sound very good to me, but I wanted to try it anyway before we went home.

After we left Drass the road was being resurfaced and was in deplorable condition. Our driver eased the bus over deep holes and high spots in the incredibly uneven road, which made us lurch from side to side. Our speed, never great, fell to a crawl and continued that way for the rest of the day.

We hadn't gone very far from Drass when the bus got a flat tire, and Windy and his assistant got out to fix it. We just happened to be at the beginning of the trail to Amarnath, where the famous ice *lingam* of Siva is located in a large cave. A steady stream of pilgrims from Hindu India were starting out on the long trail to the shrine.

A large army tent camp was also located at the spot, so there were

211

hundreds and hundreds of soldiers standing around, looking interestedly at the handful of Western tourists, especially the two young girls from Australia.

It was at that point, and in that crowded place, that I suddenly had an insistent desire to relieve myself. It was probably partly due to the tea, partly because the weather was chilly and I wasn't sweating at all, and partly simply due to the fact that it had been a long time since we left the houseboat. I knew that I had to find "facilities" immediately.

There were no trees anywhere around; in fact, there wasn't even a shrub as far as the eye could see. The only building was a little Hindu temple at the beginning of the Amarnath trail; it was on a slight rise overlooking the road. As I gazed at it, the two Aussie girls came out from behind it and started down the path toward us.

"I don't suppose there's a toilet up at that temple?" I asked them hopefully when they got within earshot.

"Naow," said Diane, the pretty dark one. "We just wint behoind it and did ah business theeah."

I considered this solution but dismissed it as sacrilegious. Then I noticed a forest of oil-drums just across the road next to the tent camp. Taking Ed with me as a guard, I made my way into the center of the cluster of drums and crouched down to do my "business." I had an audience of hundreds, but all they could see of me was the top of my head.

At last our flat tire was fixed, and we all climbed back into the bus. The scenery changed as the afternoon waned. Even grass disappeared from the stony mountainsides, and the herds of goats and yaks were things of the past. A moonland surrounded us: as stark as the Sahara, and as dry, the land on the north end of the Tibetan Plateau cannot support grazing animals. Even birds, except of course, for the occasional vulture, disappeared; there was nothing for them to eat. It was a beautiful land—pink soil lit by an ever-present sun, snow-covered peaks surrounding us on every side, and the backdrop of an indigo blue sky.

Every now and then we would come to an irrigated valley with a little town in the center. These valleys were amazingly lush. Terrace after terrace of green barley fields, poplars, and apricot trees made a vivid contrast with the bare pink slopes surrounding them. Those emerald acres of fragrant lushness were so lovely that I wanted to settle right down there and stay forever, until I remembered that for eight months of the year they were covered with snow. Sturdy peasants toiled in the fields: people with dark, leathery skin and high cheekboned faces, who wore heavy woolen clothing even while working in the sun. Their mud villages were quaint and quite charming, looking a little like the villages of the Pueblo Indians of the Southwestern United States: square, one- and two-storied houses with flat roofs, crowded together on narrow streets.

Almost before we knew it, we were approaching Kargil, our overnight stop. We were very apprehensive regarding a hotel. We had no idea where we were going to stay, and young travelers had told us that Kargil hotels were awful.

"When the bus stops, you go ahead, Bunny. You're better at choosing a hotel than I am, and anyway, I'd better stay with the luggage. And you'd better hurry, because all these people on the bus will be looking too, and I doubt that there will be very many rooms available."

I was really nervous as we bounced through Kargil. It was quite a good-sized place, located in a green and pretty valley with the Drass River meandering through it. The town itself, though, was a dirty "frontier town" peopled by mean-looking men. They were Shiite Muslims from Pakistan, with fierce black eyes and hawklike noses. They stalked the streets in pairs and stared resentfully at us ferenghis on the bus.

We pulled into a wide spot in the road in the middle of town and stopped. I flung myself off the bus practically into the arms of a hotel tout who swiftly handed me his card.

I nodded, and he motioned that I should follow him. We turned down a dirt street toward the river—a very pretty street, shaded by large trees and lined with pleasant houses. At the end of the lane, we entered a compound that contained a four-story "highrise" and a low building facing a rather weedy garden. The tout motioned me to follow him up a narrow set of wooden stairs in the taller building, where we met a nice-looking young man coming down.

"Madame, were you looking for a hotel room?"

"Yes. Do you have a double room available? My husband is waiting at the bus station." (I wanted him to know I was not alone. He *looked* all right, but I was still a little nervous in this rather sinister town.)

"Certainly, madame." He led me down a corridor and opened the door of a small but pleasant enough room, adequate if not luxurious. It smelled of fresh cement, and in answer to my question, the nice-looking young man said that the hotel was newly built (though it looked old already, in Indian fashion). It would do.

There was enough time for a walk before dinner, and we set out to explore Kargil. We walked up the long main street right to the edge of

213

town before returning. In our walk we didn't see a single woman; it was as if we had entered a strange country where they were not allowed. They must have been somewhere, for there were children aplenty, but little girls were greatly outnumbered by little boys, and then only *little* little girls were to be seen—those under nine or ten. It was eerie, and more than a bit ominous. I endured the silent stares of the men and was thankful for Ed's large, masculine presence.

The sun was setting before we returned to the hotel, and turned the peaks surrounding the little valley into a brilliant coral pink which gradually turned into mauve and then purple before darkness settled over the town.

We had to use our flashlight to find our way up the stairs and down the long hall to our room. The light switch on the wall didn't activate the naked bulb which was the only fixture, so we lit a candle from the supply that had been thoughtfully provided, and then another for the bathroom. I undressed quickly, shivering a little because it was quite chilly now that the sun was gone, and turned on the tap. Although the faucet had double handles, the water remained icy cold no matter which one I used. Damn!

Sighing, I gave myself a sketchy spongebath on the exposed portions of my body—fortunately I had been wearing trousers so only my face, neck, arms and feet really needed attention. I got into clean clothes and put on one of Ed's undershirts under my outer wear for warmth. Ed washed his face and arms, muttering curses all the while, because he hates to wash in cold water. Just as he finished, the sound of a generator started up and the lights came on.

We had a surprisingly good dinner, sitting at a single big table with a Belgian tour group, and afterwards we took our tea outside to an umbrella table on the lawn which was lit by the electric light coming through the restaurant windows. Ed nudged me and nodded toward the window.

"Look over there!"

Full in the light crouched a big rat, whiskers twitching, bright beady eyes upon us. It raised up a little on its hind legs, then dropped to all fours and scurried, in that disquieting way that rats have, to the darkness under the bushes. I shuddered, then laughed shakily.

"I'm glad we saw him *after* dinner, and not before."

By eight-thirty, we were so tired that we were drifting into sleep in our chairs, so we stumbled off to bed. Before we had crawled in and pulled the heavy covers over ourselves, the sound of the generator died and the lights went out.

Our alarm went off at three-forty, for we were supposed to be back on the bus at four-thirty. We dragged our unwilling selves out of our warm beds into the decidedly chilly, still-dark morning air, and got back into our dirty outer clothes. (We hadn't brought so many clothes that we could squander another whole set of clean clothes on another bus trip.) The town generator had not yet been turned on and it was by candlelight that we brushed our teeth, with cold tea left from last night's dinner.

Ed looked at his watch. Did we have time for breakfast before we had to be at the bus? No.

Dragging our suitcases behind us, we trudged up the dark street to the bus station. I noticed the old moon, its horns pointing upward, shining brightly in the early dawn sky, its attendant star like a diamond, framed by the black walls on either side of the street. The bus was dark and still; the driver had not arrived. Knots of people were silhouetted against the lightening street. The Australian girls were there, talking quietly and drinking chai.

"God, where did you get the chai?" I asked avidly.

"Owver theeah, across the street," said Sandy, the blond one.

We drank our tea and ate buns as the morning brightened around us. While we waited, we talked to the Aussie girls, who were both nice young things, and who seemed to be having a wonderful time. They were on an extended holiday in Asia—six months of travel—for which they had saved their money for years. They were on a starvation budget, as we discovered when we asked where they had stayed the night.

"Ow, it was owful. Sich a dirty plice—you should've *seen* the shates!"

"You should have stayed at our hotel," I said unthinkingly. "It was really pretty good—although it had no hot water."

"Haow much did it cawst?"

I did a rapid mental calculation. "Around eleven dollars U.S. for the double room."

"*Elaven dollehs!* We ownly pide tane rupees!" (Less than a dollar U.S.)

At four-fifty the driver arrived, and ten minutes later, we were jouncing through the quiet streets. How different Kargil looked, with the shops all shuttered and the streets without their hordes of hawk-featured Muslim men.

I had my window open through the town while I admired the views of still-dark valleys and sunlit snowy peaks all around us, but as we started up the mountain, a piercingly cold wind whipped through the window, and I had to shut it for a while until the sun warmed the air. Ladakh was lovely. The oases of irrigated land were even greener and more lush than

215

they had been farther west. Apricot trees were burdened with coral fruit and barley had heavy heads that billowed in the breeze. Graceful poplars pointed to the blue sky and silvery willows bent to sparkling, ice-cold streams. The mud buildings with their brightly-painted window frames had flat roofs with hay piled upon them. Suddenly, prayer flags were everywhere, for we had crossed into Buddhist India.

On the top of a steep hill, our first *gompa*, or Himalayan Buddhist monastery, came into view. It was a graceful white building with sloped sides narrowing at the top, and a dark, Chinese roof with overhanging eaves. Prayer flags fluttered from the top. A single willow tree trailed its branches over a patch of green grass at the foot of the hill. I caught my breath with delight, as somewhere celestial horns seemed to blow. Was my brain playing tricks on me?

I stuck my head out the window. Even over the noise of the bus I could hear them—the call to prayer of the great Tibetan horns. The lamas were summoning their flock to worship. I blinked back surprising tears.

"It's hard to believe that we're really here," I said. "This was always the place I most wanted to come to. The Tibetan Plateau. You know, Ladakh is the real Shangri-la. James Hilton was here when he was in the British army, and it's said that the big gompa Lamayuru was the inspiration for his book *Lost Horizon*. I want to see Lamayuru, Ed. It is near the road, but I know the bus doesn't stop there. How are we going to get there?"

"We can't, honey. There's only one bus a day that I know of, and there's no place to stay at Lamayuru. Look. I promise that we'll come back some day and go in by jeep, so we can see it." And I had to be satisfied with that.

We saw lots of Ladakhi people along the road then: proud and tough-looking lean women bundled up in their felt cloaks over very full skirts; rosy-cheeked children, bright-eyed and smiling, their beautiful teeth white in dirty faces; stovepipe hats and lots of turquoise and coral jewelry on even the small girls. Little boys were often bare-bottomed— but always sweatered! We saw one handsome old lady in full festival costume: a stiffened headpiece of leather, solidly covered with large turquoises, began low on her forehead and hung down her back to between her shoulder blades. Curly sheared lamb fur sidepieces stuck out on both sides of her head like wings, framing her high-cheekboned face. Over her colorful bodice she wore an untrimmed animal-skin cape that had long white fur on the inside surface, with the sueded leather to the outside. Her skirts were voluminous, and beneath them she wore

216

mountaineering boots. She was positively laden with heavy silver jewelry set with turquoise and coral. She was gorgeous!

We had stopped for some road construction, when two of the American boys, Jerry and Luke, approached the driver and talked to him quietly. We saw money changing hands and then the young travelers went outside. Ed followed them. In a minute he was back.

"They are going to ride over the highest pass on the top of the bus!" he whispered excitedly. "How about it? Do you want to?"

"You bet! You'd better give the driver something too. I don't think he's supposed to let people ride on top."

We gave Windy twenty rupees and went out to the back of the bus. The ladder was narrow and steep. I went up first, glad that I had worn my draw-string pants, and clambered over the lashed-down luggage, which was covered with a big canvas tarp. At the front I sat down on a convenient mound, but found I had nothing to hold onto. Luke climbed over to where I sat, and pulled at the rope which held the luggage down, loosening it.

"Here," he said, pulling the rope up over my knees. "Hold onto that."

I smiled at him gratefully, too excited to speak. Ed sat down next to me just in time, as the bus started to move. My heart was pounding and the wind whistled in my ears. We were a long way up above the road, which looked ridiculously small beneath us, and we swayed from side to side and bucked and reared as the bus maneuvered on the bumpy road. I hung onto the rope like a bronc buster in a rodeo at first, but soon found that I felt quite secure on my perch and could turn my attention to the view around us. Bright mountains surrounded us in every direction. The pink slopes rushed up to meet the snows, and thrust their icy summits high into the empty cobalt sky. There was no sound. The noise of the engine was whisked away by the wind before it reached our ears, and for me the strange silence blended with the color and the light in a kind of delirious excitement. The road looked like a ribbon beneath us, and shepherds yelled "Julay!" and waved as we passed. We felt like kings, like gods.

We zigzagged up a long, steep mountainside and came to the top of the pass, Fotu-la, at 13,469 feet above sea level. From our lofty platform there, we could see range after range of mountains marching away in the distance, fading into Tibet, into China and Nepal. We felt that we could see forever. On the other side of the pass, the road, coiling like a snake, plunged into a deep valley. Off in the distance we could just make it out, climbing yet another range of mountains.

We started down the long grade then, swaying in the wind, with the sun in our faces. We began to pass other vehicles, at first only the odd commercial truck. We would pull up behind one, horn blaring, and then fall back until the truck found a wide spot (sometimes this wouldn't occur for miles). The truck would edge out to the brink of the precipice, ever so slowly, and stop. Then we would squeeze past it, left wheel climbing the bank and right hand door handles almost grazing the other vehicle. Sometimes, frighteningly, it would be the other way around. The precipice would be on our left. (Vehicles stay on the left in India, as in Britain.) The truck would climb the bank on the right, and we would ease past it, left wheels on the very edge of an awesome chasm. As I was sitting near the edge of the left side of the roof, the view could be stupefying. Sometimes I unconsciously held my breath for so long that I became dizzy.

"Sweet Jesus!" exclaimed Jerry, from the other side of the bus.

"What?" the rest of us chorused, for his voice had been shrill.

He pointed down the road in front of us and we sat in stunned silence, pondering the significance of what we saw. A long line of trucks, dozens and dozens of them, were crawling up the road toward us. An army convoy.

All too soon the radiator of the first khaki truck appeared around the bend, and we came to a halt. The truck had the right of way because it was coming *up* the hill, and so we slowly backed up the twisting road until we came to a "wide" spot. We inched out to the very edge, dislodging some pebbles which bounced down, down, and out of sight without ever finding a resting place. Then we went forward a couple of inches closer to the edge, dislodging some more pebbles, and stopped. The truck, driven by a dashing-looking soldier with tremendous mustaches, scraped past us, its roof only an inch from ours. We could have crawled over onto it for the space of a minute or two, and then it was past. Slowly, slowly we backed up a couple of feet, then ever so carefully, Windy eased us away from the precipice, and we were safe!

We had just let out our collective breaths and hadn't gone more than a quarter of a mile, when we met another truck, and we had to go through the same process again. Over and over, that long morning, we performed our perilous dance; only once did we actually come close to disaster.

We rounded the bend, and we were again on the *outside* when we came face to face with a truck that was squarely in the middle of the road. As usual, we backed to one of those wide spots and went out to the edge, but this time the truck did not move right over to the bank. This driver wanted to stay in the middle of the road. He was an arrogant-looking fat man, and he simply sat there blowing his horn, and then actually moved forward and bumped our right fender. Windy backed closer to the edge, then forward a few inches, and then backed up again. The outside edge was on my side, and fearfully I peeked at the rear wheels, for I had heard the tell-tale fall of pebbles. The left one of the double wheels actually hung out over a drop of two thousand feet—the inner wheel supported the whole weight of the bus. I gasped and shut my eyes, and wondered what I'd do if the bus went over. Would I have time to jump free? Would Ed? Would it help?

I opened my eyes and the truck was past.

"Jesus," breathed Ed. "The bastard took off a layer of paint."

"Our wheel is over the edge," I moaned.

Then Windy eased the bus forward, away from the awful chasm, and it was over. I glanced at Jerry and Luke. They were white to the lips.

"That was as good as a laxative," croaked Luke.

I shrieked with laughter, and the tension was broken. After that nothing could scare us, and nothing did. The rest of the passings were routine, and an hour later we were free of the convoy and were sailing silently through the mountains again.

"Hey, look," said Ed in my ear. "Lamayuru."

We were in a kettle, closely surrounded by jagged peaks without a break. Ahead and slightly below us was a green, green valley, and soaring up above it, crowning a steep little mountain, was a vision of a palace. The monastery loomed above the little green valley like the Potala—like Shangri-la. I watched it hungrily as we passed. It was only half a mile away, but it was completely out of reach. I wanted to cry, but instead I made myself a promise. We'd come back.

We rolled into Khalsi, the third largest town in Ladakh, in early afternoon and the bus stopped. The four of us climbed rather shakily down from the top of the bus, and all the passengers scattered to look for one thing: a toilet. (That is a characteristic of all bus trips in Asia. A toilet, or a private place that will serve as one, is more important than a drink of tea, or sleep. More important than food. One can do without most things, we have found, but a toilet is not one of them.) The Aussie girls went along with me, and we found what we sought: a mud hut right on the edge of the road which was built out over the bank, with no door. A few boards laid across the walls served as a roof. A hole had been knocked out of the center of the floor, and through it I could see a brushy ravine below. Two of us blocked the door while one used the "facilities," taking turns. Then we rejoined Ed and looked for a tea stall.

We found Jerry and Luke already sitting at a table on a leafy terrace, drinking chai. We joined them and started to talk about our hair-raising experiences.

"Weren't you frightened when we passed that one truck?" I asked, for Sandy and Diane hadn't commented on any of the episodes we recounted.

"Way were aslape," Diane sheepishly admitted. "Averyone awn the bus was. 'Strewth, am Oy glaid."

After we finished our chai, Ed and I walked through the pretty, shady little town. A ditch ran the length of the single street, brimming with murky water. A small boy peed in it, the arching yellow stream splashing in the water just a yard from where a little girl was washing apricots. I stood there watching while she carefully arranged her apricots in a shallow box and then walked around to bus and truck windows, trying to sell them. Other children were gathering windfall apricots across the road under the trees, snatching them from under the noses of pigs and goats, and then bringing them to the ditch to wash.

Carefully avoiding the children's wares, we bought some apricots from a woman who had just picked them from the tree.

"How are we going to wash them?" asked Ed.

"I'm going to buy some more tea and wash them in that," I answered. "Tea is sterile. Anyway, we *saw* them being picked."

"I know, I know, but we also saw where those kids were washing the others."

I giggled. "Awful, wasn't it? I hope none of our companions bought any from the kids—we'd better warn them."

We all moved back into the bus for the rest of the trip. All four of us were sun- and wind-burned and squinty from our hours on top, and the bus seats (those very same bus seats we had complained about earlier) felt luxuriously comfortable compared to a pile of swaying luggage. We ate apricots washed in tea all the rest of the way to Leh, between naps.

CHAPTER 19

The Roof of the World

The Leh valley was green and pretty, with the swollen Indus River leaping and racing through the center in full flood from the melting snows. The town of Leh was snuggled against the Karakorums, a range of the Himalayas separating Ladakh from Tibet, only a few miles to the east. To the west, the Zanskar range glittered beyond the river, providing a backdrop of icy blue-white to the heavenly view of valley and mountain slopes.

The approach to the town was disappointing: a long uphill approach over bare, stony ground past the airport. A low bare hill concealed the town from our view, and the idyllic valley was behind us. Signs advertising various hotels and lodging-houses littered the roadside. The airport consisted of a single runway and a quonset hut of corrugated iron, surrounded by a chain-link fence: straight out of an old movie about the Flying Tigers. It even had a couple of rusty old planes of World War II vintage parked carelessly off to one side.

As usual, the problem of accommodations was foremost in our minds, and I was trying to read all the signs advertising lodgings. Most of the names were of Ladakhi or Tibetan origin, however, and I couldn't remember them two seconds after we had passed the signs. While I was frantically trying to memorize one or two, Ed calmly pulled out his ever-present pen and notebook and wrote down the name of a hotel that described itself as the most luxurious in Leh.

At the bus station we hired a jeep to take us to the hotel, the Tsemo La. It was one of a large American-based chain, situated in a beautiful garden blooming with marigolds and primroses. We requested a double room and were delighted when the manager, an oily type in a business suit, said that he could accommodate us. We had been warned in Kashmir that Ladakh, a trendy tourist destination, was extremely short of hotel rooms, and we congratulated ourselves on hitting the jackpot at first try. After we registered, we were shown to a charming modern room. (The toilet didn't work, but that was a minor matter which Ed put right at once.)

After baths, we went out to the garden and drank Limcas at a lawn table in the warm sun. A pair of newborn baby donkeys frolicked on the grass while their mother grazed nearby, and a couple of Ladakhi women, in colorful costumes, were hanging out the freshly washed hotel linen.

"God, this is wonderful," I breathed. "Aren't we lucky?"

Just then the manager came out to our table.

"I am so sorry, but we cannot accommodate you tomorrow night. I will find you hotel to stay at, do not worry. Then you come back for the rest of stay."

We looked at each other in dismay.

"You are sure that you will find us a hotel for tomorrow night?" I asked anxiously.

"Certainly, Madam. Do not worry at all."

"Oh. All right then."

Taking the manager's promises at face value, we went for a short walk around our end of town, panting from the elevation—which was just under twelve thousand feet.

At seven o'clock we changed into our nicest clothes and went to the dining room, but a waiter intercepted us before we could enter.

"So sorry, but the dining room is full. You wait until eight o'clock, then you eat."

A little bewildered and very hungry, we returned to our room. Just before eight we re-entered the dining room, which by then was practically empty of people.

The room looked like a food-fight had taken place in it. The plates had been cleared away, but food and crumbs in revolting quantities covered every table. There were even scraps of food all over the floor. We chose the cleanest table we could find and sat down. A waiter approached and brought us folded napkins and glasses of water. I opened the napkin and started to drape it over my lap, when I noticed that it hadn't been laundered since it was last used, and the bits of food had actually dried on it. Curious now, I brushed the tablecloth and found that food had dried on it too.

"This is really disgusting, Ed," I said. "I think that it is more than just one night's accumulation."

"It's pretty bad, all right, but Bunny, I'm starving. Let's go to the buffet and see what there is to eat."

But when we got our plates—fortunately they were clean—and looked

222

into the silver chafing dishes, we found that there was nothing left. A bit of gravy here, and a slice or two of carrot there—there was one dish with a little rice pilau in one corner. The staff had even snuffed out the flames under the dishes. Ed summoned the waiter who had prevented us from entering earlier, and demanded food.

"You said eight o'clock, goddammit, and we were here at seven fifty-five. There is NOTHING LEFT!" I have seldom seen him so angry. His eyes were like ice-blue slits and his hair, normally bushy, literally stood on end.

The little waiter scurried away and returned bearing a chafing dish nearly half-full of macaroni and cheese, placed it in the holder, and lit the flame underneath. He sidled away as if expecting Ed to hit him, and disappeared, returning with another tray a quarter full of creamed chicken. We served ourselves and returned to the table. I picked up the tablecloth by both corners and folded it halfway back to expose the clean underside. Then I rummaged through my purse for kleenex to use as napkins, and we sat down along the clean side and ate our dinner.

"It's delicious, I must admit," I said placatingly.

"You know what's happened," Ed growled. "This is a goddam tour group hotel, and we don't count. We get what they leave and the management won't even let us eat with them. And that's what happened with our room, too. They had a cancellation and that's why we got the room, but they'll kick us out tomorrow, and I'll bet that son-of-a-bitch won't get us another hotel room, either."

"You think so?"

"Damn right. And you notice he didn't tell us until after we were all settled in. He figured we wouldn't want to move then, and he was right. Goddammit." Ed has always fallen back on profanity when annoyed—he says it helps a lot.

When we went outside, the temperature had dropped sharply. It hadn't been very chilly when we started out for dinner, but now the cold poured over us like ice-water, and we hurried to our room. It was pretty chilly in there too, so after undressing quickly, I burrowed into my bed and pulled up the spare thick wool blankets that had been folded at the foot. I lay there shivering but with burning hot cheeks, a little feverish, probably from the altitude. When he was ready for bed, Ed turned out the lights and pulled back the drapes. That's when we saw the stars. I got up, wrapped my blanket around me, and stood at the open window.

The moon wasn't up, but a gentle radiance lit the town and the ghostly mountains beyond. A billion stars pulsated there in the velvet black sky, hundreds of times brighter than I had ever seen them before. I forgot about our troubles with the hotel. I forgot my annoyance over our disastrous dinner. I even forgot that we might have to sleep in the street the following night. We were as close to heaven as it is possible to get on earth. I felt that I could almost have touched the stars. We watched them for a long time before we climbed back into bed and went to sleep.

We woke early and decided to climb up to the Red Gompa that loomed a thousand feet above the city. The gompa had been built in 1430; a small stone building crowning an incredibly steep hill that overlooked Leh and the City Palace.

We stopped by the desk to ask what time we had to be out of our room, and whether the manager had arranged for accommodations for us that night. The manager couldn't be found, but we were informed that one o'clock was the check-out time, so we had to be content with that. A short walk took us to the beginning of the trail that passes the City Palace on its way to the Red Gompa far above the town.

We started up the steep, crumbly path that zigzagged back and forth across the face of the mountain. It was slow going, very steep, and hot in the sun. The altitude made itself felt; we had to take deep breaths to keep ourselves in oxygen, and it was necessary to place one foot ahead of the other very slowly, with a breath at every step. The crumbly rocks and pebbles were loose and mixed with sand, and my sandals scooped them up, causing me to kick each foot every couple of steps, as I've seen cats do, walking in dewy grass in the early morning. Step, breathe. Step, breathe, *kick*.

It took us well over an hour to reach the top. The last few yards of trail ended at stairs that wound between large boulders with the gompa walls rising steeply above. Prayer flags by the hundreds fluttered overhead, and lots of them lay in the dirt underfoot. They were made of coarse, translucent cloth of loose weave and a grey color, and the Buddhist prayer—in Tibetan script—*Om Mane Padme Hum* (The Jewel In the Eye of the Lotus)—was often faded so badly that it could not be made out. Ed picked one up that was lying half-buried by the side of the trail, shook off the dirt, and tucked it into his pocket for a souvenir.

The last few feet were agonizingly steep, and we had to force our unwilling legs to make the effort; but at last we were on the platform of the gompa. We turned to face the town from which we had come. It lay far below us; its downtown center a rabbit warren of huddled mud and stone buildings, surrounded by emerald fields and trimmed with poplars and willows. The wind whistled in our ears, and our faces were flushed from our exertions. Our backs were hot from the sun and our fronts were chilled by the wind, caused by the thinness of the air. We found a sunny corner that was sheltered from the wind and sat for a long time on the warm stones just resting and contemplating the trail we had climbed up. Far below us, two climbers looked like ants crawling slowly upward.

When we were rested, we searched for the door into the gompa, but the only one we could find was locked and padlocked. A tattered piece of paper nailed to the dark-red painted wood indicated that the gompa would be open to visitors at five o'clock in the afternoon. There was no sign of life anywhere except a lone vulture that circled in the infinite blue of the sky.

"Well, that's that," said Ed. "We're not going to see the inside of *this* monastery."

Looking down that trail I had to agree with him. The Japanese have a saying: "A man is a fool not to climb Fuji. He is a bigger fool to climb it twice."

Going back was easy. It was steep and my sandals scooped up even more sand and pebbles, but we skidded and slipped down effortlessly. Ed even pretended to ski down a particularly steep slope, his weight propelling him along over the pea-sized pebbles. Near the bottom of the slope, a Ladakhi woman had evidently seen us coming, and she and her little daughter had spread out a piece of old brocade on a flattish spot on the ground beside the trail. On it were her wares—old temple items like bells and exquisite wooden teacups decorated in silver, turquoise and coral. Naturally we couldn't resist a teacup, and one more item caught my eye: a beautifully worked round copper reliquary heavily decorated with Buddhist symbols, with a bit of old glass set into the middle, under which was a piece of paper with the Buddhist prayer on it. The copper top had been made to fit an ordinary flat red tin can bottom (such as chewing tobacco used to come in), with screw threads on it. A ring had been soldered to the can, and the whole was suspended by a long piece of cotton gauze that was black with dirt from having hung around someone's neck, no doubt for years and years.

"How much?" I asked, indicating the reliquary.

The woman held out ten fingers, then five. Fifteen rupees, about a dollar and a half. I nodded happily and pulled the money out of my pocket.

Ed said, "Aren't you going to bargain?"

"No. It's cheap enough—I'd feel sleazy trying to get the price down. You get to pay for the teacup." All the money came from the same pot, but we have always wrangled over who pays for what—a harmless diversion for people married a long time.

"What time is it?"

Ed glanced at his watch. "Twelve. Holy smoke, let's get going. Check out time is one o'clock."

We hurried back to the hotel, getting there with twenty minutes to spare, to find our suitcases standing outside the door, and our tooth-brushes, hair brushes and soap piled on top of them. Rather grimly we packed our toilet articles and then dragged our cases down to the office. The manager was there.

"Have you found a place for us to stay tonight? And can we have the same room back tomorrow?"

The manager slid his eyes away. "So sorry, we cannot accommodate you. We are full all week."

"You said we could come back tomorrow." Ed's voice had an edge to it.

"So sorry."

I quickly interrupted, before Ed could explode. "Did you find us a hotel for tonight?"

"I will try now." He picked up the phone and dialed. Turning his back on us, he spoke rapidly in Hindi. Long pause. Then he hung up and dialed again. Another rapid conversation. He hung up and faced us, all smiles.

"I have good news for you. There is a room at the Indus Hotel." He got up and quickly left the room.

"Son-of-a-bitch. It's just as I said before—he just wanted to fill his empty room for one night and he never had any intention of accommo-dating us longer than that!" Ed gritted his teeth in fury.

"I know. But at least we've got a room. Where's the Indus Hotel?"

"I have no idea."

Luck must have been with us, for we were able to make the first taxi driver we found understand that we wished to go to the Indus Hotel. We climbed into the jeep-taxi and bounced away from the Tsemo La.

"I hope the dining room is better at the Indus," I said with feeling. "But where *are* we going?" We had left the downtown area and had turned south away from familiar territory. The road stretched out before us through a barren and desolate area littered with occasional mud huts. We drove for what seemed like an age but was actually about five or six miles before we dropped down close to the banks of the Indus River where the emerald fields and poplar trees began again. Then we turned off the main road onto a tiny jeep track that took us almost to the edge of the river. We crossed a log bridge and pulled up at a green lawn surrounded by buildings that looked somewhat like army barracks.

"How are we ever going to get back to town?" I asked Ed. "It's too far to walk, and I don't see any taxis hanging around."

"It's pretty late to go anywhere today anyway, but I'll ask the driver if he'll pick us up tomorrow morning. Let's go to Thikse tomorrow. We should start at six—the morning service at Thikse starts at seven."

Ed talked to the driver while I went up to the lobby. There I discovered that our troubles were not yet over, for the manager apologetically said that while he could accommodate us for that night, the following night he was expecting a tour group that would fill up the entire hotel.

"Manager at Tsemo La said you only need room for one night." But then he added comfortingly, "But tour group will not come until late tomorrow, so you can stay until five o'clock. If there is a cancellation in tour group, then you can have room for the rest of your stay."

I relayed the worrisome news to Ed, but he took this final blow remarkably calmly.

"Hell, if they throw us out tomorrow, we'll go to a monastery. Luke told me the monks will let tourists sleep there if they ask. Let's not worry about it."

A young man showed us to our room. It was primitive—unpainted cement walls with roughly hand-hewn window casements and doors—but very clean and nice. I crossed the room and pulled back the drapes. The mighty river was only a few feet away, racing by the window. Across the river was a group of low buildings surrounded by poplars, and behind that rose the mountains, with their sugary tops touching the blue, blue sky.

We went for a walk before dinner, along one of the irrigation canals that branched off the river. Each canal had a footpath on the top of one bank, keeping pedestrians out of the barley fields. The water in them was ice-cold and clear, and the current was slow, waving the long water-grass that grew along the bottom. We were accompanied by one of the hotel dogs, a cute little black mutt who looked as though he was part scotty—he had one ear that stuck straight up and one that folded and dangled rakishly over one eye, and a wiry, curly coat. He looked to be in good condition, and he was cheerful and lively, but he had parasites of a kind we had never seen before: horrid, brown, spider-like ticks that crawled around his eyes and nose. They were big and active, but they didn't seem to bother our little doggy friend, and he trotted along with us as if he belonged to us.

227

Along the road stood a fence of piled stone, and we noticed that each stone was beautifully carved on its flat side with the Buddhist prayer; the Tibetan script was elegant in design and powerful in execution, every stone a small work of art. There were hundreds, thousands of them, piled along the roadside. Occasionally yak horns or bones substituted for stones.

"Just think of the labor involved," I said wonderingly. "What an incredible act of devotion it is."

"They spend their winters carving stones," said Ed. "I've read of it—but seeing them here, piled up like that—I realize now what winters must be like up here: so cold that the people must stay in their huts, with nothing to do but carve stones . . ."

That evening we had dinner in the dining room, a screened pavilion on one side of the lawn. The food was good and everything was clean and sparkling. We ate with two tour groups, one French, one Belgian, and the service was impeccable.

Lying in my snug bed that night, I found myself unable to sleep. Were we going to find a place to stay? If not, *would* the monks let us sleep in a monastery? Where would we sleep—on the floor? On a straw pallet? Would there be bedding? Would we end up in the bus station, like other travelers we'd seen, rolled up in our extra clothes on the floor, like the street sleepers of Delhi and Calcutta?

I heaved a sigh and turned over. In the next bed, Ed did the same.

"Can't you sleep?" I whispered.

"Hell, no. I keep wondering where we'll sleep tomorrow night."

"I thought you weren't worried."

"I lied."

I got out of my own bed and crawled into his, snuggling up to his back. His nearness was comforting, and in a few minutes I was asleep.

In the morning, in the first light of dawn, I had just finished shivering my way through a dipper bath in the chilly bathroom when Ed stuck his head in the door.

"Come and hear this, Bunny."

He led the way to the window which was wide open, letting in the morning chill, and also admitting strange sounds from across the river. I stuck my head out and listened. Chanting and the peculiar sounds of musical instruments that we had never heard before floated in, as distinct as if the invisible orchestra had been on our side of the river, instead of a hundred yards away and separated from us by a noisy river that should have drowned out all but the most persistent noises. We could just see the monks through the bushes that lined the river, slowly walking in single file toward a low building that lay across from the hotel. They were chanting as they walked. The trees behind the gompa were almost black in the pale light, and a mist lay over the water. In the background, looking like a painted backdrop, rose the icy range of mountains.

"I think our luck has changed," I said softly. "What a wonderful morning."

The jeep taxi came for us promptly at six, rattling over the bridge and bouncing to a stop beside the lobby. Our driver, a Tibetan with a face wreathed in smile creases and a woolen toque on his head, let down the back of the jeep for us and we climbed in, settling ourselves on the two little benches that faced each other behind the driver's seat. The way to Thikse was short, and we spotted its Potala-like silhouette in a very few minutes. The monastery crowned a steep hill that rose abruptly out of the barren plain. Little mud houses clung to the hill under the benevolent protection of the gompa which loomed high above them. We bounced to a stop at the crossroads, and our driver twisted around to tell us that the road to the gompa had been washed out the previous year and that we would have to walk to the top. Then he pulled his hat over his eyes and prepared to sleep away the hours before we returned.

Two slender poles laid side by side bridged a stream that ran through the village at the foot of the hill. The sandy path started there and ran up between the little houses. Prayer-stones lined the path as it zigzagged steeply up toward the gompa. The altitude bothered us less than it had the day before, and we had breath enough to admire the view when we emerged above the village and approached close beneath the monastery.

A marvel greeted us there at the switchback—a little plot of soft green grass edged with willows and planted with red and pink hollyhocks, which contrasted strangely with the barren moonscape beyond and below us. A tiny spring seeped out of the rock there and dampened the ground enough to sustain the tender green plants. I could smell the richness of the wet earth, and for some reason that and the realization that some monk had loved the little green plot enough to plant it with flowers, caused my eyes to blur. It was the sweetest place I had ever seen.

Suddenly from above the melodious horns announced the beginning of puja.

"Come on, Bunny. We're going to miss the service."

I followed Ed up the last steps and we entered the wooden gateway into the gompa. In the narrow courtyard, ranged along one wall, were a

229

hundred prayer wheels, and beyond were the steep stone steps leading to the sanctuary. Already we could hear the chanting of the monks at prayer, so we dragged ourselves up the stairs and crossed the long verandah that set off the entrance to the sanctum. A sign in English and Hindi warned that flash pictures were not permitted inside. Beneath the sign, a jumble of shoes and boots told us that other tourists were already there. Quickly we added our shoes to the pile and crossed the threshold. Benches had been set up near the entrance, and they were filled with Westerners, nearly all male. We took places at the extreme right-hand side where there was enough room for us to sit.

It was dim inside; dim and cool. The smell of butter permeated the place; later we found out that the floors of the monasteries were polished with it. I noticed the slight tackiness of the satiny boards beneath my bare feet. The monks sat serenely on three low platforms at right angles to the door, each with a narrow-leaved book before him whose pages he turned as he chanted. Behind the chanting monks on the left was an "orchestra": several monks seated against the wall with musical instruments on the floor in front of them. Holy water containers made from human skulls lined the back wall and their silver rims gleamed dully in the gloom. Three little acolytes bobbed around, carrying enormous copper kettles full of tea, with which they continually refilled the wood and silver teacups that sat before every monk. These teacups were continually brought to monkish lips between chants and needed the frequent attention of the tea servers.

The chanting was soft and rhythmic, hypnotic in its effect on us, especially in combination with the flickering butter lamps which were the only illumination except for the dusty daylight which slanted in from the doorway. I was just sliding into a trance when the orchestra suddenly gave out with a cacophany of strange sounds, where clangs and the sawing of stringed instruments blended with eerie horn music, rousing me with a start. The lively music continued for some time while the monks ate breakfast and rested from their devotions. Each took out a leather pouch filled with parched barley flour (*tsampa*, or *champa*) which was mixed with the butter tea into a paste with the fingers and then scooped into their mouths. During this interval, the little boy monks also had a chance to drink some tea and have a bite of breakfast. The lively little boys proceeded to have a food fight, scooping out gobbets of porridge and throwing them at each other. The older monks blandly ignored this evidence of high spirits and calmly went on eating their own breakfasts.

We had noticed several of the other tourists moving around annoyingly during the service, and at this point we were appalled to see a young Japanese man march boldly into the center of the room and start taking flash pictures of the monks. His example encouraged others, and one blond young European, wearing boots which he had not bothered to remove, actually stepped over one of the platforms to take a picture, causing the nearest monk to lean to one side to avoid being jostled. I could feel my face burning; it made me ashamed of being white and a tourist, of being associated with people so arrogant and so unfeeling.

"How can they?" I whispered. "Didn't they see the sign? And those boots!"

"Bastards!" growled Ed succinctly.

Fortunately, the entire group of tourists, who were evidently on an arranged tour, left in a body shortly afterwards, and we alone remained in the dim room with the monks and the butter lamps and the chanting. I noticed one young monk staring at us with his bright black eyes. Each time I looked his way his eyes were upon us, and I wondered whether he resented us—whether he grouped us with the terrible tourists who had just left; but after a while I decided that he was just curious, for there was a cheerful benignity in his stare.

The service lasted for perhaps another twenty minutes, and then the monks rose from their platforms with that graceful motion that people who habitually rest in the lotus position seem to achieve, and shuffled quietly out into the courtyard. After leaving an offering of rupees on the altar, we followed, still slightly dazed from the hypnotic chanting, into the blinding sunlight. The monks had dispersed, so we thought we'd explore a little. We poked around the foot of the stone building that contained the sanctuary until we found a doorway from which issued a stream of woodsmoke. Peering into the dark and smoky room, we saw several little boys tending a crackling fire. They beckoned to us and we entered, bending our heads to clear the lintel of the doorway. When our eyes became adjusted to the dim light, we could make out the details of a Ladakhi kitchen. Copper utensils with black bottoms lined the walls on wooden shelves. A large stone stove was in the center of the room, with an opening in front like a fireplace. Brushy sticks were burning in it, producing a hot fire. On the stove sat a huge iron pot which was being vigorously stirred by a kid of ten or so. I went over and peered into the pot. It was filled with a murky liquid that smelled rich and buttery.

"What is it, butter tea?"

"I think so. I wonder if they'd let us have a taste."

231

Before we could ask, one of the little boys scooped out a tin cupful and handed it to Ed. He tasted it gingerly.

"How is it?"

"Not bad at all. Here, have a sip."

It *wasn't* bad—just strange. The butter taste was strong, and it was quite salty. Oddly, the tea flavor didn't clash with the butter, but melted into it to produce a rich and smooth liquid. It was unlike anything I'd ever tried before. I could imagine that one could get to like it very much, especially in cold weather. It was a bit rich for summer drinking.

Leaving the kitchen, we returned to the courtyard and climbed a waiting stairway up to the roof. There, overlooking the mud village, were two spires, or finials, of pure gold, overlaid on wood. Their tops were dulled with the dust of centuries, but their bases were rubbed shiny from the caressings of many pilgrims. At the base of one rested the horns we had heard announcing the service. There were two, each about five feet long, tapering, of copper banded with heavy silver wrought into gorgeous designs.

Beyond stretched the Leh Valley, its rich green barley fields, which bordered both sides of the silvery Indus, a counterpoint to the stark slopes beyond. Across the broad valley rose the Himalayas in frosted splendor. The air was so clear that we could see every ripple on the glaciers slanting down the mountainsides, and every kite that soared on the updrafts.

"Allow me to show you Kali," said a soft voice behind us. We turned to see the young monk who had stared at us during the service.

"I speak English, so I will be your guide this morning," he continued. "Kali is covered up now; not for nine years can we see her again. Every eleven years we take the cloth from her face. Many people come to Thikse then; many pilgrims even from Thailand, and Sri Lanka. So many that the line of people goes down to bottom of this hill, or further. Thikse is very famous for the statue of Kali."

As he spoke he led us up another stairway and paused to unlock a dusty wooden door. We followed him into a dark and mysterious cubicle that reeked of butter. When our eyes had accustomed themselves to the gloom, we became aware of a veiled figure against one wall. Eight black arms extended from a torso beneath a head that was covered with ancient, heavy hangings. It was the goddess Kali, the same Kali that had impressed me so vividly in Calcutta with her malignant stare and her necklace of human skulls. How strange to find her here, in this austere bastion of Lamaism, nearly cheek to jowl with the gentle Buddha. I knew from my reading that Lamaism was mostly Buddhism with a

232

touch of Hinduism, but until then, I hadn't realized that Kali was a part of it.

We left two more rupees on the silver and gold altar which stood on one side of the room, covered with the paper money of a dozen countries, and followed our young monk outside. After we donned our shoes, he gravely shook our hands.

"I am happy to meet you who are interested in our beliefs," he said. "Some tourists are not very nice." He grimaced in remembrance and then smiled at us. "I must go back to my studies. I am studying so that I can translate the writings of Buddha into English." He bowed and was gone, his feet making no noise on the stones.

We retraced our steps back down to the courtyard and surveyed the long row of prayer wheels.

"I promised Jack at home that I would spin a few for him," I said, "and then I'll spin a few for myself." And I went down the row spinning each in a clockwise direction until I reached the end. With a shamefaced grin, Ed followed me.

"Jeez, do I feel foolish," he said. Nevertheless, he finished the whole row as I had done.

We started out the gate but turned when we heard someone call from behind us.

"You must see the great Lord Buddha!" said a thin, middle-aged monk, beckoning to us. He led us to a newer building than the others and we climbed the steps to the door. The usual shoe-removal ritual followed and then we were ushered into a bright and cheerful room dominated by a golden Buddha so large that his hips and feet were on a lower floor and his head and chest extended up through the second floor to the ceiling. He had a jeweled headdress on his head, and colorful silken draperies partially covered his golden chest. Offerings of flowers rested on his upturned palms. Behind this resplendant figure the walls were brightly painted with scenes from Buddha's life. Light flooded in from large windows, and the whole scene was as different from the Kali sanctuary as it was possible to be. In front of Buddha, a butter lamp containing forty kilograms (eighty-eight pounds) of butter flickered, emitting a rich scent. A score of small butter lamps added their aroma and light to the scene, and another gold and silver altar bore its burden of paper money in the center.

"When was this Buddha built?" asked Ed of the monk, who was busying himself replacing wicks in the small lamps.

"In 1979," he answered. "Very new. Very beautiful, yes?"

"Yes," we said, heartily.

On our way back down the path, we came upon two monks sitting on the stone coping at the first switchback. One was a bony old man whose flesh drooped on his arms and whose withered face was creased by a thousand wrinkles, and one was a little boy whose dirty face betrayed a mischievous spirit. The old man reached out to us as we passed, and we stopped to see what it was he wanted. He handed me a paper on which was written the single word *aspirin*. As I looked back up at him, he touched his elbow joint and grimaced as if in pain. Arthritis. I was carrying only a tiny purse containing my sunglasses, tissues, and a lipstick. Ruefully, I turned it out for him to see, shaking my head as I did so.

"I'm so sorry," I said. "I didn't bring any with me." I knew he couldn't understand me, but my tone of voice told him what I wanted him to know.

"I have some," said Ed, unexpectedly. "I've been carrying these around for quite a while, but I don't suppose he'll be too particular." He brought out a grubby envelope which obviously had been in his pocket for weeks. In it were four aspirins, two anti-histimine pills, half a dozen antacid tablets, and several Pepto Bismol tablets in their cellophane wrappers. All were slightly worn from being rubbed together, but they were recognizable. "I thought they might come in handy sometime," he said, smiling.

"You don't ever take aspirin," I said in surprise.

"You do."

"You're wonderful."

Ed gave the aspirin and a ballpoint pen to the old man, who clutched his hand in gratitude.

"I wish I'd brought more—those won't last long. Poor old guy."

I handed a pen to the little boy, who grinned from ear to ear.

"How old are you, honey?"

He stared at me uncomprehendingly.

I wanted to try sign language, but at first I couldn't think of any way to ask the simple question. Then I pointed to myself, and held out all the fingers of both hands four times, and finally held up eight. Then I pointed to the little boy.

"You?" I asked, with a rising inflection. Then I held up the fingers of both hands, guessing him to be about ten.

He grinned and held up both hands and then one finger.

I smiled, then pointed to the old man. "You?"

He held up the fingers of both hands seven times, then added two.

234

We started back down the trail. When I looked back they were both busy inspecting their pens. The little boy was writing with his on the corner of his red robe.

Waiting at the jeep were three of the dirtiest and most unkempt little urchins I had ever seen, even in the worst of the slums of Bombay. A little girl of no more than six carried her baby brother on her back in a Chinese sling. Her hair hung in filthy strings around a face that was crusted with dirt, and she had smeared her runny nose with her arm. She wore a pair of red polyester knit pants that were too small for even her tiny frame, held up by a rope that was pushed through holes in the fabric. There were large holes in several places, including one in the center of the rear, through which her little buttocks showed. She had a pair of dreadful leather sandals on her feet which were much too large for her, and a tattered sweater, once yellow, hardly covered her chest. Her baby brother sported two heavy streams of snot on his round, dirty face. He was about ten months old, bright-eyed and cheerful, dressed warmly in several filthy sweaters and wearing a knitted cap. Accompanying this pathetic duo was a tyke of three or four, comparatively well dressed in a pair of bright orange split pants (Indian children do not wear diapers) and a red striped T-shirt that was more or less in one piece. He was, however, even dirtier and snottier than the other two. They approached us and smiled winningly.

"Rupees!" the older two whined in concert, "rupees, mister!"'"

They grinned at us, showing beautiful white teeth in those filthy faces, their bright Tibetan eyes sparkling.

"Give them something, Ed," I said. "They are so cute I can't resist them. But I want to take their picture, so they don't get something for nothing."

I squatted and snapped a couple of pictures as Ed pulled out his money.

"Woops. All I've got are ten-rupee notes. I got rid of all my smaller stuff at the monastery." He showed me the money he had left.

The little girl was an interested spectator. When she saw Ed's money, she promptly pulled a wad of bills out of her pants pocket, peeled off seven one-rupee notes, and held them out to him. He laughed aloud and gave her the large note, accepting the seven in change. The baby on her back smiled broadly and held out his fat little hand too.

"By God," Ed chuckled, after we had climbed into the jeep and were on our way, "there was a good businesswoman."

"How about the baby? He wasn't bad either."

"What shall we do this afternoon in town, Bunny? Any other

sight-seeing to do in Leh? I thought we should save Hemis for tomorrow."

"Sure. There are a couple of minor monasteries, but what I'd really like to see is the City Palace, and also the antiques market. What do you want to do first?"

"Antiques."

"I thought you didn't want to buy anything more. You'll have to carry whatever we get, because I haven't a square inch of room left in my suitcase."

Ed looked sheepish. "We'll only buy small things."

We spent the whole afternoon prowling the stalls of the outdoor market, fingering silver and turquoise beads, admiring the larger items, and finally buying a few trinkets. The day flew by as if the hours had been minutes, and we emerged at four o'clock to meet our taxi without having seen the City Palace, or even thinking about it.

On our way back to the Indus Hotel, our precarious situation regarding lodging came to mind, and my hands were ice-cold when we entered the lobby to speak to the manager. I hadn't let myself think about where we would sleep that night, and as usual, thoughts and feelings repressed for a while gathered force when allowed back in. I was actually in a state of panic when he approached the desk.

"I have good news for you," the manager said with a broad smile. "The tour group had two last-minute cancellations, so you may stay in your room. How many nights do you want to stay?"

"Only two—tonight and tomorrow," I said, relief flooding through me so that I felt light-headed. "We have plane reservations on Friday to Srinagar."

That night I was just drifting off, my mind at ease for the first time in days, when I became aware that Ed was tossing and turning in the other bed.

"What's the matter, honey?" I asked. "Our troubles are over."

"Not quite. I was surprised today when I counted my money after we got through shopping. It's a good thing we didn't buy much, because I've only got one more traveler's check, and it has to last until we get home."

"Well, that's all right, because our plane tickets back to Delhi and then home are all paid for, and there's only one more night in Delhi—don't you have any rupees left? We still have to pay for this hotel. Oh, yes, and one more night on the houseboat."

"I only have eight hundred rupees cash. Enough to pay for the hotel and our food, but we'll have to change our last traveler's check in Kashmir.

I've been thinking: we were going to go to Hemis tomorrow, but the taxi will cost about two hundred and fifty rupees for the day. Hemis is quite a long way from here. I think we'd better just go into town for the day and skip Hemis."

I shut my eyes and lay there thinking.

"How about taking the taxi into town and then catching the public bus into Hemis? I know that it only costs about six rupees each. What time is the taxi picking us up?"

"Eight o'clock. That's a great idea. Then in the afternoon we'll go and see the City Palace." The other bed creaked as Ed turned over, and within a minute or two he started to snore gently.

I lay there for a little while, enjoying the sense of well-being that an unworried mind produces. We had enough money. Not a lot, but enough. We had our houseboat and a room in Delhi already reserved and waiting for us. Another thought intruded: in four days we would be home. Quickly I pushed that thought away. I didn't *want* to go home. Sighing, I turned over. I thought that sleep would be hard to achieve, but I was away before I knew it.

SRINAGAR

DELHI

CHAPTER 20

The Long, Long Trail

We were at the bus station at nine o'clock in the morning, half an hour before the bus to Hemis was supposed to depart. The station was closed, and only two or three people stood around in the dusty lot. A couple of rusted old buses sat sadly to one side, one of them with eight flat tires, and the other with no tires at all. It was rather a depressing place, at the very edge of town, with only a few commercial corrugated iron huts scattered around on the sandy, barren ground. There was no place to sit and no window at which to buy tickets.

After twenty minutes people started to arrive with startling suddenness, and we jockeyed for position, hoping to be in the right spot to be able to board the bus before it was filled, for there was no line and no attempt at order.

When the bus approached, Ed and I ran alongside it, for we were wise in the ways of Asian buses; and we were first in line when it stopped. A group of French tourists who had been waiting with us stood back instead of fighting for a place as we did, and I wondered why they weren't trying to get in, but I was too busy with immediate concerns to worry about them. I was directly in front of the door when it opened, but had to step aside to let the people inside get off the bus, and I noticed that Ladakhi men were climbing in through the open windows.

As soon as I was able, I squeezed in, only to find that most of the seats were already taken possession of by young male locals who had climbed in, and that two whole rows of three seats each had young Ladakhis blocking them, saving the seats for someone else. A glance out the window at the complacent French travelers, who were standing back, chatting and laughing, told the whole story. In an instant, without even thinking about it, I stepped to the nearest block of empty seats, grasped the surprised little Ladakhi by the hand, and pulled him away. I took the window seat, and Ed, who was right behind me, sat down in the middle

238

one after offering the aisle seat to an old lady who was pathetically grateful for such unexpected good luck. The Ladakhi smiled and shrugged, and left the bus. Meanwhile, the aisles filled with local people who hadn't the nerve or the strength to dislodge the other "saver" as I had done, and the French travelers got on board leisurely, pushing through the crowd to reach their "reserved seats." The young threesome, two young men and a girl, who had "reserved" ours were furious and frustrated, for the Ladakhi had left, of course, without returning the money they had paid him.

Local people and other travelers continued to board the bus until it literally could hold no more. An old man joined the old lady at the end of our seat—we squeezed as close together as we could get to make room for him—and the aisles were packed so tightly that no one could move. At last, at nearly ten o'clock, the bus groaned out of the bus station and started down the road to Hemis. Once we were on our way, the conductor started to collect money for the tickets. After trying and failing to push through the impenetrable crowd, he simply climbed up onto a seat back and then crawled over the shoulders of the seated, calmly making change and handing over the tickets as he went.

It was a wonderful trip, even though I had to bend over to see out of the lower part of the window, the part that was open. The upper part was opaque dirt. We passed Thikse, rising magnificently out of the plain; then we bumped along past the beautiful emerald barley fields along the river. The river, turgid and murky with silt, thundered and leaped along.

We slowed down and stopped at a wooden shack situated at the side of the road amid a tangle of barbed wire. A sentry stood at attention, his bayonetted rifle smartly shouldered.

The conductor shouted something in Ladakhi, and one of the local young men translated for the foreigners.

"Everybody off for border inspection."

We filed off the bus, and took our places at the end of a rather long line, and then realized that we were expected to show our passports, for the foreigners among the passengers were hauling them out of backpacks and neck pouches.

"I didn't bring ours along," whispered Ed.

"Good God. What are we going to do?"

"I don't know. Stay here and I'll see what I can find out."

He went up to the shack and held a quiet conversation with the official at the door. After a while he came back smiling.

239

"It's okay. We can just tell them our passport numbers."

"I don't know mine."

"Jesus Christ. I *told* you to memorize it. Try to remember."

By this time we were through the door, and Ed wrote on the sheet that lay on the desk. Behind the desk sat a fierce-looking official with a great deal of gold braid on his shoulders and a truculent scowl on his brow.

My head was whirling with the effort to remember my number, and I was almost overcome with despair. All I could remember was the first letter—the official was looking at me expectantly—when all of a sudden inspiration came to me. Ed handed me the pen, and I bent over the desk and simply made up a number, using the real letter and the same number of digits as there were in Ed's number on the line above. My hand was shaking, but the official didn't seem to notice, and in a moment I was safely out the door.

"Thank God you remembered it in time," said Ed, smiling with relief.

"I didn't. I made it up."

He shouted with laughter. "I hope there's no master list of numbers."

I hoped so too. I certainly didn't want to spend time in an Indian jail.

Soon we started up the long, steep series of hairpin turns that led to Hemis. The bus parked far below the gompa, which was located high on the mountain above the bank of a rushing stream.

We entered the large, rather tumble-down courtyard through a crumbling gate. The yard had paintings all around the walls and a row of prayer wheels, some fallen into disrepair, along one side. It was full of people.

We went through an imposing front door and entered the sanctuary, where a great, golden Buddha sat in front of an altar made of silver and gold. The altar was studded with enormous turquoises and coral and the stuff they call amber but which is very heavy, unlike the amber we are familiar with. Two red-robed monks were chanting. Butter-lamps and incense were burning everywhere, and offerings of sweets and fruit lay in front of the Buddha. One of the monks rose and asked in excellent English if we would like to see the rest of the monastery. We were led upstairs to two "*puja* rooms," one of which had a very fine altar of gold, silver and jewels, and a large glass case with an elaborate *mandala*, or Tibetan calendar, made of colored butter. The monk explained that butter sculptures lasted for years in Ladakh, for temperatures in the shade were always cold enough to keep butter firm.

We were taken into the quarters of the head lama, the *rimpoche*. It was quite a sumptuous apartment, as warm and luxurious as the rest of the monastery was cold and austere. It contained nicely-upholstered furniture, thick carpets, bright hangings, and the temperature was about seventy degrees, in contrast to the rest of the building, where it must have been about fifty-five.

"Where is the Rimpoche now?" asked Ed.

"He is with other high lamas praying for rain," answered our guide. "There is not enough snow at the higher elevations, and we fear a drought later this year."

He asked if we would like to see the precious Tibetan writings that were stored at Hemis. Of course, we said we would like that very much, and he took us to another large room, lined with cabinets containing yellow-wrapped packages of uniform size. The packages contain the Tibetan scriptures, which are written in exquisite golden script on black paper. They had been smuggled out of the Potala when the Chinese invaded Tibet in 1950, and brought secretly to Hemis, where they are carefully protected and maintained. Hemis Gompa is now the largest living Himalayan monastery.

When we left the golden rooms and holy atmosphere of the building, we were astonished to find that clouds had gathered overhead and a gentle, cold rain was falling. The whole aspect of the place had changed. A certain gloom had settled over the scene, and the empty courtyard was slowly turning into mud.

"We have another hour before the bus leaves, but I think we should be back early, or we'll never get a seat. We have time for a cup of tea in that 'Camping Place and Restaurant' that we passed on our way in."

"I thought it never rained in Ladakh," I said musingly, as we picked our muddy way downhill to the 'camping place.' "I thought our book said it gets less rain than the Sahara."

"That's what the book says, but in reality it looks like the Rimpoche's prayers are being answered. You know, Bunny, I sure hope the rain stops, because we're supposed to fly out of here tomorrow morning, and I understand that any kind of bad weather will cause the cancellation of all flights. At this elevation, surrounded by such high mountains, they don't take any chances."

I didn't answer. I didn't want to think about what would happen if our flight was cancelled. I would pray—that's what I'd do. I'd pray really hard that the rain would stop. (Here I had to smile in spite of the situation. Did I think my prayers would take precedence over the Rimpoche's?) I looked up at the uncompromisingly cloudy sky, getting

241

raindrops in my face as I did so. Already I was thoroughly wet, and very cold.

At the camping place we all huddled together under a canvas awning and were grateful for the warmth of the tea. Most of the young travelers were actually camping there, and I didn't envy them their damp and chilly accommodations.

"Hurry up," I said nervously. "Let's get back to the bus before it's filled up."

The bus was indeed nearly filled when we reached it, but we found a couple of seats together right in the front row. Before long the bus was jammed, but people kept getting on, even after I would have sworn that it was stuffed to capacity. A thin old man squeezed next to me; even though I moved over against Ed as closely as I could, there was no more than a four-inch space for him; no matter—it was a space. Soon people were actually sitting upon our laps, and then people were sitting on *their* laps. The interesting thing was that, bathless or not, the Ladakhi people had no body odor. My lap-sitter was wearing a heavy, brown felt cape over several layers of clothing, and the interior of the bus was by no means cold, but though my nose was pressed firmly to his back near his armpit, the only smell about his person was the fragrance of woodsmoke. My vision was restricted to a square foot of the back of my lap sitter, and a few square inches of the grey cloak that covered the person of Ed's lap sitter. We were weighed down so that we literally couldn't move. It seemed to be a long way back to Leh.

When we creakily dismounted at the bus station, we saw that the sun was shining in the customary blue sky.

"Look, honey. The clouds are gone."

Ed shook his head. "The clouds aren't gone, they just haven't reached here yet. Look south. It's still socked in down there."

Resolutely I turned my face towards Leh. I wasn't going to spoil my last day in Ladakh—almost the last day of my precious trip—worrying about the weather.

"Come on. Let's go up to the City Palace."

We walked up the colorful main street and looked for a way up to the beautiful stone building that soared high above the town. After a couple of false starts, we found the beginning of a path—a garbagey area full of dried and semi-dried human shit, over which we carefully picked our way. We were on the rear pathway to the palace instead of the main one, and it was obviously used by the lamas for their needs, no doubt due to a lack of plumbing in the ancient building.

We went up some very steep steps, and then simply up over the rocks, a precarious path indeed. Lingering in the few flat spots was inadvisable, due to the previously mentioned embellishments and accompanying smell. At last we found our way around the building to the palace door, but to our dismay, it was closed and locked.

"Oh, damn it. I did so want to see it. What bad luck!" I said, almost tearfully. Really, our luck *had* been rather poor since we had arrived in Ladakh.

Sadly we turned and started down the steep path. As we went down we noticed a fine-looking youngish man cleaning brass pots in a courtyard below us.

"Would you like some chai?" he called up to us.

"Yes," we answered, realizing that we were thirsty, and glad that there was a chai stall nearby.

We found a path between the ruined stone buildings that clung to the hillside under the palace, and emerged into the courtyard we had seen from above. The provider of chai proved to be a lama who was inviting us into his monastic cell to have tea with him. Ed was curiously reluctant (I think he felt that we were imposing) but I was thrilled to have a chance to see how the ordinary monks lived, and I accepted happily before Ed had a chance to refuse. The lama held aside a cloth hung over a tiny doorway that was only about three feet high and raised two feet above the ground level.

We had to step up and crouch down at the same time to get in, and then crawl down a dark little passage for several feet before emerging into a tiny room measuring about seven feet by eight. A bed stood on one side, with a little altar at the head of it. A tiny window was located next to the altar, its cracked glass looking out over the town far below. Several large metal boxes containing the lama's personal belongings sat beneath the window, and atop these were other possessions—a picture of the Dalai Lama, a vase of plastic flowers, several cups and dishes, candles, two large thermos jugs decorated with brightly printed flowers. A padded mat was against the wall opposite the bed; this was his "chair" for meditation and prayer. A primus stove was on a low shelf on the remaining wall, with shelves above it for foodstuffs and pans. Soot from the stove had deposited a shiny black coating on the ceiling of branches and twigs above it, and right in the center of the room was a smoke hole with a stream of sunshine pouring in, so thickly filled with dust motes that it was almost palpable. From the hole dangled a single light bulb. The bed was covered with a colorful spread, and ruffled valences of red

243

and yellow material were suspended from the tops of the single door and the window. A "bolo" drum and horn made of a human shin-bone rested on a pile of bedclothes at the head of the bed and completed the list of our lama's belongings.

His name was Nawong Dorje, he told us, as he bustled about, making tea with canned milk over the primus stove, nodding and smiling as he chatted with us all the while. His heavily accented English was difficult to follow, but listening hard, we managed to catch the drift of his conversation.

He told us that he was one of only four lamas who looked after the holy rooms in the palace. His favorite activity was to go to Hemis Gompa for a puja now and then, and his ambition was to go to Daramsala where the Dalai Lama lived. He was happy living in Leh, he told us, but it was a lonely life, and he enjoyed inviting people to tea for the sake of their company. He was a handsome man, with the beautiful teeth and rosy cheeks of his people; he was cheerful and very kind.

When we had finished our tea, he took down the two instruments. First he blew the horn to signal the opening of his prayers (it was made from the shin-bone of a high lama, he told us, and over two hundred years old). Then he played the drum, accompanying his chant with quite a catchy cadence. He closed his eyes as he sat in the half lotus position, and his voice was resonant and thrilling. I think I have never enjoyed myself so intensely as I did that afternoon, in a lama's cell in the heart of the Himalayas.

When we got outside, we asked if we could take his picture, and he insisted on changing into his proper monk's red robes for it. Then he led us up to the Palace door and called to another lama, who opened it and guided us through the holy rooms (which are the only ones that are being maintained).

"Palace is falling down," the new lama said. "Public not allowed in anymore."

He showed us the beautiful murals far up on the wall beneath the high log ceiling, and the ancient masks before the altar, whose gargoyle faces had been exquisitely painted by hands long dead. We had been lucky after all.

That night we packed in silence. I looked up to see Ed holding the faded prayer flag that he had picked up out of the dirt at the Red Gompa.

"I don't think we'd better take this with us," he said. "The book says we'll get in trouble if we try to take any holy object out of Ladakh." He carried it outside and laid it on the grass near the river, then came back in and silently resumed his packing.

I wondered what Ed was thinking. Did he hate to leave as much as I did?

"A penny for your thoughts."

"Listen. It's raining."

"It'll stop by morning."

"I hope so."

In the morning, a weak sun was shining through the window when we awoke. Relieved, we bathed sketchily (no wonder the Ladakhis never washed—it was *cold*) and hurried through our breakfast. By the time our taxi arrived we were ready and waiting and trying to ignore the clouds that once again were threatening to blot out the sun.

At the airport, the weather improved, and the sun shone with more strength than it had all morning. We underwent the most rigorous search we had ever endured. We were frisked, and then our suitcases went up on counters to be examined.

"What is this, madam?" the pretty Ladakhi woman asked, holding up my nail clippers. I told her.

"You give to me?"

"Okay." I showed her how to operate them.

"Lipstick?"

"Yes."

"You give?"

"No."

And so it went, item by item, through all our possessions. The customs people were curious about each unknown item, and cheerfully tried to talk us into giving them any little trinket that caught their fancy. Officially, of course, they were looking for holy items out of the monasteries, and we silently thanked God that we hadn't kept the prayer flag.

Finally we were seated in the holding area, waiting to board the plane. We sat for an hour, but no plane landed. At last a young woman in uniform came into the roomful of anxious people and announced,

"The flight to Srinagar has been cancelled because of the weather. We are very sorry, but there will be no flight until Tuesday."

Ed took my hand and we looked at each other in dismay. The worst had happened, and it was hard to take it in. We were supposed to leave Srinagar the next morning for Delhi. Our flight to San Francisco would leave in the late afternoon. Unless we could somehow manage to get back

245

to Srinagar before eleven o'clock the next day, we would miss the flight to Delhi, and our flight home.

Ed went into the baggage area to retrieve our luggage, and my mind raced, all the dreadful possibilities of our situation haunting me. Would the airline honor our tickets if we missed our homeward flight? Would we have to buy new tickets home? I knew that buying a ticket on short notice meant that there would be no excursion fare. It would be *full price*. The enormity of this hit me with the force of a blow. We had no money left. Hell, we didn't even have that kind of money in the bank at home! The sheer awfulness of our situation numbed my brain. I coped by simply turning it off and refusing to think about it further. Getting up, I went into the baggage area and found Ed, who had gathered our stuff together. We dragged it all outside, under the shelter of the edge of the roof, for it was starting to rain again.

"What shall we do?" I asked humbly.

"Hire a taxi to take us to Srinagar. If we drive all night we might still make the flight."

"We don't have enough money."

"We still have our American Express card and one big traveler's check. We can get it cashed in Srinagar and pay the driver. I'll see about a taxi. You stay with the luggage." He started up the road toward town, for every taxi at the airport had already been taken by disappointed passengers going back to Leh.

In an hour he returned in the passenger's seat of a jeep-taxi driven by a reckless-looking youth.

He swung out of the seat.

"Hop in. I'll ride in the back with the luggage." He started to heave the bags into the back compartment.

"No, honey. I want to ride in back with you. We can put the two big bags in the passenger's side in front."

Within two minutes we were careening down the road toward Kargil.

"Sorry I took so long to get back," Ed said, "but there was no gasoline available in Leh, and this guy had to go home where he had a cache of gas laid away for emergencies. The worst part is that he just came up from Srinagar today and he hasn't had any sleep. But he's the only one I could find who would agree to go—the rest of them didn't have any gasoline. It'll cost us two hundred and fifty dollars. We'll have to get Amin to accept our American Express card and pay the driver for us." He grinned at me.

Suddenly it was an adventure, and I grinned back. Surely we'd be able

246

to make the flight if we drove all night, I thought. It was going to be okay.

Our driver, Sadiq, was a maniac—young and fast, and always keeping to the wrong side of the road. We had a near head-on collision right at the outset, and I kept thinking of the road ahead *at night*. The jeep had two slightly padded benches facing each other in the back where we sat, accompanied by some of our luggage and two jerry cans of gasoline (which leaked a little). We couldn't quite sit upright, and we could only see out the rear opening, the flap of which was thrown up over the top and somehow managed to stay there. Fumes from the exhaust wafted in from the back and that, mixed with fumes from raw gasoline, made a heady brew.

At Khalsi we stopped so that Sadiq could have tea, and we each downed a cup as well. I bought packaged cookies to see us through the night, and then distributed wet towelettes to the little children who clustered around us, and showed them how to wash their faces and hands. Instead of following my directions, they smelled the damp tissues with obvious pleasure, and then folded them reverently and tucked them away in their pockets.

As soon as our driver had finished with his tea, we got back in the jeep and were off. We bounced and swerved through the late afternoon to a little restaurant within sight of Lamayuru, where we had some soup and chow mein for supper. While we ate we gazed at the unattainable Shangri La so close to us and thought about the night ahead. The road beyond Lamayuru was the narrow and twisting section over Fotu La where we had met the convoy coming in. Only now it was getting dark. Suddenly it began to rain, at first a few drops, and then in torrents, and thunder shook the building.

We got back in the jeep and spun our wheels getting back onto the road. It was quite dark by then and the weak headlights barely lit up the road ahead, rain streamed down the windshield, for there were no windshield wipers (it never rains in Ladakh), and the windshield steamed up on the inside. Sadiq did not deign to slacken his pace for such trifles, and continued to take every curve at breakneck speed.

"Do you think we'll survive the night?" Ed asked.

To take my mind off what I knew was the awful abyss a few inches away on our left, I started to sing 'The Thinnest Man,' a comic song Ed had taught the kids when they were little.

> . . . thin as the glue on a postage stamp,
> the skin of a new potater,
> for exercise he used to dive

247

through the holes in a nutmeg grater . . .

Ed joined in and soon we were singing songs we hadn't sung for years. It kept us awake and probably kept our driver awake too, for we were certainly noisy if not particularly melodic.

Near Kargil we came to a screeching stop at a barrier across the road (driving the Srinagar-Leh road at night is officially prohibited), but fortunately we didn't waken the sentry who was dosing in the shack alongside. Ed got out and lifted the barrier while we drove underneath it, and then hopped back in for the final couple of miles. By then it was nearly two o'clock in the morning, and we had decided to stop in Kargil so that Sadiq could get a few hours sleep. We would have to get started again at five to get to the airport in time to make the plane, but even three hours' sleep was better than none.

We pulled into the courtyard of the Greenland Hotel and woke up a porter who was sleeping on the porch. Within five minutes we were asleep in the same room we had had before. I don't even remember getting undressed.

When the alarm went off, we were instantly awake. Even in our sleep we had been poised to get going again, so worried were we about missing that flight. We stumbled outside and found that our driver was already up and fussing with the innards of the jeep. He turned to us with a broad smile.

"We go now?" He downed the remains of a cup of chai and stuffed the last of a chapatti in his mouth.

"Geez, I'm hungry," complained Ed. "Are there any of those cookies left?"

"A few." I wished we hadn't eaten so many the night before. It had been a way of passing time then; now we needed the food. I divided them and we spun them out, chewing them slowly and making them last.

It was a cold, cloudy and cheerless morning. The road was wet and bumpy, and we slewed around the curves. Now that the time was so short all we could think about was making haste, and the reckless speed with which Sadiq drove suited us perfectly. We were just beginning to relax, sure that we would make the flight in time, when we rounded a bend just south of Drass and drew up short behind a stalled convoy of at least a hundred army trucks. They stretched ahead of us for miles. Undaunted, Sadiq pulled off the road onto the slippery bank on the right hand side, and eased the jeep slowly past three, four, then twenty trucks, until the bank became too steep to traverse, and he was forced to crowd us in between the trucks again. We sat there, fuming, until the convoy started up, and then we passed them perilously, one by one.

After half an hour had gone by, the convoy stopped again. The soldiers all got out and lit cigarettes, and lounged about, leaning on the fenders of the vehicles, peeing on the roadside, and sometimes squatting comfortably at the edge of the abyss, chatting. It was impossible to pass at that point, and we were forced to remain inactive, as the little numbers on Ed's digital watch succeeded each other relentlessly. The morning slowly evaporated while we either ground along at eight or ten miles an hour behind the behemoths and risked life and limb to pass them; or sat helplessly while they took their smoke breaks. Except for the enforced rests, we stopped for nothing. I saw a hundred men casually take a pee but I couldn't do it myself—not with half the Indian army watching.

We passed the vanguard of the convoy just before we reached Sonnmarg, and from there we almost flew along, no doubt breaking every speed law in Kashmir.

"Bunny, we don't have time to stop at the houseboat to get money from Amin. We'll have to see if we can get cash with our American Express card in town on the way to the airport."

"Sadiq, do you know anyone who can get us cash with our American Express card?" Ed had to repeat this several times and wave his arms around before Sadiq finally understood what he was saying.

"Uncle give you money, okay. No problem, sir."

We careened into Srinagar and took a corner on two wheels. At a souvenir shop on one of the side-streets, Sadiq's uncle, with maddening slowness, made out a charge on his American Express machine and gave us a double handful of rupees, less his small percentage for the service. We rushed out, tumbling back into the jeep. As Sadiq threaded through the pedestrians, we counted out his fare in preparation (two hundred and fifty dollars is an *awful* lot of rupees) and finally we were almost free of the town on the road to the airport.

Suddenly we stopped.

"Sorry, not go to airport. You take other taxi."

"But Sadiq! We must get there quickly! Please take us."

"I not go to airport." And from that position he would not budge, though we wasted several precious minutes pleading with him.

"No gas," he said at last, tears standing in his eyes, for he saw that Ed was becoming angry.

"Honey, he's really upset. Let's find another taxi, because we're just wasting time. Give him a tip too—he's been so good and tried so hard to get us here on time."

Wrathfully Ed paid him and hauled our luggage out of the jeep. Before very long, a regular taxi came along and we piled in.

"Jesus, that was all we needed." Ed shook his head as we sped along toward the airport. "I think I know why he wouldn't take us, though. I'll bet the local taxi-cabs have the airport run sewed up. Those Ladakhi taxi-drivers don't have licenses to operate here in Srinagar, and he was afraid of getting in trouble." Later we found that Ed's surmise was correct.

The clock in the terminal said eleven-fifteen when we pushed our way to the desk through a large crowd of people. Our plane was due to leave at eleven-forty-five.

Breathlessly I shoved our airline tickets in front of the ticket agent. He looked at them cooly, then pushed them back at me.

"So sorry. It is too late. Next!"

Unbelieving, I thrust them back.

"Please, there is still time. We have to catch our flights home to America today!"

"Sorry, madam." He turned to a man standing to my left and took his tickets. Stamping them, he picked up the man's luggage and put it on the scale.

"Your flight will leave at one o'clock, sir. Gate 3 to Amritsar after security."

"Please . . ." I began.

"Next."

Ed took my arm and led me away from the desk. The room was swimming through my tears. We had come so far, and tried so hard . . . I wanted to sit down on the floor and howl.

"It's no use, honey," Ed said, and squeezed my shoulders. "Let's go."

I didn't trust myself to speak, but I allowed myself to be led outside. After a few minutes I was able again to control my voice.

"Why didn't they let us on the flight?" I was still bewildered.

"Because there was no time to go through security. We were supposed to be here two hours before flight time. I wasn't thinking about that in all the rush. You know how security-conscious the Indian airlines people are, all those body-searches and all the rest of it. Impossible to do in half an hour. Don't worry. I'm sure Air India will honor our tickets, and if we're a day or two late for work, well—it's not the end of the world. Come on, let's see if we still have our room on the *New Texas*."

We managed to get a seat on the airport bus back into town, and were deposited back at the familiar bus station. After collecting our bags we trudged out to the street to look for a taxi. Majid stood there at the gate and broke into a wide smile when he saw us.

"We worried," he said, and gathered us into a waiting taxi. "Room all ready."

Back on the *New Texas*, Amin was assuring us that Air India would honor our tickets.

"It is not your fault that flight from Leh was cancelled," he said. "Flights often cancelled because of weather. Do not worry. My father will go to the Air India office in Srinagar with you this afternoon. He will help you."

At the offices of Indian Airlines we were assured by the ticket agent that we needn't worry.

"No problem, madam. Air India will protect you. We will get you out of Kashmir tomorrow. But flights out of India are very full. You may have to stay in Delhi for several days until seats can be found for you."

The next morning we said goodbye all over again to the whole family at the houseboat.

"We'll come back," we said, and meant it.

A chilly rain was falling as we crossed the lake. Drops dimpled the water and a fine mist drifted among the poplars and obscured the wooded hill above the boat landing. Amin sat in the front of the shikara looking wistful.

"Someday I would like to visit you in America," he said. "I would love to travel, but it is so expensive. It is hard for Indians to travel to America or Europe because we can only take five hundred U.S. dollars with us. Not enough unless we stay with friends. No one in my family has ever been outside of India—I have only been as far as Delhi."

"You will always be welcome at our house, Amin."

Before we landed in Delhi, the captain announced that the ground temperature stood at thirty-five degrees Celsius (ninety-five degrees Fahrenheit). When we descended the steps to the tarmac, the heat enfolded us and the aroma of dung smoke and with it, faintly, a whiff of incense, reminded us that we were back in India proper.

"It feels good," I said wonderingly. "It really feels good. I've been a tad chilly for the last month or so. I must have become used to the heat before we left for the Himalayas."

For the next two days, while we waited for Air India to find us a seat on a San Francisco-bound plane, we shopped in the bazaars, visited museums, and simply wandered the streets. We weren't sorry to have received the gift of time, even though the giving of it had been so painful. It was a last-minute reprieve, a delicious extension of pleasure before we had to resume our everyday lives.

At last the time came when, strapped into my narrow seat, I gazed down at a darkening landscape below. The smoky ground of India fell away as the plane climbed into an indigo sky . . .

On cold and rainy nights in America, when I am in my comfortable bed, it seems to me that the sun is slanting through the trees and the scent of dung smoke is in the air. Slender girls like butterflies cross a field with their water-jugs on their heads, and in my dreams I am, once again, in India.

This book has been typeset by
American-Stratford Graphic Services, Inc.
of Brattleboro, Vermont.
It has been printed and bound by
McNaughton & Gunn, Inc.
of Ann Arbor, Michigan.